CONTENTS

INTRODUCTION

From camel milk chocolate in Dubai to honeycomb chocolate in Australia, single-origin chocolate ice cream in San Francisco and chocolate-covered blueberries from Trappist Monks in Quebec, the world of chocolate has never been more diverse...or more delectable. Innovative chocolatiers are thinking up novel ingredient combinations from Ho Chi Minh City to Texas and finding new means of sourcing from and supporting small cacao farmers in the race to elevate each bite into chocolate heaven. Yet not every chocolate destination in this book is a craft bean-to-bar maker; beloved Hershey's Chocolate World, chocolate-themed hotels and classic old-world cafes serving famous chocolate cakes all earn a mention as well, and we didn't entirely leave out nostalgic childhood favourites either. Tastes for chocolate vary from region to region, but inventiveness can be found everywhere, alongside old, delicious standbys like *chocolate con churros*. Or maybe you fancy attending the fashion show at the annual Salon du Chocolat in Paris?

We couldn't cover every worthy Swiss chocolatier or incredible Parisian chocolate boutique, but we included favourites from Lonely Planet writers across the world. The major cacao-growing countries are represented as well, often with tours of cacao farms where it's possible to see the crop as it's grown and harvested. While most production of chocolate is done elsewhere and growers in places like Côte d'Ivoire and Costa Rica primarily export the raw crop without much in-country chocolate production of their own, new bar-makers are popping up all over to challenge the traditional paradigm and capture more of the revenue from the chocolate trade domestically.

Within each of the countries in this book, we've organised the attractions alphabetically by region. Each entry suggests must-try chocolate specialties at the profiled shop, as well as local sights to visit after your tour, tasting or treat. You'll find pointers on tracking down the best Black Forest cake and discover which chocolate makers are the most serious about ethical sourcing for their cacao. Enjoy!

THE B

For chocolate, it all starts with the bean. Cacao beans grow on trees, and they have a long cultural heritage in certain parts of the world. Today, chocolate is produced across the globe, but it was once reserved for kings and conquerors.

ORIGIN

The cacao bean is the seed from *Theobroma cacao*, a tree that is native to the Brazilian Amazon basin. Cacao has been domesticated for over two millennia, and consumption dates back to the Olmec, Aztec and other major civilisations through the centuries. Prior to the Spanish conquest of the region, cacao beans were often used as currency.

After the arrival of the Spanish, chocolate was introduced to the rest of the world, at first as a drink. It became a popular beverage by the mid-17th century, and the Spanish began introducing the cacao tree across other equatorial growing zones around the world. Its spread would continue in fits and starts for centuries.

EANS

VARIETY

The three main varieties of cacao plant are Forastero, Criollo and Trinitario. Forastero is the most widely used, comprising 80–90% of the world production. Criollo is a rarer and much lower-yield cacao pod and is considered a delicacy due to the low volume it produces. Trinitario is a hybrid between Forastero and Criollo, improving the yields of Criollo while still maintaining its rarity and quality.

FLAVOUR PROFILE

If you've ever eaten a cacao bean, you might wonder how something so bitter and astringent could become the world's favourite sweet. Raw cacao beans are slimy from their surrounding pulp and hard, much like eating a nut in its shell. Their flavour is sour and wholly different from the sweet flavours of chocolate. All of the flavour of chocolate we're familiar with comes from the production process.

PROCESSING METHOD

Much like coffee, the final product is the result of many involved parties and specific steps. As detailed further on the following pages, turning cacao beans into chocolate is a complex and still mostly manual process. Cacao beans are harvested, fermented, roasted, and then undergo a series of processes to create the right mixture of byproducts that give you the perfectly creamy milk chocolate or slightly bitter dark chocolate you enjoy. To ensure the highest quality chocolate, many farmers and manufacturers still use few machines in the process.

1 HARVESTING

On the cacao farm, workers cut the bean pods from trees and split them open to reveal the beans inside. For the most part, this process is still manual to reduce damage to the trees and ensure the highest harvest of cacao beans from each pod.

2 FERMENTATION

The cacao beans are then left to sit and ferment for 5 to 8 days. This allows the yeasts, bacteria and enzymes in the pulp around each cacao bean to ferment and add flavour to the bean.

CACAO TO C

12 PACKAGING

The final chocolate products are packaged and shipped to consumers.

11 MOULDING

The tempered chocolate is moulded into various shapes for the final product, including chocolate bars, chocolate layers in other sweets, and other shapes. Sometimes the final product after tempering is covered in couverture, a glossy chocolate with a higher cocoa-butter content.

9 CONCHING

The mixture is stirred continuously for several days to ensure a smooth, even mixture that gives chocolate its creamy consistency.

10 TEMPERING

The chocolate mixture is allowed to cool slowly while still being mixed, then is brought back up to temperature again to make it tempered; this will preserve the chocolate's appearance and keep it shiny.

GLOBAL CHOCOLATE TOUR

3 DRYING

Following fermentation, the cacao beans are spread out and allowed to dry for between 5 to 12 days. This ends the fermentation process before the beans are shipped to a chocolate manufacturer.

4 ROASTING

After being shipped from the cacao farm, the cacao beans are sorted and roasted at between 120 and 149°C (250 to 350°F) for 30 to 90 minutes. This is part of what gives the chocolate its colour and flavour.

HOCOLATE

5 CRUSHING

The beans are then crushed to release the internal cocoa nib. This nib is the only part of the massive bean pod that's used to create chocolate.

8 MIXING

Depending on the type of chocolate being manufactured, the cocoa butter and cocoa mass are combined in various proportions with other ingredients. See more about this on the following pages.

6 GRINDING

The cocoa nibs are ground up to create a brown mixture called cocoa mass. In a solid or semi-solid state, this is also called chocolate liquor. This mixture is roughly 55–60% cocoa butter with particles of cocoa mixed in.

7 PRESSING

The cocoa mass is then pressed to separate the cocoa butter and cocoa powder. Both ingredients are used in the manufacturing of certain types of chocolate in different proportions.

TYPES OF CHOCOL

1 DARK CHOCOLATE

At one end of the spectrum, dark chocolate is the result of mixing cocoa butter and cocoa mass with no additional milk added to make the flavour more creamy or smooth. Also, sugar is added in a lower amount than other flavours of chocolate. This creates a chocolate that is very dark in colour, and has a more brittle, flaky or even chalky texture.

Dark chocolate retains much of the original bitter and roasted flavours of the original cacao bean from the early fermenting and roasting process. Dark chocolate is almost always sold with an indication of the cocoa percentage in it, typically between 70 and 100%, which will help you gauge exactly how bitter the chocolate will be.

2 BITTERSWEET/SEMISWEET CHOCOLATE

Sometimes, dark chocolate is also called bittersweet or semisweet chocolate to indicate the amount of sugar added to the product during the mixing and conching stages of chocolate production. Typically, bittersweet has less sugar added than semi-sweet chocolate, though this isn't consistent between chocolate manufacturers, and the amount of sugar and cocoa that each manufacturer dubs 'dark,' 'bittersweet' or 'semisweet' can vary. Bittersweet and semisweet chocolate must have at least 35% cocoa in it.

F ATE

Everyone has their own favourite type of chocolate, and these preferences aren't arbitrary. Whether you prefer the bittersweet flavours of darker chocolates or the creamy smooth sweetness of milk or white chocolate, you're tasting the different proportions of ingredients in each chocolate. Chocolate products are generally comprised of four main ingredients· cocoa butter, cocoa solids, milk and sugars. The proportions of these four ingredients make all the difference in chocolate colour, texture and taste – and why each person prefers their own favourite kind.

MILK CHOCOLATE

Milk chocolate, as the name suggests, is a chocolate product with added milk. This gives it a rich, creamy and smooth texture. Milk chocolate is also typically far less bitter flavour than dark chocolate, because the milk solids help soften the flavours of the cocoa. Milk chocolate is the most popular type of chocolate produced across North America and Europe.

Milk chocolate in the United States must have a minimum of 20% cocoa in it; in Europe, milk chocolate has a minimum of 25% cocoa in it.

WHITE CHOCOLATE

White chocolate sits at the opposite end of the spectrum from dark chocolate. Unlike dark chocolate which is made of cocoa butter, cocoa solids, and sugar with no milk, white chocolate is made from cocoa butter, sugar, and milk with no cocoa solids. This lack of cocoa solids is why white chocolate is a different colour from all other chocolate products. White chocolate has a similar texture to milk chocolate.

In the United States, there are minimum regulations for the composition of white chocolate: it must be at least 20% cocoa butter, 14% total milk solids and 3.5% milk fat, and no more than 55% sugar. White chocolate is also sometimes flavoured with other ingredients, most commonly vanilla.

GLOSSARY

Baking Chocolate - A type of dark chocolate also referred to as bitter, cooking or unsweetened chocolate, used for baking.

Bean to Bar - The process of converting cacao beans to chocolate products such as bars or candies.

Bittersweet Chocolate - A type of dark chocolate indicated by the amount of sugar added during the mixing and conching stages of production. Sometimes called semisweet chocolate, but typically has lower sugar content than semisweet.

Cacahuatl - The Aztec word for chocolate.

Cacao Bean - The dried and fermented seed of *Theobroma cacao*, the cacao tree, from which cocoa solids and cocoa butter can be extracted during the bean-to-bar process. It is typically grown in equatorial regions around the world and harvested manually for chocolate production.

Cacao Pod - The pod which contains cacao beans and a pulp substance, which is harvested as part of the chocolate making process.

Cocoa Butter - The vegetable fat product extracted from cacao beans as part of the bean-to-bar process. One of the primary ingredients in chocolate.

Cocoa Liquor - Cocoa mass in its solid or semi-solid form.

Cocoa Mass - Also called chocolate liquor, the product extracted from pressing cacao beans, which can be separated into its two primary components: cocoa butter and cocoa solids.

Cocoa Solids - The dried non-fat product extracted from cacao beans as part of the bean-to-bar process, responsible for giving chocolate its colour.

Conching - The specific process of mixing and heating cocoa butter and cocoa mass to create the chocolate for final production.

Couverture - A high-quality chocolate that contains a higher percentage of cocoa butter than baking or regular eating chocolate.

Criollo - One of the three types of cacao, the most rare and coveted, but which produces less chocolate per bean than other types.

Dark Chocolate - A chocolate product made of cocoa butter, cocoa mass and sugar, which contains little or no milk product.

Forastero - The most common of the three types of cacao.

Milk Chocolate - A chocolate product which contains milk in addition to cocoa butter, cocoa mass and sugar. Different countries have different standards for the proportion of milk to other ingredients in the final product.

Nibs - A smaller portion of a cacao bean.

Semisweet Chocolate - A type of dark chocolate sometimes called bittersweet chocolate but which typically has more sugar content.

Tempering - The process of heating, cooling and reheating the chocolate mixture to ensure consistency and shine before moulding.

Trinitario - A hybrid form of cacao, which takes advantage of the rich flavours of Criollo but has better production value.

Virgin Chocolate - Chocolate made with unroasted cacao beans.

White Chocolate - Chocolate which is made of cocoa butter, milk and sugar, but which does not contain any cocoa mass and thus no brown colour.

Xococatl - The Mayan word for chocolate.

AFRI
THE MID

TOP COCOA GROWERS

CA &
OLE EAST

GHANA

Next time you eat a bar of chocolate, think of Ghanaian agriculturist Tetteh Quarshie. The man who arguably did the most for modern chocolate production brought seeds of *Theobroma cacao* home from the island of Fernando Po (now called Bioko) in 1876. Planting them in Mampong, he made Ghana a primary cocoa exporter – Ghana produces about 20% of the world's cocoa.

CÔTE D'IVOIRE

Together with Ghana, Côte d'Ivoire produces over 50% of the world's cocoa crop, and the export is a pillar of the country's economy. A 2019 agreement set a floor price for a tonne of cocoa to capture back some of the global chocolate market's worth, only a small proportion of which goes to the farmers. Small-batch local chocolatiers are starting to take advantage of the access.

GLOBAL CHOCOLATE TOUR

CÔTE D'IVOIRE

How to ask for hot chocolate in the local language? *Je voudrais un chocolat chaud, s'il vous plait.*
Signature chocolate flavour? *It's all about the local beans.*
What to order with your chocolate? *Local coffee.*
Do: *Buy local chocolate.*

It's likely that the last morsel of chocolate which melted softly in your mouth was created from cacao beans harvested in Côte d'Ivoire: the West African country is the largest cocoa-producing country in the world. Situated along the equatorial belt of West Africa, Côte d'Ivoire's cacao beans are grown inside pods which turn shades of orange, yellow or red when ripening before falling from the cacao tree. Local farmers use knives or machetes to crack open the cacao pods, which are technically fruits, releasing about 40 almond-sized beans. Each one is covered in a sweet, sticky like mucilage. The gooey goodness is fermented under plantain leaves for days, dried away from sunlight and turned every few days. When the cacao beans crackle in the farmer's hands, it's just about ready to be packaged and sold. Nestlé, Hershey and Cadbury are some of the major chocolate companies using cacao beans harvested from this West African nation.

Cacao, as it's called in the French -peaking country, is the country's top export. However, it's not without controversy. Allegations of child slavery within the cacao farms plague the industry here. Furthermore, while over 30% of the global supply of chocolate comes from Ivorian cacao beans, the farmers face pervasive poverty. To counter this, in 2019 Ivorian farmers joined forces with fellow cocoa-producing country Ghana, to set a fixed increase per-tonne chocolate price for their top crop. Many farmers and most Ivorians cannot afford to taste their premier product in its chocolate form. Actual chocolate can also be rare to find in the world's leading cocoa country.

Within the past few years, a handful of Ivorian chocolatiers started buying locally sourced beans for their ventures into Côte d'Ivoire chocolate, producing homegrown products for the first time ever. These local entrepreneurs such as Mon Choco and Instant Chocolate, both in Abidjan, are trying to change access to chocolate within their country, hoping that in the future not all the raw product will be exported and expanding the chocolate economy to include bean-to-bar makers. Ivorian chocolatiers are using Ivorian beans to make chocolate affordable for consumers at home and change the conversation.

INSTANT CHOCOLAT

Cocody, 1194 Abidjan; www.facebook.com/instantchoc;
+225 72 60 50 81

◆ Roastery ◆ Classes
◆ Shop

In 2015 Axel Emmanuel, Yvan Patrick and Marc Arthur co-founded Instant Chocolat in Abidjan's Cocody district, intending to transform Ivorian cacao beans into an affordable, chocolate delight. Though Cote d'ivoire is the world's largest cocoa-producing country, finding cocoa in its chocolate form within this West African nation is rare. The chocolatier trio is pioneering locally made chocolate with unique flavours like Aboki coffee milk, with 'bursts of organic coffee'. Their P'ti Cola' boasts of being a 'perfect balance between bitterness and sweetness' with 75% cocoa in their dark chocolate. Another tasty twist to their chocolate is their Black Ginger flavour, called Gnamakou. And by making their sweets, the Instant team is reminding the world that Ivorians deserve a bigger slice in the chocolate industry pie, starting with locally produced African chocolate.

THINGS TO DO NEARBY

Panaf
If you're looking for culinary adventure, Panaf is your spot. The culinary campus features Pan-African cuisine, reflecting a diverse array of spices and flavours from the African diaspora. *www.facebook. com/PanafAbidjan*

Galerie Cécile Fakhoury
Artists featured at this gallery dismantle and challenge 'geographical stigmatisation' through contemporary art that brings together complexities of the past with hope for the future. *cecilefakhoury.com*

GHANA

How to ask for hot chocolate in the local language? English is the official language and great for requesting your cocoa.
Signature chocolate flavour? *Bissap*, or hibiscus flower.
What to order with your chocolate? Pre-game dessert with a dish of red-red bean curry.
Don't: Skip touring Tetteh Quarshie's cocoa farm.

Ghana is the second-largest cocoa-producing country in the world thanks to its prime real estate for cacao cultivation. Warm temperatures, heavy rainfalls and sprinkles of rainforest trees for wind protection add up to an environment where cacao trees thrive. They are most plentiful in the Ashanti, Western and Eastern regions of the country. Local farmers fertilise the soil while blocking excess rays of sunshine to the cacao trees, allowing for healthy harvested pods in four to five years. Each tree has a 30-year life spa, and a pod sprouts about 30 cacao beans.

Ghanaian cacao beans brag of a decadent flavour due to the farmers' maintaining their old-school tradition of the post-harvest process. The beans are covered with banana or plantain leaves for up to a week. The top layer ferments, further marinating the cacao bean. It's sundried for a few more days before they are packed and sold. After export to the world's biggest chocolate producers, the harvested beans are transformed into your favourite chocolate morsel, making the world a happier place – at least for the consumers.

The Ghanaian cocoa producer has a harder situation. Cacao beans are produced in some of the poorest parts of the country. Cocoa is Ghana's chief agricultural export, but the wages for harvesting the world's favourite sweet treat haven't kept pace with the chocolate market's value. The Ghana Cocoa Board is asking for higher wages from the international chocolate manufacturing community for producing their premium crop. From cacao beans grown in the country's remote regions to neatly wrapped chocolate confections, everyone desires to reap the benefits of gastronomic pleasure packed inside a Ghanaian cacao pod.

Increasingly, local Ghanaian entrepreneurs like the Addison sisters are making it their mission to 'revive Ghana's can-do spirit' by keeping more of the raw beans here and producing fine chocolates within Ghana, made from the country's own crop.

'57 CHOCOLATE

19 Pawpaw Street, East Legon, Accra;
www.57chocolategh.com; +233 504 736 539

◆ Tastings

Kimberly and Priscilla Addison are sisters in chocolate. Disheartened by the lack of African chocolatiers after a taking chocolate factory tour in Switzerland, the entrepreneurial Pan-African duo quit their professional careers and relocated to their native Ghana. In 2016, the sisters launched '57 Chocolate, named after the year Ghana earned its independence from colonial British rule. Their handmade, bean-to-bar brand makes chocolate from Ghanaian beans. Having no background in the culinary arts, the Addison sisters studied cocoa production and the facets of the chocolate-making industry prior to setting up shop in their mother's kitchen, finding a cacao bean producer in Eastern Ghana to deliver beans to the Addison home just a few hours away in Accra. Visitors can contact '57 Chocolate to schedule tastings in their home factory; chocolates are poured into different traditional Adinkra symbol moulds.

THINGS TO DO NEARBY

Labadi Beach
People flock to Accra's most popular beach to play ball games, frolic in the surf, go horse riding along the sand or party to loud dance music in the bars and restaurants on the shore.

ANO Centre for Cultural Research
This arts institution, whose name is from the word 'grandmother' in Akan, has just opened a well-curated permanent space for exhibitions and screenings.

© Gallo Images / Getty Images

ISRAEL & THE PALESTINIAN TERRITORIES

How to ask for hot chocolate in Hebrew? *Shoko kham.*
Signature chocolate flavours? Hints of orange, za'atar and Dead Sea salt.
What to order with your chocolate? Cinnamon rugelach.
Do: Bring an insulated pouch to keep your chocolate purchases intact in this sunny clime.

Cacao isn't grown in the land of milk and honey. But the innovative spirit that turned Israel into a high-tech powerhouse and foodie destination has oozed over into a burgeoning boutique chocolate scene enlivened with bold local flavours such as passion fruit, pistachio, halvah cream and za'atar – a hyssop-oregano-thyme-sesame-sumac spice blend. For the first 40 years of the state's existence, virtually the only choice in chocolate was the Elite mass-market brand – call it the Hershey's of Israel – still selling strong in supermarkets. Praline pioneer Ornat introduced handmade kosher chocolate confections in 1988. In 1996, Max Fichtman and Oded Brenner founded Max Brenner, which grew into a global brand. Soon, Israelis started hopping over to Europe to train with master-chocolatiers before returning home to open their own chocolate businesses and win prestigious prizes.

Among those holding International Chocolate Awards medals are Ika Cohen of Ika Chocolate in Tel Aviv (za'atar ganache); Yulia Freger of Bruno Chocolate in Rehovot (strawberry cheesecake white chocolate truffles); and Ronen Aflalo of Emilya Chocolate Passion in Givatayim (raw tahini bonbons). By 2015, 28 Israeli chocolate makers were exporting around $10 million worth of the sweet stuff to 42 countries – including Belgium, one of Israel's main sources for cocoa nibs, cocoa liquor and cocoa butter. But the smaller players only sell domestically, so the only way to sample their gourmet wares is to visit in person. While you're here, join the locals in one of their favourite chocolate pastimes: expressing their out-of-the-box creativity in the hands-on workshops available at chocolateries across the country.

SWEET'N KAREM

2-3 Mevo Ha-Sha'ar St, Jerusalem; www.sweetnkarem.co.il;
+972 (0)77 200 6660

◆ Food ◆ Tour ◆ Takeout
◆ Shop ◆ Bar ◆ Rooms

THINGS TO DO NEARBY

Ruth Havilio Tile Artist
For 28 years, Havilio's studio next to local landmark St John the Baptist Church has sold hand-painted ceramic tiles in delightful designs for useful and decorative purposes.

Eden-Tamir Music Center
Located near Mary's Spring holy pilgrimage site, Eden-Tamir is a focal point for music activities, recitals and chamber-music concerts performed by Israeli and overseas musicians.

Christian Historic Sites
Walk around the pastoral Ein Karem neighbourhood to see its Christian sites: Mary's Spring, Church of the Visitation, Monastery of St John in the Mountains and others.

Haya White Watercolorist
The home gallery of Haya White sells gifts, originals and small prints of her watercolour and mixed-media paintings of Jerusalem gardens, people, pets and landscapes.

The Sweet'n Karem chocolate and gelato shop sits centrally amidst artist studios, trendy restaurants and historic Christian sites in the pretty village-within-Jerusalem that is Ein Karem. Pilgrims, artists, musicians, monks, photographers and tourists stream daily to this pastoral place believed to be where the pregnant Virgin Mary visited her cousin Elizabeth, mother-to-be of John the Baptist. As visitors walk past the little shop run by Ofer Amsalem since 2008, the aroma draws them in to admire rows of gorgeously displayed gourmet treats. Packaging adorned with charming depictions of Ein Karem by local painter Haya White envelops unique chocolate souvenirs such as a gold-wrapped 'Walls of Jerusalem' chocolate tablet hand-inscribed on the spot with Hebrew blessings; velvety handmade truffles and pralines infused with locally produced cream laced with signature Mideast flavours like cinnamon-tinged sachlav and sesame halvah candy and rosewater; plus a vegan chocolate bar studded with market-fresh sunflower seeds, tahini and pink Himalaya salt.

In the factory around the corner in a renovated 12th-century structure, chocolate-making workshops send you off with a kilo of pralines. Dine in the adjacent Sweet'n Karem kosher cafe and then retire upstairs to dream choco-latey dreams in the owner-operated Chocolate House B&B with rooftop spa.

CHOCOLATE BY THE BALD MAN
MAX BRENNER

MAX BRENNER

Rothschild Blvd 45, Tel Aviv;
maxbrenner.com; +972 3-560-4570

- ◆ Food
- ◆ Transport
- ◆ Shop
- ◆ Cafe

Today Max Brenner has gone international, with locations from Australia to New York, Singapore to Russia, but it was founded in Israel (in 1996), and its heart remains here. For the local experience, start at the Chocolate Bar and restaurant on trendy Rothschild Blvd in the heart of Tel Aviv, where the variety of chocolate creations is dizzying, decadent and, above all, fun. Treats come in forms from sharable to sippable, pourable to dippable and dunkable; even 'injectable'. Cradle a signature 'hug mug' filled with Max's famous hot chocolate, or sip milkshakes from exclusive 'Alice cups' ceramic vessels with 'drink me' written down the side. Crunch a praline cigar with chocolate dipping sauce. A chocolate pizza is topped with chunks of milk and white chocolate. Typical regional ingredients like coriander also find their way in.

THINGS TO DO NEARBY

Carmel Market
This market is a foodie's dream: block after covered block of produce, hummus, deep-fried goodness, beer and juice bars and the aroma of fresh-baked bread permeating the air.

Tel Aviv's coastline
After your chocolate fix, tour Tel Aviv's coastline, 14km of beaches with family-friendly, gay-friendly and sport-friendly options, all lined with bike- and footpaths.

SÃO TOMÉ & PRÍNCIPE

How to ask for hot chocolate in the local language?
Chocolate quente por favor.
What to order with your chocolate? Island-grown Arabica coffee.
Signature chocolate flavour? Coffee, naturally.
Do: For safety, use a guide when visiting abandoned roças.

With a sobriquet like the 'Chocolate Islands', you'd expect this miniscule twin-island country off equatorial West Africa to be a fascinating destination to explore cocoa production. And you'd be right. Portuguese colonists brought Forastero seedlings from Brazil here in 1822 to replace the faltering sugar crop, and within a century the islands became the world's largest cocoa producer on the backs of indentured labourers. Jagged volcanoes, rising like Easter egg shards, bequeathed fecund soils and dappled rainforest shade that fostered bumper cacao harvests and enabled Portuguese colonists to develop prosperous roça (plantations) enriched by the exploitation of slavery.

But like pistoles of tempering chocolate, global domination melted away. Around 1909, Quaker-owned British chocolate giant Cadbury boycotted cocoa from the islands, citing the practice of indentured labour, and production further waned after the Portuguese abandoned São Tomé and Príncipe in 1975. 'Everything collapsed after the Portuguese left,' remembers Joao Qatarina-Conceicao, an elderly ex-employee at Roça Porto Real. 'The roça were like small cities but we were slaves'.

Now São Tomése cocoa is being reinvented. The UN's International Fund for Agricultural Development (IFAD) identified the islands as ripe for organic fair-trade production, given its unbroken lineage of superior Forastero untainted by chemicals or pesticides, with a richly intense taste with refreshing citrusy notes. French biological-chocolate producer Kakao has a partnership with a cooperative of cocoa farmers (CECAB), and now 15% of the population is employed in its organic production, lifting families out of poverty. Kakao guarantees a 40% price above market value to local cooperatives who roast the beans for export.

'Our people can now afford to educate their children and move on from the slavery cocoa brought,' says Alberto Luis from a CECAB cooperative. Small scale bean-to-bar production has been pioneered by São Tomé island's only local chocolatier, Italian Claudio Corallo, nicknamed the 'King of West African chocolate'. More recent investment by South African billionaire and astronaut Mark Shuttleworth has transformed Roça Sundy on Príncipe into a five-star resort with a functioning roça that has attracted internationally acclaimed chocolatiers like David Greenwood-Haigh.

CLAUDIO CORALLO

Av 12 de Julho 978, São Tomé, São Tomé Island;
www.claudiocorallo.com; +239 9916815

◆ Tastings ◆ Tours
◆ Roastery ◆ Shop

 Since abandoning coffee-growing in Zaire in 1992, the quixotic Claudio Corallo has flown the flag for the island's cocoa production and pioneered chocolate making. Beans from his Terreiro Velho plantation on Príncipe are transported to Roça Nova Moca on São Tomé for hand-preparation and then lovingly blended into chocolate at his factory and shop overlooking Ana Chaves Bay. Corallo has long experimented with flavours and roasting techniques to produce world-class luxury chocolate. His fascinating tour includes a tasting of the whole gamut of chocolate products, allowing visitors to savour 73.5% cacao chocolate bars spiced with candied ginger and smoky home-grown Arabica coffee beans encased within a dark chocolate coating.

THINGS TO DO NEARBY

Roça São João

Innovative chef João Carlos Silva has transformed Roça São João into an artistic hub, restaurant and gastronomy school. Overlooking Santa Cruz Bay, it's a great spot for lunch.

Pico Cão Grande

Get up close to São Tomé's most iconic landform, a rather phallic-looking volcanic pinnacle within Obô National Park's rainforest, which is a haven for hiking and endemic birds.

SUNDY PRAIA

Roça Sunday, Principe;
sundyprincipe.com;+239 9997000

◆ Tastings ◆ Classes ◆ Cafe
◆ Roastery ◆ Shop ◆ Rooms

 Mark Shuttleworth's restoration of Roça Sundy has breathed new life into a dilapidated plantation (itself the site of 1919's Eddington Experiment confirming General Relativity) to create a luxury tented beach-camp bringing much-needed local employment to Príncipe. Chocolate lovers may tour an active plantation and factory producing innovative treats like cocoa vinegar or high-cocoa-butter couverture for tempering into bars. Sundy Praia offers a chocolate ritual spa treatment and weekly chocolate dinner featuring dishes like beef carpaccio with a garlic and cocoa cream. They run a seven-day Tropical Chocolate Safari out of Sundy Praia: the itinerary for sweet-toothed foodies includes roça visits, chocolate-making, and writing classes, most recently with *Chocolat* author Joanne Harris.

THINGS TO DO NEARBY

Praia das Bananas

Spend a day at the beach – and what a beach! Praia das Bananas' golden foreshore is so sublimely perfect that in the 1990s it featured in Bacardi's rum advertising campaign.

Turtle Nesting

Take a nocturnal walk with local conservation rangers to witness leatherback and hawksbill turtles come ashore to lay eggs on Praia Grande between September and March.

SOUTH AFRICA

How to ask for hot chocolate in the local language?
In Afrikaans: *Warm sjokolade asseblief.*
In Zulu: *Itiye elinoshokholethi ngiyacela.*
Signature chocolate flavours? Amarula.
What to order with your chocolate? A cup of locally roasted coffee.
Don't: Miss a wine and chocolate pairing around Cape Town.

South Africa can tell its history of European settlement through chocolate, starting in 1652 with the foundation of Cape Town as a refreshment station for Dutch East India Company ships, which carried spices used to flavour chocolate from the East Indies to Europe. Appropriately, this bygone maritime trade is celebrated in the name of Spice Route wine estate, home to De Villiers Chocolate. Mass-produced bars by the likes of Cadbury and Nestlé have long filled sweet-shop shelves, but it wasn't until the country entered global commerce at the end of apartheid that highbrow confectioners such as Lindt entered the market.

Since Nelson Mandela walked free from prison in 1990, South African producers have learnt much from other countries and unleashed the strengths of their own people and environment. With their Mediterranean climate, Cape Town and the surrounding Winelands are now a world-class foodie destination, offering an unlimited menu of wine estates, food markets, microbreweries, coffee roasters and craft distillers. Artful chocolate makers have also popped up everywhere from Johannesburg's regenerated industrial spaces to the small towns of the Western Cape. South African producers generally take an ecological bean-to-bar approach, helping Africa by sourcing beans on the continent and creating jobs locally. Honest Chocolate, for example, shifted its cacao source from Ecuador to Tanzania, while chocoholics snack with a purpose at Cocoafair, which sells boxes of 500 mini-chocolates emblazoned with '500 for social change: 1 box, 6 jobs, 6 happy families'. Given its lively food culture, South Africa produces an experimental flavour for every classic Belgian slab, evolving a chocolate scene with its roots in family experiences of snack-bar sundaes, *padkos* (packed lunch) treats and bedtime hot chocolates.

CHOCOLOZA

44 Stanley Ave, Braamfontein Werf, Johannesburg, Gauteng; www.chocoloza.co.za; +27 10 900 4892

◆ Tastings ◆ Classes
◆ Cafe ◆ Shop

Jozi chocoholics love this Belgian-inspired, 100% South African chocolatier, which uses local farm products in its treats. Even the furniture, handcrafted from reclaimed pallet wood in Pretoria, is local – perfect for savouring a hot drink and perhaps an Amarula chocolate, incorporating South Africa's Baileys-like marula cream liqueur. Conveniently, *lekker* means the same (tasty) in both Dutch and local lingo Afrikaans; the word comes in handy for describing the creamy coffee pralines and cappuccinos, bursting with beans from Bean There Coffee, South Africa's first fair trade coffee roaster. Vicki Bain helms the all-female team, having learned her trade at the fine Belgian chocolatiers Demeestere and Neuhaus. Catch one of Chocoloza's legendary Chocolate Adventure Evenings.

THINGS TO DO NEARBY

44 Stanley
Lounge under olive trees at this shopping arcade in repurposed industrial 1930s buildings, home to the Chocoloza mothership, Bean There Coffee, boutiques and cafes.
www.44stanley.co.za

1Fox
This regenerated gold-rush mining camp and tram depot hosts the excellent Mad Giant craft brewery (try the Jozi Carjacker IPA) and a food market.
www.1fox.co.za

COCOAFAIR

Old Biscuit Mill Block-C, Woodstock, Cape Town,
Western Cape; www.cocoafair.com; +27 021 447 7355

◆ Transport ◆ Shop
◆ Roastery

Heinrich Kotze left the corporate world for Cocoafair in 2009 with the genius idea of making excellent chocolate and improving society at the same time. Now employing over 20 people and supplying 200 outlets, they try to do, rather than be, the best, following the social entrepreneurship model of creating jobs for underprivileged people. Staff start as chocolate novices and learn everything from packing to hand-tempering. Only then can they wear Cocoafair's cool red overalls, while producing creative confectioneries from passion fruit and pepper white choc-olate to citrus and cardamom dark chocolate. Cocoafair's responsible ethos carries through to buying cocoa directly from growers, to ensure the beans have been organically cultivated and the workers have not been exploited.

THINGS TO DO NEARBY

Old Biscuit Mill
Cocoafair's home is this converted biscuit factory in vibey Woodstock, which houses arty shops, restaurants and the lively Neighbourgoods Saturday food market. *www. theoldbiscuitmill.co.za*

The Kitchen
Add some wholesome greens to all that chocolate with a lunch plate at Karen Dudley's beloved cafe-deli in Woodstock, where Michelle Obama stopped for lunch in 2011. *www.lovethekitchen.co.za*

DE VILLIERS CHOCOLATE

Suid Agter Paarl Rd, South Paarl, Western Cape;
www.dvchocolate.com; +27 021 874 1060

◆ Tastings   ◆ Classes   ◆ Cafe
◆ Roastery   ◆ Shop

It's the perfect setting for De Villiers' bean-to-bar, single-origin chocolate, most of which supports fellow Africans by sourcing beans from small-scale Ugandan farmers. Making the chocolate directly from the cacao bean and controlling all the processes, including sustainable bean selection, roasting, grinding, refining and conching, allows De Villiers to develop interesting flavours from orange peel and vanilla to peppermint and macadamia. There are several ranges and products, including the African Collection, an organic single-origin range and drinking chocolate. Don't miss a turn of the tasting stations, nibbling on tantalising juxtapositions such as sea salt and caramel or cinnamon and ginger.

THINGS TO DO NEARBY

Spice Route
More family funfair than wine farm, De Villiers' home base has shops, mountain bike trails, a kids' 100m-long 'choc-o-trail' and a pizzeria.
www.spiceroute.co.za

Fairview
Under the same ownership as Spice Route, this wine estate offers tastings of its 50-plus artisanal cheeses, some produced with milk from the estate's goats.
www.fairview.co.za

Afrikaans Language Monument
Rising needle-like from Paarl Rock, one of the world's largest granite outcrops, this modernist monument celebrates the Dutch-derived local *taal* (language).

Babylonstoren
Even among the Cape's paradisiacal wine farms, this rustic estate stands out as a delightful haven with its Cape Dutch–style garden, which supplies the restaurant and cafe.
babylonstoren.com

Approaching Pieter de Villiers' Cape Dutch chocolate lab, it's easy to get excited. For starters, there's the glorious setting of Spice Route wine estate, its vineyards leading the eye to a many-layered mountain range and resident artisanal producers offering tastings from biltong to schnapps. Then there's the multi-roomed temple of delights within, its doorways opening onto a choc-packed shop, a factory of fire-engine-red mixing machines, a tasting room and a confectionery bar with a cacao flavour wheel. Cacao contains over 600 flavour components, making it the world's most flavourful food – who knew!

GABOLI CHOCOLATES

2037 Delport Rd, Betty's Bay, Western Cape;
www.gaspardbossut.wixsite.com/gabolichocolates;
+27 082 394 1016

◆ Tastings   ◆ Classes
◆ Roastery   ◆ Shop

 GaBoLi, which stands for Gaspard Bossut Limited, is the brainchild of a Belgian-born chef-turned-chocolatier who learnt his tricks at a British confectioner supplying London's Harrods department store. Gaspard can be found among the machines and vats in his kitchen in the Cape Whale Coast town of Betty's Bay, where he handcrafts Belgian chocolate treats from truffles and pralines to glazed fruit. Flavours include classics (hazelnut, coffee liqueur), South African favourites (Amarula, brandy) and taste-bud trips to adventurous realms (blue cheese and biltong, grappa, limoncello, local fynbos). Diabetics and dieters are catered for, too, with truffles and bars that taste indistinguishable from other chocolate, thanks to the use of maltitol natural sweetener instead of usual sugar substitute xylitol.

THINGS TO DO NEARBY

Stony Point Nature Reserve
This former whaling station in Betty's Bay is home to one of the largest breeding colonies of cute African penguins, as well as three types of cormorant. *www.capenature.co.za/reserves/stony-point-nature-reserve*

Hermanus
Follow Clarence Drive, one of the world's most beautiful coast roads, from Betty's Bay to Hermanus, the world's best land-based whale-watching spot (between June and December).

HONEST CHOCOLATE

64A Wale St, Cape Town, Western Cape;
www.honestchocolate.co.za; +27 076 765 8306

◆ Food   ◆ Classes   ◆ Cafe
◆ Transport   ◆ Shop

Just off Cape Town's foodie Bree Street, Honest's courtyard cafe is a peaceful city-centre nook for enjoying truffles, tarts and cakes with a hot chocolate or coffee. Dairy-free milkshakes and local Sorbetiere ice cream appeal to lactose-intolerant and vegan sweet tooths, while house specialities include banana bread bunny chow – a lighter remix of Durban's trademark dish of curry in a hollow bread loaf. Then there's the chocolate, whether it's the 70% slab bars, bonbons, nibs, spread or drinking powder, all made with organic Tanzanian cacao beans. Having started by experimenting with raw cacao, owners Anthony Gird and Michael de Klerk espouse the bean-to-bar approach with their 'chain of positivity', ethically sourcing raw materials to produce 'honest chocolate' that showcases its ingredients.

THINGS TO DO NEARBY

Secret Gin Bar
Try the local craft gin, flavoured with the Cape's indigenous fynbos, at this speakeasy sharing Honest Chocolate's Mediterranean-style courtyard.
www.theginbar.co.za

Bo-Kaap
Continue up Wale Street from Honest Chocolate to this pastel-painted neighbourhood, the traditional home of the Cape Malay people, for a coconut-sprinkled *koeksister* doughnut.

UNITED ARAB EMIRATES

How to ask for hot chocolate in the local language? *Talab shukulatuh sakhina.*

Signature chocolate flavour? Camel's milk chocolate is a classic choice.

What to order with your chocolate? A 'camelccino' (camel milk cappuccino) goes well with chocolate cake.

Do: Keep your chocolate bar out of the desert heat.

The United Arab Emirates (UAE) is known for the endless pursuit of over-the-top opulence. In the shadow of the world's tallest building and beyond the shimmer of the infinity pool, chocolate is no exception to the bigger-is-better luxury trend. In the Alserkal Avenue arts district, Dubai's first bean-to-bar chocolate factory, Mirzam, has sprouted amidst the galleries. The art of crafting fine chocolate is taken very seriously at this high-tech factory, where all stages from roasting to

handwrapping the product take place behind glass walls. Only single-origin beans from such locales as Madagascar, Papua New Guinea, Vietnam, India and Indonesia are used.

Even the Fairmont Dubai got into the chocolate game, creating a gigantic chocolate egg to sit in the hotel's atrium ahead of Easter 2018. Dubbed 'Dubai's biggest chocolate egg,' it was made from 80 kg (176 lbs) of 55% dark chocolate and stood at 2.5m-tall (8-foot-tall), taking four weeks to craft. But there are more down-to-earth chocolate trends as well, particularly the growth of the local camel milk chocolate industry. Bedouins have known it for centuries, but the health benefits of camel milk have started to make international headlines, and local products use it in abundance: camel cheese, chocolate and ice cream are now staples on supermarket shelves. Visitors can discover the distinctive, salty camel milk for themselves.

AL NASSMA

Financial Center Rd, Dubai Mall; www.al-nassma.com;
+971 4 333 8183

◆ Transport   ◆ Shop

THINGS TO DO NEARBY

Burj Khalifa
The world's tallest building glitters above Dubai Mall and the cooling fountains at its base. The view from the top is dazzlingly dizzy. *www.burjkhalifa.ae/en*

Mall of the Emirates
Probably the most famous mall in the Middle East, notable for its an indoor ski slope, complete with snow. *www.malloftheemirates.com*

Frying Pan Adventures
Get to know Dubai's super-diverse foodscape by foot on fascinating tours around the city's older quarters. Wear stretchy pants. *www.fryingpanadventures.com*

Camelicious
This 4000-head dairy is not open routinely to individual visitors; you can arrange a group tour to learn all about the mighty beasts. *camelicious.ae*

En route to sprawling, sparkling Dubai Mall's immense luxury shoe shop or its dazzling aquarium, you might miss the tiny Al Nassma kiosk on the ground floor. And even if you notice the 'camel milk chocolate' sign, you might assume it's a dull tourist gimmick: milk chocolate in the shape of a camel.

There is indeed camel-shaped chocolate – but the milk in the chocolate is in fact from camels, which are raised at Camelicious, in the desert just outside the city. At the state-of-the-art dairy operation, the beasts of burden are fed hay and carrot-date protein bricks, and milked every afternoon. The milk is portioned out: some is sold on Dubai's supermarket shelves; some is made into ice cream and beauty products. And some is shipped to Austria, where it is blended with chocolate by expert chocolatiers. Then the milk chocolate is shipped back to Dubai, where it's moulded and flavoured, and eventually sent to the upscale mall kiosk of Al Nassma.

The gold-wrapped camels make a great gift, but the best treats are the flavoured bars. The 'Arabia' variety is flecked with cardamom and other spices. Even better is the bar studded with chunks of Emirati dates, the perfect foil for the uniquely sweet-salty taste of camel milk. Good luck finding this specialty anywhere else.

With fiery spices and liberal splashes of liqueur, different countries bestow their own distinctive flair on this classic winter warmer. Snuggle up with these 10 hot chocolate varieties from around the world.

10 DISTINCTIVE HOT C

© HighImpactPhotography / Getty Images; © Tonglin Lin/EyeEm / Getty Images; © Andrey Shtanko / Shutterstock; © Lindsay Lauckner Gundlock / Lonely Planet

Green Chaud, France

Freezing temperatures call for potent hot drinks. In the French Alps, 'green chaud' is created by fortifying chocolatey milk with a generous splash of Chartreuse liqueur. A herbal intoxicant originally devised by monks as a health tonic, nowadays it's a steamy favourite of après-ski revellers.

Chocolate Santafereño, Colombia

Salty white cheese adds a contrasting flavour to Colombian hot chocolate. A small wedge of cheese is usually served on the side, to dip in the chocolate at the drinker's leisure. Occasionally the cheese is dropped in, melting away at the bottom of the foamy concoction.

Paprika Hot Chocolate, Hungary

The signature spice of Hungarian cuisine is paprika, which adds unmistakable smokiness to dishes like chicken paprikash and goulash. So popular is this peppery flavour that many Hungarians can't resist sprinkling paprika to give their *forró csokoládé* (hot chocolate) some nostril-flaring heat.

Churros con Chocolate, Spain

Spanish hot chocolate is almost too thick to sip. Fortunately it comes accompanied by churros, batons of dough fried until they're crunchy on the outside and yieldingly soft within: the perfect vehicle to dip into rich, dark chocolate.

Champurrado, Mexico

Blended with corn flour, sugar and evaporated milk, champurrado is thick and nourishing, almost like a hearty chocolate soup. This comforting brew has its origins in Meso-American cultures; modern-day drinkers in Mexico riff on the classic recipe by whisking in vanilla and cinnamon.

10 DISTINCTIVE HOT COCOAS

Berry Hot Chocolate, Poland

In keeping with the Polish love for berries, wine-drenched raspberries and other juicy fruits add tart flavour to hot chocolate; sip it at E Wedel cafes from Poznań to Białystok.

Tsokolate, The Philippines

Chocolate lovers here start early: tsokolate is served for breakfast. A strong, slightly grainy drink made by dissolving tablets of cocoa in hot water, its kick is softened by a splash of milk.

Chocolate Chai, India

Perennial favourite masala chai, an aromatic and milky black tea, is given a delicious twist in chocolate chai, which incorporates cardamom and pepper into a sweet chocolatey beverage.

Peanut Butter Hot Chocolate, USA

American palates can't resist the sweet-salt marriage of peanut butter and chocolate, so naturally peanut butter's satisfying protein hit has melted its way into hot chocolate recipes.

Tote Tante, Germany

The name 'dead aunt' doesn't sound too nourishing, but in this northern German (and Danish) hot chocolate, a generous slug of rum is added to hot chocolate and a decadent dollop of whipped cream dropped on top.

OCOAS
AROUND THE WORLD

THE
AMER

TOP 3 CHOCOLATE ICE CREAMS

...RICAS

HELADERÍA EMPORIO LA ROSA, *SANTIAGO, CHILE*

Pair your chocolate gelato here with one made from a local fruit, or order a scoop of the choco-chili variety of this extra-creamy handmade ice cream, which has been known to cause addiction. Ever-expanding, there are now a dozen branches across town. Flaky *pain au chocolat* is another reason to station yourself at the chrome tables and indulge.

VAN LEEUWEN, *NEW YORK CITY, USA*

This stalwart of the Brooklyn artisanal food movement started with a truck and now boasts half a dozen stores across Manhattan and Brooklyn. Their chocolate ice cream is made from cocoa supplied by French chocolatier Michel Cluizel, all from biodynamic, organic plantations. Their mint-chop flavour, meanwhile, uses single origin 72% chocolate chips from renowned Missouri chocolate maker Askinosie.

SMITTEN ICE CREAM, *SAN FRANCISCO, USA*

A chocolate ganache ice cream made with 61% Guittard cacao? Fifth generation San Francisco chocolate maker Guittard supplies the chocolate, supplemented with their Cocoa Rouge cocoa powder for extra-chocolatey flavour. Before working with Guittard, Smitten sourced from Berkeley-based chocolatier TCHO. Locations can be found in the Bay Area.

ARGENTINA

How to ask for hot chocolate in the local language? Order a *submarino*, an Argentine hot chocolate made from a chocolate tablet dissolved in hot milk.

Signature chocolate flavours? *Dulce de leche* is a prominent ingredient in the country's decadent chocotorta, a popular *postre* (dessert).

What to order with your chocolate? Churros are a must.

Do: Visit the Argentine Swiss-German villages that carry on European chocolate-making (and eating) traditions.

Argentines in general are definitely not afraid of sugar consumption. Breakfast begins with *medialunas* (sweetened croissants), *café con leche* with sugar, and any time of day seems appropriate for gelato. In northern Patagonia there's a strong Swiss influence which has helped the neighbouring towns of San Carlos de Bariloche and El Bolsón become the epicentre of artisanal chocolate production in the country. Bariloche even has a street aptly referred to as 'The Avenue of Chocolate Dreams'.

To communicate your preference, state how bitter you like your chocolate. A higher cacao content is *chocolate amargo*, semisweet is *semi-amargo*, and milk chocolate is *con leche*. Ultra-dark chocolate is difficult, although not impossible, to find here, as the local tastes ride more on the milkier side of things. A traditional hot chocolate is *chocolate caliente*, but do not confuse this with the more common *submarino* – frothed milk with a small piece of chocolate on the side to drop into the hot drink. It melts, leaving a puddle of goopy chocolate at the bottom of the glass.

Because Patagonia is the focal point of Argentine chocolate, popular flavours often include regional ingredients like walnut, cassis, and homemade *dulce de leche*. Bariloche and Buenos Aires-based chocolatier Rapanui is famous for their raspberries first dipped in white chocolate, then in dark chocolate, then frozen. Mamuschka is a dizzying (in the best way possible) locale filled with cases of hundreds of chocolate combinations and they are very generous with their free samples. When in outdoorsy El Bolsón, check out the Lida stand at the central artists' market, run by a no-nonsense grandmother who makes an intense dark chocolate-covered cherry filled with her rather potent homemade cherry liqueur.

JAUJA

Av San Martin 2867, El Bolsón, Río Negro;
www.heladosjauja.com; +54 294-449-2448

◆ Tastings   ◆ Classes   ◆ Cafe
◆ Roastery   ◆ Shop   ◆ Transport

In a mountain valley of northern Patagonia known for small-scale organic farming and the hippie lifestyle of the locals, Jauja arrived on the scene in 1980. Committed to using zero artificial flavours, the owners create their chocolates around the freshest regional ingredients such as currant, blackberry, calafate berry, *dulce de leche* and walnut. There is a dedicated chocolate shop, but in the summer the lines are long for their homemade gelato sold next door. The Mousse de Piltri flavour celebrates the nearby towering peak Mt Piltriquitrón with a *dulce de leche* mousse filled with caramelised almonds, and Profundo y Contradictorio is a bitter 80% cacao gelato generously packed with homemade meringue and *dulce de leche*.

THINGS TO DO NEARBY

Mt Piltriquitrón
Paraglide over and around Mt Piltriquitrón, the dramatic backdrop for downtown El Bolsón. On a clear day you can see all the way to the volcanoes in neighbouring Chile.

Rio Azul
Raft the family-friendly, class II Rio Azul. Stop on a sheltered riverbank midway through the trip to snorkel and watch trout swimming through the transparent water.

MAMUSCHKA

Mitre 298, San Carlos de Bariloche, Río Negro;
www.mamuschka.com; +54 294-442-3294

◆ Tastings   ◆ Cafe
◆ Roastery   ◆ Shop

THINGS TO DO NEARBY

Lago Nahuel Huapi
This is Bariloche's key tourist attraction: a mythical mountain-ringed glacial lake with crystal-clear water spreading out from the city's edge.

Cerro Catedral
This mountain outside Bariloche is South America's top winter sports destination, with world-class ski facilities and superb summer hiking.

Cerro Tronador
The best way to appreciate Bariloche's majestic mountain surrounds is from atop the region's tallest regional peak, Cerro Tronador (3554m, or 11,660ft), with seven glaciers on its slopes.

El Bolsón
It's not just Bariloche making chocolate hereabouts: 120km (70 mi) south, this pretty town with a relaxed hippy vibe also obliges. Phenomenal cheeses and craft beers are also produced.

 'El chocolate mas rico' (the richest chocolate) is some statement to make in this Argentine lake district city that, thanks to an influx of sweets-savvy Swiss immigrants in the 19th century, is festooned with chocolate shops. But Mamuschka lives up to the claim. It is one of the longest-running chocolatiers on the Bariloche street Argentines endearingly call 'The Avenue of Chocolate Dreams', and the very mention of the name (Ma-musch-ka) makes mouths water and eyes glaze over nostalgically across Latin America. With a bright red-and-gold old-timey sweet shop vibe, its chocolate store is an enticingly presented wonderland with a try-before-you-buy policy that keeps the place constantly crowded.

Spring for their *corazón de avellana*, a rapturous hazelnut homage of a choc stuffed with Patagonian hazelnuts and their bestselling Mamusch cream, a chocolate spread

itself concocted with Peruvian or Ecuadorian chocolate and, yep, tons of hazelnuts. Then again, the *timbal de dulce de leche*, layered with the caramel-like spread Argentina is famous for, is a big temptation. Their cafe is filled with temptations, in fact; here you can slurp on one of the thickest hot chocolates your palate ever will ever encounter, and at their ice cream shop just down the road, almost all the flavours have some inclusion of chocolate. Now do you see why the bonbon buffs are queuing up?

BELIZE

How to order chocolate in the local language? English is the official language of Belize, but if you're doing any of the chocolate tours down south you'll impress the heck out of any Maya you meet by greeting them with a hearty *Yo'os* (Hello).

Signature chocolate experience? You can mix luxury with chocolate at Toledo's Cotton Tree Lodge, which also has its own chocolate kitchen.

What to do besides eat chocolate? Toledo's annual Cacao festival is a multi-day celebration of cacao and Maya culture held during the third week in May amidst the ruins of the ancient Maya city of Lubaantun.

Do: While cacao beans were used as currency by the ancient Maya, modern Maya prefer cash. Luckily, most Belizeans will accept Belize dollars or American ones.

Belize, considered the jewel of Central America by its people, has lured travellers for decades with its alluring jungles, pristine beaches and super-laid back vibes. Before Belize was Belize – or even British Honduras – it was part of the vibrant Maya civilization, to whom chocolate was food, medicine and sacrament. So it's hardly a surprise that chocolate tourism has been added to the already ample list of reasons to visit Belize. Being both a noted producer of cacao beans and home to a number of amazing bean-to-bar chocolate producers, Belize offers a wide variety of choco-late-themed experiences ranging from tasting to farm tours. A warm country (in both temperature and temperament), your best bet in Belize is to do your chocolate sampling as close to the source as possible.

In Placencia Peninsula, don't miss out on trying the many varieties offered by local chocolate powerhouse Goss Chocolate. If you find yourself in Ambregris Caye's San Pedro, Belize Chocolate Company offers handmade dark and milk chocolate confections under the Kakaw brand that are as delicious as they are hard to find off the island itself. Truly dedicated chocola-tourists will want to head south to Belize's southernmost (and least visited) district, Toledo. In addition to being the nation's primary cacao growing region, Toledo is also home to a number of unique family-owned farms offering Maya-culture-infused tasting tours, cooking lessons and more. Toledo farmers offering tours include Agouti Cacao Farm in San Pedro Columbia and Ixcacao Maya Belizean Chocolate in San Felipe, while Toledo's Maya Mountain Cacao is a Belizean bean leader.

GOSS CHOCOLATE

Placencia Rd, Seine Bright, Placencia;
www.goss-chocolate.com; 501-523-3544

◆ Tastings   ◆ Shop
◆ Roastery

THINGS TO DO NEARBY

Playa Placencia
The Placencia Penisula
is home to Belize's
best beaches (no small
distinction), which visitors
can stroll and swim to their
heart's content.

Chill in Placencia Town
Placencia has everything
you'd want in a Caribbean
beach town, including bars,
restaurants, live music,
soccer fields, yoga studios
and more.

Lola Delgado's Studio
The renowned Belizean
artist (whose artwork
graces various Goss
products) Lola Delgado is
a Seine Bight native. A visit
to her studio lets you see
(and even purchase) her
paintings up close.

Garifuna Music
Distinctive Garifuna beats
are a highlight of Seine
Bight village in the centre
of Placencia Peninsula;
drum maker Bobby offers
lessons in the traditional
local music. Hopkins also
has a drumming centre.

Visit any grocery store in Belize and chances are good that you'll notice shiny foil bars in the refrigerator bearing the label Goss: Organically Grown. These lovingly crafted chocolate bars all come from one small family-operated enterprise on Belize's super-laid-back Placencia peninsula. Operating since 2007, Goss makes their chocolate from Fair Trade certified, 100% organically grown Belizean cacao beans, Belizean cane sugar, natural whole vanilla bean (minus artificial flavours, fillers or colours) and not much else. The result is an authentically Belizean bar with a deep, rich flavour that's as warm and inviting as the Caribbean nation itself. You'll find a variety of Goss products on offer in stores and coffee shops in the country, including varying shades ranging from milk chocolate to extra-dark, as well as truffles, drinking chocolates and a few other specialty items. Family-owned Goss is about as local as local can get (even the artwork on their posters and packaging comes from local Belizean artists such as Lola Delgado), making the chance to try Goss Chocolate one more reason among many to book a trip to Belize. During the cooler months they do a brisk mail order business for folks not lucky enough to make it to Belize for their wholesale open office hours each Wednesday.

BRAZIL

How to ask for hot chocolate in the local language? *Um chocolate quente cremoso, por favor.*

Signature chocolate flavours? *Suco de cacau* (a refreshing juice made from the cacao fruit).

What to order with your chocolate? *Pudim de leite* (a flan-like dessert).

Don't: Don't pass up a homemade *brigadeiro* (a truffle-like sweet made of cocoa powder and condensed milk) when dining at someone's home.

A little over a century ago, Brazil was one of the leading producers of chocolate in the world. Then in the 1980s disaster struck. A fungus known as *Vassoura de Bruxa* (Witches Broom Disease) hit the region and destroyed the vast majority of the cacao plantations in Bahia – home to more than 80% of Brazil's chocolate production. Many farms never recovered, and the collapse of cacao production had widespread ramifications – devastating the local economy and leaving some 250,000 workers without jobs.

Things started to turn around at the dawn of the 21st century, with the rise of small growers and bespoke chocolate makers more interested in quality than the budget cacao and chocolate of generations past. Brazilian consumers also drove the rise of a homegrown market, nurturing a small industry of entrepreneurs. Today there are more than 40 bean-to-bar producers in Brazil, and pioneering chocolatiers now gather annually in São Paulo for the Bean to Bar Chocolate Week, an event that first launched in 2018.

Cacao production in Brazil is also deeply connected to the issue of sustainability. In the Amazon, depleted lands previously cleared for cattle ranching are currently being replanted with cacao (*cacau* in Portuguese) in an unlikely partnership between ranchers and environmental organizations like the Nature Conservancy. As these plants require shade, taller native tree species – such as mahogany and ipe – are also planted, helping to bring biodiversity back to a barren landscape. Over 1700 sq km (656 sq mi) of degraded cattle pastures have already been transformed into cacao plantations, with many more on the horizon.

From left: © agustavop / Getty Images; © marchello74 / Getty Images

CHOCOLATE Q

Garcia d'Ávila 149, Ipanema, Rio de Janeiro;
www.chocolateq.com; +55 21-2274-1001

◆ Tastings ◆ Classes ◆ Cafe
◆ Roastery ◆ Shop ◆ Transport

THINGS TO DO NEARBY

Gilson Martins
Rio's iconic landscapes are transformed into eye-catching silhouettes emblazoned on handbags, wallets and other accessories at Martins' flagship store in Ipanema. *www.gilsonmartins.com.br*

Lagoa
The saltwater lagoon just above Ipanema makes a fine spot for a jog or bike ride along the extensive paths. Waterfront outdoor bars like Palaphita Kitch make a memorable setting for a drink.

Zazá Bistrô Tropical
Dine on creative Brazilian fare with Asian accents at this art-filled villa one block from the beach in Ipanema. *www.zazabistro.com.br*

Polis Sucos
You can't leave Brazil without trying one of its myriad tropical juices (like cacau!) at a juice bar. This one is is a local institution. *www.polissucos.com.br*

Best known for its captivating beachfront, Rio's upscale neighbourhood of Ipanema is also home to one of Brazil's best chocolate shops, run by Samantha Aquim. Stepping inside is like entering a tiny jewel box — albeit one deeply imprinted with the heavenly scent of rich, dark chocolate. The shelves are lined with beautifully packaged bars, which feature colourful illustrations of the flora and fauna found in the Atlantic rainforest (think bromeliads, imperial palms, toucans, armadillos). You can stop in for a one-hour guided tasting, with knowledgeable staff describing the chocolate-making process and the origin of the beans as you sample your way through Q's premium delicacies, starting at *suave* (soft, aka 55% pure cacao) and ending at *intenso* (intense indeed at 85% pure cacao that's a must for dark chocolate-loving purists).

The family-run Chocolate Q sources its beans from a single, environmentally conscious grower – the Fazenda Leolinda, located in pristine *Mata Atlântica* (Atlantic Rainforest) in Bahia. Just like a fine wine, these chocolates embody 'terroir', with subtle notes of tropical fruit (like dried banana and jackfruit) in every bite. Q lets the chocolate speak for itself: there's no added flavourings: just pure cocoa, cocoa butter and sugar. While you'll want to take home a few artfully wrapped chocolate bars, be sure to order a decadent hot chocolate from the on-site cafe.

CANADA

How to ask for hot chocolate in the local language? *Chocolat chaud* in Québec, hot chocolate elsewhere.
Signature chocolate flavours? Anything with maple syrup.
What to order with your chocolate? A Nanaimo bar, a uniquely Canadian dessert that layers custard and chocolate on a graham cracker crust.
Don't: Mix chocolate and *poutine*.

Canada may not be widely known for its chocolate – yet – but just as microbrewing, craft distilling, third-wave coffee and the local food movement have swept across this vast country, so too has the artisanal chocolate trend. Canada got its commercial chocolate start in 1873, when Ganong Bros Ltd launched in St Stephen, New Brunswick, claiming the title of Canada's oldest independently operated chocolate company. Chocolate moved west in the 1880s, when Charles and Leah Rogers opened a grocery store in Victoria, British Columbia, initially selling chocolates that they imported from San Francisco, before Charles began making his own. The company that became Rogers Chocolates still produces the 'Victoria Cream' created by Charles decades ago.

These days, you'll find chocolatiers in all the major Canadian cities selling bean-to-bar chocolates – many sourcing beans from small-batch, organic farms – and crafting bonbons in a range of creative flavours, in addition to small makers in towns in every province. Locally produced maple syrup and honey are popular additions, as are blueberries, raspberries, cherries and other fruits grown during the long days of the northern summers.

Hot chocolate has always been popular, particularly after ice skating or skiing in winter, and rich espresso-style chocolate shots are appearing on cafe menus. Chocolate is also a well-loved ice cream flavour in Canada, with artisanal producers offering ever-darker blends. Perhaps because of the country's francophone roots, you'll find bakeries selling *pain au chocolat* (chocolate-filled croissants) in many areas. And now that Canada has legalised cannabis consumption, the next new trend may be chocolates infused with marijuana.

THE CHOCOLATE PROJECT

Victoria Public Market, 1701 Douglas St, Victoria;
www.chocolateproject.ca; no phone

- ◆ Classes
- ◆ Shop
- ◆ Transport
- ◆ Tastings

David Mincey is passionate, even obsessive, about chocolate. His goal? To protect the world from industrial producers and help chocolate artisans around the globe earn a living wage. The owner of Victoria's Chocolate Project works directly with more than five dozen small bean-to-bar chocolate producers worldwide, many of whom he has visited in person. He brings their chocolates – more than 300 different bars – to his small stall inside the Victoria Public Market, where he'll eagerly talk your ear off about chocolate in any form. His most distinctive product might be the customised 'party packs' that he assembles for at-home chocolate tasting parties. Tell him your budget and the kind of chocolates you prefer; he'll put together a selection and provide tasting tips.

THINGS TO DO NEARBY

The Pedaler

See, and sample, Victoria on a guided cycling tour, from the 'Eat. Drink. Pedal' rolling food fest, to the 'Hoppy Hour Ride' exploring Victoria's craft beer scene.
www.thepedaler.ca

Royal BC Museum

Trace British Columbia's natural and cultural history at this well-designed museum, which has particularly strong exhibits about the region's indigenous peoples.
www.royalbcmuseum.bc.ca

CHOCOLATE TOFINO

1180A Pacific Rim Hwy, Tofino;
www.chocolatetofino.com; +1 250-725-2526

◆ Shop ◆ Transport
◆ Cafe

 The motto at this tiny chocolate maker on Vancouver Island's west coast is 'save the whales – unless they're chocolate', a fitting maxim for a region known for its migrating cetaceans and popular whale-watching excursions. Naturally, among their small-batch handmade goodies, they make whale-shaped chocolates. You can watch the production process in their deliciously aromatic shop. Owners Kim and Cam Shaw relocated from Saskatchewan to the beach town of Tofino to surf and craft chocolate. You'll be glad they did when you sample their 'Island Flavours' trio:

a blackberry buttercream made from locally foraged berries, lavender truffle and wildflower honey ganache (with island-sourced honey). The extra dark 'Midnight Marauder' gelato is perfect for recovering from your adventures on the water.

THINGS TO DO NEARBY

Chesterman Beach
Take a picnic (or your chocolate) to this 2.7-km (1.7-mile) expanse of sand, a Pacific Ocean beach that's popular with surfers. Sunsets seen from here are especially epic.
www.tourismtofino.com

The Wolf in the Fog
Sip a craft cocktail and sample anything with local seafood at this second-floor bistro that serves some of Tofino's most creative dishes.
www.wolfinthefog.com

WILD SWEETS

12191 Hammersmith Way, Unit 2145, Richmond;
www.dcduby.com; +1 604-765-9507

◆ Roastery ◆ Classes ◆ Tastings
◆ Transport ◆ Shop ◆ Shop

Dominique and Cindy Duby are husband-and-wife pastry chefs and chocolatiers who go a little 'wild' with their creations, crafting one-of-a-kind chocolate designs in their workshop, tucked into an industrial park in the Vancouver suburb of Richmond, near historical Steveston. Several times a year, they host 'Meet The Makers' experiences, where you can taste chocolate at different stages (from roasted cacao beans to cocoa liquor to single origin bars); sample pastries, ice cream, and other chocolate confections; and pair chocolates with wine, beer and spirits.

The rest of the year, they open their 'Atelier' Factory Store to visitors for limited hours (generally on Friday, Saturday and Sunday), where you can see what they're up to. Be sure to sample the bean-to-bar chocolates, crafted in-house.

THINGS TO DO NEARBY

International Buddhist Temple
Recover from your chocolate rush with a stroll through the ornate halls of worship and serene gardens at this Chinese Buddhist temple.
www.buddhisttemple.ca

Mama's Dumplings and Coffee
This Chinese eatery specialises in Shanghai-style pork buns, *xiao long bao* (soup dumplings), plus espresso drinks.
www.mamasdumpling.com

GANONG CHOCOLATE MUSEUM & GANONG CHOCOLATIER

73 Milltown Blvd. St Stephen; ganong.com,
www.chocolatemuseum.ca; +1 506-466-7848

◆ Tastings   ◆ Shop
◆ Classes

Forget your newfangled passion fruit-pink-peppercorn-matcha truffles and get back to the classics at this old-fashioned chocolatery. Ganong Brothers is the oldest chocolate company in Canada, opened in 1873 in the amiable New Brunswick border town of St Stephen. The associated museum is housed in the former Ganong factory. It walks you through Ganong's cocoa-dusted history, with antique roasting machines, vintage candy boxes and interactive displays on the chocolate manufacturing process. Taste Ganong legends like the 1920 Pal-o-Mine peanut fudge chocolate bar or the oddly addictive 1885 Chicken Bones, oblongs of crunchy cinnamon hard candy filled with chocolate 'marrow'. They're a time-honoured Christmas stocking stuffer hereabouts. The gift store abounds with peanut clusters, chocolate-dipped cherries and caramels.

THINGS TO DO NEARBY

Ganong Nature Park
Once owned by the Ganong family, this 140-hectare (350 acre) park is located outside the town limits of St Stephen, overlooking the cross of the St Croix River and St Croix Island.
ganongnaturepark.com

St Andrews By-The-Sea
Half an hour from St Stephen is this refined resort town, one of North America's oldest, with elegant inns overlooking the Bay of Fundy.
standrewsbythesea.ca

ALICJA CONFECTIONS

829 Bank St, Ottawa; www.alicjaconfections.com;
+1 613-884-5864

◆ Tastings   ◆ Classes   ◆ Cafe
◆ Roastery   ◆ Shop   ◆ Transport

What's the best kind of postcard? A chocolate postcard, of course! Alicja Buchowicz, who owns this cheerful chocolate shop in Canada's capital city, not only makes some of Canada's most vibrantly coloured bonbons, she also packages her chocolate bars in sweetly designed, ready-to-mail 'postcards'. Buchowicz began making chocolate as a hobby, and when one day she set a bar on a stack of envelopes, inspiration struck. What if you could package chocolate bars in envelopes and actually send them through the mail? The postcard bar was born. Opened in Ottawa's Glebe neighbourhood in 2017, Alicja Confections now sells more than two dozen varieties of postcards, from the Hippy bar with goji berries, cacao nibs and chia seeds, to the Nicholas, a milk chocolate bar with potato chips, named after Alicja's husband. The shop even sells stamps.

THINGS TO DO NEARBY

Parliament Hill
The must-see attraction in Canada's capital is the stately national parliament. A multiyear restoration is in progress, but you can still book a free tour online. *visit.parl.ca*

Rideau Canal
Stroll along the tree-lined banks of North America's oldest continuously operating canal. In winter, it freezes to become the world's largest ice-skating rink.

SOMA CHOCOLATEMAKER

32 Tank House Ln, Toronto;
www.somachocolate.com; +1 416-815-7662
◆ Tastings   ◆ Classes
◆ Transport ◆ Shop

THINGS TO DO NEARBY

The Distillery District
SOMA's flagship shop
is located in the historic
district – once home
to the Gooderham &
Worts Distillery – that
now houses galleries,
cafes and shops. *www.
thedistillerydistrict.com*

St Lawrence Market
Formerly Toronto's City
Hall, this 19th-century
building morphed into a
jam-packed food market.
One vendor, Carousel
Bakery, sells a classic
peameal sandwich. *www.
stlawrencemarket.com*

Underpass Park
This outdoor gallery of
murals, sculptures and
street art was created
beneath a web of roadway
overpasses, east of the
Distillery District. *www.
explorewaterfrontoronto.
ca/project/underpass-park*

Sugar Beach
Fanciful pink umbrellas
draw Torontonians to
this urban beach fronting
Lake Ontario, named for a
nearby sugar factory. *www.
explorewaterfrontoronto.
ca/project/canadas-sugar-
beach*

Back when few people, at least in Canada, were talking about bean-to-bar or small batch chocolate making, Cynthia Leung, a former architect, and David Castellan, a former pastry chef, immersed themselves in the world of chocolate. Inspired by Maricel Presilla's book *The New Taste of Chocolate*, the pair began researching the cacao world with the goal of producing very small batches of chocolate with cacao sourced from around the globe. In 2003, they launched SOMA Chocolatemaker in Toronto and released their first single-origin bar.

At their flagship shop in Toronto's Distillery District (and at their branch at 443 King Street West), you can now enjoy the fruits of the partners' extended research – in truffles, drinking chocolates, cookies, gelato and a selection of microbatch chocolates – or book a guided chocolate tasting

to learn more. And stay tuned: SOMA is launching a new 'Cacao Bean Lab' in their Parkdale chocolate factory, where they'll offer more tastings and other chocolate workshops.

In the meantime, try one of their small-batch, bean-to-bar chocolates, like Guasare, a 70% dark bar crafted from cacao that was grown on four small farms in Venezuela's Rosario de Perijá region – one more delicious result of Leung and Castellan's chocolate obsession.

AVANAA CHOCOLAT

309 Rue Gounod, Montreal, QC; www.avanaa.ca;
+1 514-618-4305

◆ Tastings   ◆ Classes   ◆ Transport
◆ Roastery   ◆ Shop

Catherine Goulet named her business for an Inuktitut word meaning 'coming from the North', when she became one of Canada's first bean-to-bar chocolate crafters. The former geologist says she fell for local craft chocolates while working in Peru and then spent a year travelling the globe, exploring the world of chocolate, before opening her own shop back in Montreal.

She sources her cacao from small producers in Ecuador, the Dominican Republic and Colombia, and handles the entire process, from sorting and roasting to grinding, tempering and packing, in her Villeray workshop. She's happy to tell you all about her products' origins and flavour profiles as you sample the results. Goulet's current top pick? The Crunch Bar – creamy dark chocolate with cacao nibs.

THINGS TO DO NEARBY

Marché Jean-Talon
Opened in 1933, this year-round, open-air market hall is one of North America's largest, purveying produce, cheeses, baked goods and prepared foods. *www. marchespublics-mtl.com*

Bar St-Denis
This cool late-night hangout near Jean-Talon Market pairs a long list of wine, beer and cocktails, with a short menu of inventive small plates. *www.barstdenis.com*

CHOCOLATERIE DES PÈRES TRAPPISTES DE MISTASSINI

100 Route des Trappistes, Dolbeau-Mistassini; www.chocolateriedesperes.com; +1 418-276-1122

◆ Food   ◆ Classes   ◆ Cafe
◆ Roastery ◆ Shop   ◆ Transport

In the wooded countryside above Lac Saint-Jean, in the Saguenay region northwest of Quebec City, a group of monks has been running a chocolate factory since the 1940s. Their specialty is a seasonal one – chocolate-covered blueberries produced only between July and September when the region's fresh berries are harvested. Saguenay is so noted for its blueberries that local residents are nicknamed *les bluets,* and a regional cycling route that takes you past this chocolate maker is called *La Veloroute des Bluets*. The monks and their staff here produce chocolate bars, chocolate-covered cranberries and other sweets year-round, which you can purchase in the shop on the monastery grounds. But try to time your visit for blueberry season to sample their berry sweets.

THINGS TO DO NEARBY

Parc National de la Pointe-Taillon
This pleasant park on nearby Lac Saint-Jean has sandy beaches, extensive cycling and hiking trails and campgrounds. *www.sepaq.com/pq/pta*

Musée Amérindien de Mashteuiatsh
In an indigenous community on Lac Saint-Jean, this museum features the cultures of the local Pekuakamiulnuatsh people and other Quebec First Nations. *www.cultureilnu.ca*

ÉTAT DE CHOC

6466 Blvd St-Laurent, Montreal; www.etatdechoc.com;
+1 514-657-6466

◆ Tastings   ◆ Classes   ◆ Cafe
◆ Roastery   ◆ Shop   ◆ Transport

 'I never thought I would own a chocolate factory', says État de Choc founder Maud Gaudreau, a former business consultant who saw that consumers were becoming increasingly 'sensitive to ethical and environmental causes, and at the same time passionately gourmet'. Determined to offer ethically sourced artisanal chocolates, Gaudreau launched this high-style Little Italy chocolate shop in 2018. État de Choc sells their own chocolates (including some with unusual ingredients like corn and chili, hops or Sri Lankan curry), along with bean-to-bar varieties from producers around the world. Shoppers can refresh with hot chocolate in winter and iced chocolate or cacao juice mocktails during the warmer months. For serious aficionados, they offer tasting workshops and make-your-own chocolate classes. The must-try? The signature 'bean-to-bonbon' Grands Crus Lingots.

THINGS TO DO NEARBY

Alambika
Calling itself a toy store for cocktail lovers, this boutique stocks artisanal bitters, syrups and shrubs, plus high-quality glassware and other bar essentials.
www.alambika.ca

Le Butterblume
When you're ready for brunch, head down the Main for inventive morning meals, from housemade granola with kumquats and puffed quinoa to a zucchini tartine. *www. lebutterblume.com*

CARIBBEAN

How to order a hot chocolate in the local language? With hot weather year round, you might skip the hot drinks here.
Signature chocolate flavours? Nutmeg; tropical fruits.
What to order with your chocolate? Rum for the of-age.
Don't: Limit yourself to visiting one island.

With cacao first widely used just to the west over the water in Central America, it's no surprise that chocolate crops thrive across the islands of the Caribbean. The sunshine and rich, volcanic soil on many islands is ideal for nurturing the trees, a fact readily exploited by the colonial powers that historically tussled over the region. The Spaniards first planted cacao in Trinidad in 1525. From the late 16th century, as European demand for the crop grew, more slaves were shipped over from Africa to the West Indies to work the fields and satisfy a distant continent's growing chocolate cravings.

The abolition of slavery hit the profit margins of growers, and the exportation of cacao trees to the likes of India and Africa gradually reduced the importance of the Caribbean plantations, eventually resulting in a crash in prices and dramatic drop in cocoa production in the region. But the 21st century is seeing a resurgence, this time in local hands. As the world starts to care more about food quality and provenance, smaller-scale producers are transforming the industry, looking to both create premium products and to do well by their workers. A more artisanal, full bean-to-bar approach is proving beneficial for everyone, from grower to eventual eater.

The amount of cacao coming out of the Caribbean now is still small, but is high-standard – indeed, most of the world's best chocolate originates here. Caribbean farmers mainly grow Criollo and Trinitario cacao trees, which produce fine cacao noted for its sophisticated flavour palette: fruity, floral, herbal, nutty, woody, caramel. While the region may only produce around 5% of the world's total cocoa, it produces the vast majority of its fine stuff. The challenge is to raise awareness of what fine cacao is, and to persuade consumers to enjoy chocolate in a more engaged way – and pay more for quality – to drive an industry capable of sustaining future farming generations.

Another challenge is the diversity of the Caribbean, with different islands pursuing the growth of their chocolate sectors for different reasons. On some islands it is more of an agritourism product, tied in with attracting visitors with tours and tasting experiences; in Grenada, Barbados and Jamaica, it's a way of empowering women farmers; in Trinidad – arguably the major industry player – chocolate is seen as a potential way to replace the country's fast-diminishing gas and oil revenues. But, despite this, over the past few years, Caribbean countries have begun collaborating in

5 TOP LOCAL SPOTS

1. AGAPEY, BARBADOS

The Agapey Chocolate Factory in Bridgetown uses Caribbean beans and Bajan cane sugar to make its bars; its Mount Gay Rum Caramel is infused with local rum. Tours available. *www.agapey.com*

2. JOUVAY, GRENADA

Working out of an 18th-century rum distillery, Jouvay uses Grenadian cacao to produce six bars, including one with Grenadian nutmeg. *www.jouvaychocolate.com*

3. ANTILLIA BREWING COMPANY, ST LUCIA

This craft brewery produces an award-winning Chocolate Stout, made using local fresh-roasted organic cocoa nibs. *www.facebook.com/antilliabrewing*

4. TOBAGO ESTATE, TRINIDAD & TOBAGO

Tobago Estate's Laura 45% Dark Milk bar – with its hints of honey, nuts and toffee – has scooped numerous International Chocolate Awards. *www.tobagococoa.com*

5. EMERALD ESTATE, ST LUCIA

Cacao beans grown on this estate are hand-harvested, slow roasted and stone ground to produce premium bars with intense flavours, ranging from 60% to 92% cocoa. *www.emeraldchocolate.com*

ASHLEY PARASRAM
founder and CEO of the Trinidad & Tobago Fine Cocoa Company

'The origin, the terroir, the genetics, the history and the heritage – with all these components, Caribbean chocolate has some fantastic stories to tell.'

order to jointly put Caribbean chocolate back on the map.

For instance, in the past chocolate was rarely produced here; rather, the beans were shipped off to be processed elsewhere. Now, companies such as the Trinidad & Tobago Fine Cocoa Company and the Grenada Chocolate Company are completing the whole bean-to-bar process on-island, directly connecting growers and producers, and keeping the value of the product in the country. The result is a mix of extremely high-quality chocolate being produced in state-of-the-art facilities to be used in the kitchens of Michelin-starred chefs as well as more rustic, small-batch operations making great-tasting bars that you can buy in the shade of the cacao grove from which they were created. Ultimately though, it's win-win: the farmers are feeling the financial benefits while chocolate aficionados are discovering the full taste potential of the great Caribbean bean.

BOIS COTLETTE

Roseau, Dominica; www.boiscotlette.com;
+1 767-440-8805

◆ Food   ◆ Tours   ◆ Tastings

THINGS TO DO NEARBY

Pointe Baptiste Estate
This guesthouse near Calibishie also has a small family-run chocolate factory making bars spiced with flavours such as ginger, nutmeg, hot pepper and cloves.
www.pointebaptiste.com

Banana Lama Eco Villa
This rustic-chic riverside hideaway is ideal for relaxing amidst nature. Desserts often involve chocolate, which owner Melissa makes herself.
www.bananalamaecovilla.com

Secret Bay
Stay in a villa at this boutique eco-resort and book a cooking class to learn to create dishes from sustainably caught lionfish or edible flowers from the garden.
secretbay.dm

Cocoa Cottages
Aptly named, this artsy guesthouse is renowned for its rainforest views and its homemade chocolate, made using organic cacao from its own garden and local growers.
www.cocoacottages.com

Bois Cotlette is the oldest surviving estate on Dominica – people have been producing cocoa, coffee and sugar cane here for around 300 years. Though when American business exec Jonathan Lehrer first found the place in 2011, it was a little worse for wear. First settled in the 1730s by a French family from Martinique, Bois Cotlette was still owned by descendants of the original settlers, and had been largely neglected. But, since Lehrer decided to swap the corporate world to turn farmer and chocolatier, the estate has been back in business. As well as growing his own food and generating his own green energy, Lehrer is growing organic cacao. Chocolate tours explore the site's legacy of cacao cultivation; there's also the chance to process a pod into a bar, with plenty of tastings and a focus on the differences in flavour between artisanal and mass-produced chocolate. Most fascinating, though, is exploring the site itself. Because the estate is tucked into a volcanic valley, sheltered from the worst of the tropical weather, its 18th-century buildings and layout remained relatively well intact, allowing Lehrer to restore the place as authentically as possible. Archaeologists have made some fascinating finds – including a whole slave village – which provide unique insights into the complex history of chocolate making.

GRENADA CHOCOLATE COMPANY

Upper Hermitage, St Patrick Parish;
www.grenadachocolate.com; +1 473-442-0050

◆ Roastery   ◆ Tours
◆ Shop

The Grenada Chocolate Company is a leading light in ethical – and delicious – chocolate production. In 1999, an Organic Cocoa Farmers' and Chocolate-Makers' Cooperative was set up by visionary American Mott Green and Grenadian farmers Doug Browne and Edmond Brown. It proved a game-changer, demonstrating that it was possible to produce chocolate on Grenada while also benefitting local people. Now, more than 80 hectares (200 acres) of organic cacao farms are part of the cooperative, and farmers are paid around 65% more than market price for their crop. The company's success has led to the island becoming a real hub for the sweet stuff, inspiring other artisan chocolatiers and, in 2014, the founding of the Grenada Chocolate Festival, held each May in St George's.

THINGS TO DO NEARBY

Belmont Estate
Founded in the 16th century as a coffee and sugar plantation, this organic farm now produces chocolate in its own factory and runs bean-to-bar tours. *www.belmontestate.net*

Crayfish Bay Estate
An organic cocoa estate, Crayfish Bay produces small-batch single-source bars; there's a rustic guesthouse too. *www.facebook.com/ crayfishbaygrenada*

House of Chocolate
This mini-museum, store and cafe in capital Georgetown stocks the island's top choc producers, and gives some backstory on cacao farming. *www. houseofchocolategnd.com*

True Blue Bay
Every week this resort hosts rum and chocolate tasting at its Dodgy Dock Bar, a chance to try samples and learn about cocoa production and distillation. *www.truebluebay.com*

Make the lush, hilly drive to the Grenada Chocolate Company's bonbon shop (open weekdays and Sundays), which shows a video about the chocolate-making process as well as selling handmade truffles and award-winning bars – a collection of dark chocolate varieties, including the 71% Salty-Licious, made with Caribbean sea salt, and the punchy 100% pure cocoa, so strong it's almost savoury. Tours of the small factory (with its solar-powered machinery) are possible too, so you can see where the beans are fermented.

GINA'S CHOCOLATE TRUFFLES

Goodwood Park, Diego Martin, Port of Spain;
www.facebook.com/ginaschocolates; +1 868-794-6202

◆ Tastings   ◆ Shop

THINGS TO DO NEARBY

Ariapita Avenue
'De Avenue' is the place to eat and 'lime' (that's slang for hang out, for non-natives) in Port of Spain: pick up a Trini gyro (stuffed flatbread) from a stall or eat creole at Veni Mangé.

Santa Cruz Green Market
Just north of Port of Spain, this community Saturday market is a great place to pick up organic Trini produce, fresh fish and local crafts. *www.greenmarketsantacruz.com*

Trinidadian-Singaporean law graduate Gina Hardy was high-flying in finance before getting sucked into the sweet stuff. Having completed her Advanced Chocolatier Training in Belgium, she now makes show-stopping truffles and slabs using 100% local, single-origin Trinitario cacao beans and employing some unusual flavours to create what she calls her 'little drops of heaven'. To make her decadent truffles, she melts the chocolate and mixes in ingredients such as local rum and coffee, toasted coconut, nuts, fruits and spices. She's created more than 50 flavours to date: her Taj Truffles combine pistachio and cardamom, while Passion Unleashed is a 12-flavour collection that sees passion fruit combined with everything from rose and banana to soursop and prosecco. She's doing something right: Gina's Truffles have been relished by a range of VIPs, including Queen Elizabeth II and President Barack Obama.

TRINIDAD & TOBAGO FINE COCOA COMPANY

Hilton Trinidad, Lady Young Rd, Port of Spain;
www.ttfinecocoa.com; +1 868-225-2182

◆ Cafe ◆ Tours
◆ Shop

The amount of cocoa produced annually in Trinidad & Tobago has dropped by 98% in the past century. But the Trinidad & Tobago Fine Cocoa Company (TTFCC) is looking to reverse the decline, with a focus on sustainability and quality. Trinidad cultivates 100-plus distinct varieties of Trinitario cacao, which the TTFCC uses to create premium chocolate as complex as wine; their aim is to deliver both better flavours for consumers and higher margins for local farmers. TTFCC works with several plantations; at the 200-hectare (494-acre) La Reunion Estate it has a modern processing factory that produces award-winning chocolate; some is even shipped to Harrods. Tours can be arranged. The best place to buy on-island is The Chocolate Box at the Hilton, which sells handmade TTFCC truffles in chai-spiced rum, pineapple and piña colada flavours and holds tastings.

THINGS TO DO NEARBY

Ortinola Estate
The TTFCC works with this 18th-century estate, which runs hands-on cocoa and chocolate experiences, where you can try making your own bars. Visits must be pre-booked.
www.ortinola.com

Cocoa Research Centre, University of the West Indies
Learn all about chocolate by touring the International Cocoa Genebank, one of the world's most varied collections of cacao trees.
www.sta.uwi.edu/cru

CHILE

How to shop for chocolate in the local language? *¿Me muestras los chocolates?* (Can you show me some chocolates?)

Signature chocolate flavour? *Alfajores con manjar* (chocolate dipped cookies filled with caramel).

What to order with your chocolate? *Una caja de regalo* (a gift box).

Do: When buying handmade chocolates, it's important to store them in a cool place.

Chile is a curious country, long and lithe as a runner's leg that stretches from the Atacama Desert to Cape Horn, the last windblown stop before Antarctica. This narrow ribbon is bordered on one side by the Andes mountain range and the Pacific Ocean on the other. This unique geography means that wherever you go, you will find mountains to climb and waters to explore, making Chile the destination in South America for outdoor adventure. Of course, it's easy to work up an appetite. No surprise that Chileans also nurture a voracious sweet tooth.

Chocolate culture is new to the country. Long addicted to hefty Nestlé bars, the local populace has finally started to acquire a taste for the finer stuff, thanks in part to economic and cultural changes. Enter the gourmet market for artisan chocolate, finally catching up to Chile's renowned winemaking. The trend has spread from the savvy capital of Santiago to Puerto Varas, a waterfront resort town in the heart of the Lakes District.

Puerto Varas, population 25,000, now boasts as many gourmet chocolate shops as gas stations. Perhaps choco-mania spread over the border from nearby Bariloche, Argentina, a Swiss-founded mountain hub that is well-known for its chocolaterías. Warming and sustaining, hot chocolate is also the perfect compliment to trekking in the temperate rainforest or braving the breeze plying through the Patagonian fjords on a ferry. It's no wonder that Chile leads South America when it comes to chocolate consumption.

CHOCOLATERIE DOMINIQUE

Walker Martinez 239 B, Puerto Varas;
chocolateriedominique.com; +56 9-9788-9532

◆ Tastings ◆ Classes ◆ Cafe
◆ Roastery ◆ Shop

THINGS TO DO NEARBY

Vicente Perez Rosales National Park
Chile's most-visited park has Osorno Volcano's perfect cone over Lake Llanquihue. Hike, ski or soak in hotsprings. *www. conaf.cl/parques/parque-nacional-vicente-perez-rosales*

Teatro del Lago
Take in a concert at this world-class performance hall built over Lake Llanquihue with outstanding acoustics; the fine craftsmanship features local beechwood.
www.teatrodellago.cl

Birds of Chile
Sustainable tour operators Birds of Chile can take you in Charles Darwin's footsteps for full-immersion nature experiences in the temperate rainforest.
www.birdschile.com

Mesa Tropera
This boisterous brewery jutting out over the lake is the perfect gathering spot any night of the week, with a casual menu and killer views, plus 12 taps of house-brewed craft beer.
www.mesatropera.cl

For Dominique Vergeynst, becoming a chocolatier meant choosing a profession that gave her happiness. A native of the Congo (DRC) and Belgium, she had come to Chile's Lakes District for love but ended up an entrepreneur, handcrafting the one product that the region lacked: chocolates made with local berries and Chilean hazelnuts, an exquisite, warming treat in the temperate rainforest. There's equal artistry in the packaging, with gorgeous chocolate gift boxes stencilled with naturalist drawings that are 100% biodegradable. Even the clear wrappers can be composted.

It has been eight years since Dominique started adapting recipes learned in a Belgian Chocolate Academy in a closet-sized kitchen. Now her shop with an open-view workshop has an adorable main street address and a faithful clientele. Knowing both the global market and Chile's rampant sweet tooth, she tries to nurture new tastes by offering samples ranging from 54% to 85% cacao. Travellers shouldn't skip the regional classic of alfajores, chocolate-dipped cookies filled with locally made *dulce de leche*. Dominique's signature chocolate is simply called 'Mmhh', a velvet ganache of praliné over a cinnamon biscuit dipped in milk chocolate. It's a scrumptious reward to fortify your intrepid exploration into the region of lakes and volcanoes.

COSTA RICA

How to ask for chocolate in the local language? *Chocolate por favor.*

Signature chocolate flavours? *Trinitario cacao.*

What to order with your chocolate? The strong international influence and growing cafe culture means you can have hot chocolate with French croissants, American brownies, or Italian biscotti.

Do: *Tour a cacao farm.*

'It was impossible to find any decent chocolate here when I first moved to Costa Rica in the late 90s', says Juliet Davey. 'Trees grew in the region but the only chocolate available was imported, cheap and unhealthy.'

Boy, how things have changed.

Now, in the towns around foggy, volcanic La Fortuna, you see 'Chocolate Tours' advertised everywhere. (We've chosen the coolest and longest-running one to feature.)

Even the pueblito of Bijagua, near the crystal blue waters of Tenorio. Guatuso, is home to ASOPAC (80 producers of cacao in Northern Costa Rica under the umbrella Asociación de Productores de Cacao Agro Ambientalistas en Costa Rica), who have spun off a consortium of female chocolate-treat-making businesswomen.

Sibú (named for the creator god in BriBri legend), a larger maker founded in 2008 by historian Julio Fernandez Amón and journalist George Soriano, has won awards for innovation and environmental ethics, while Nahua, founded in 2011, promises their Trinitario cacao beans produce 'a strong cacao flavour with a balanced combination of yellow fruits, red berries and caramel notes'.

At the heart of the national scene are small batch producers like Juliet Davey, aka Mamá Cacao, a one-woman whirlwind of chocolate-and-cacao related events, and Two Little Monkeys, a bean-to-bar producer in San Carlos (near Guatuso). Adding local tropical fruits and coconut to their mixes lends a Tico touch. Davey's homage to the magic cacao bean is the annual Salón de Cacao festival in Parrita. A lecture on Quetzalcoati and the mythological origins of cacao: why not? 'Costa Rican cacao is experiencing something of a rebirth and quickly gaining a reputation for its fine, bright and fruity flavour notes', says Davey.

DON OLIVO

Via 142, La Fortuna; www.donolivochocolatetour.com;
+506-2469-1371

◆ Tastings ◆ Classes ◆ Cafe
◆ Roastery ◆ Shop ◆ Transport

© travelview / Shutterstock

THINGS TO DO NEARBY

La Fortuna Pub
Just up the block from La Fortuna's main square, this pub offers flavourful home brews, satisfying bar food and occasional music. *www.facebook.com/lafortunapub*

Bike Arenal
Quality road bikes to hit the challenging ascents around the volcano. Available for day rentals, or explore the country more on one of their multi-day trips. *www.bikearenal.com*

Volcano & Hot Spring Hike
See the best of La Fortuna on an all-day hike; Red Lava Tours seem to have the most fun. You can also hike overnight all the way to Monteverde, camping out in the forest. *www.redlavatouristservicecenter.com*

Night Frog Tour at Arenal Oasis
A trained naturalist takes you along the trail to see the shimmering red eyes of nocturnal amphibians and maybe a few other creatures. *www.arenaloasis.com/frog-watching*

Getting greeted by a machete-bearing grandfather isn't everyone's idea of a Tico welcome. But consider it in context: before tourism sprung up like a multi-headed hydra to dominate Costa Rica's economy, Don Olivo and family ran a simple farm outside of La Fortuna. And they still do: three generations of growing fruits, spices, coffee, and – need we mention – cacao?

Seeing the cacao process from beginning to end isn't unique to Don Olivo's, but combining all these flavours and fragrances into one sensory-overload of a tour is: coffee, organic fruit, spice (vanilla, pepper and sugar cane with obligatory rum shot) all are flavour notes to the #1 attraction here, the chocolate tour. Many have copied the formula, but few have the authenticity of Don Olivo's earthy farm. (Did we mention the machete?)

The kid-friendly tour wends through trails that pass by 37 varieties of fruit trees, as well as a garden of medicinal plants. You'll taste the fruit of the vine (banana, mango, papaya), and the sugar cane juice as well as its distilled, devilish cousin, demon rum (!) and finish off with a cup of steaming cocoa which may remind you of the wispy fuma-roles puffing out of nearby Volcán Arenal.

MAMÁ CACAO

Parrita; www.facebook.com/pages/
category/Company/Mama-Cacao-Choco-
late-171192356238905; +506 8383-5910

◆ Tastings ◆ Classes
◆ Roastery

THINGS TO DO NEARBY

Oceans Unlimited Diving
Explore beneath the waves
with this environmentally
conscious, fully PADI-
certified team of divers.
*www.scubadivingcostarica.
com*

**Manuel Antonio
Surf School**
South of Quepos, attentive
surf instructors help you
ride waves confidently.
*manuelantoniosurfschool.
com*

**Manuel Antonio Parque
Nacional**
One of the country's most
beloved, and visited, parks,
replete with monkeys,
sloths, birds and nearby
waves beckoning.

Titi Canopy Tours
Named for the monkeys in
the treetop canopy, Titi is
close to downtown Quepos,
with rappelling and a
Tarzan swing, too.
www.titicanopytour.com

A trip to Juliet Davey's jungle-dense hillside Finca Alcazan, on the steamy Central Pacific coast, is nothing less than a religious experience. Davey, disappointed by the dearth of quality Costa Rican chocolate in the 1990s, found some cacao growing wild on a friend's *finca* (plantation) and took the initiative to cultivate it and harvest it herself, making rustic truffles and selling to local farmers markets, bakeries and hotels.

These days Juliet is better known as Mamá Cacao, spreading the gospel of Tico chocolate across the globe. She makes small batches of fine chocolate bars for the local market – you'll taste them here – as well as a range of truffles, cacao drinks and cacao beans.

Mamá Juliet hosts workshops, chocolate tastings and even three-course cacao-centred cuisine. You may arrive to a cacao ceremony by Alejandro Quiros of the Bagaci tribe, accompanied by traditional instruments (to the Bagaci, cacao represents lifeblood).

Her brownie is unique, and to die for: a cacao beans, eggs, black beans, coffee, vanilla and cardamom combo you might think fell from heaven, but really, just came out of her oven. During Mama Juliet's two-hour workshop you will delve into the legends, history and spiritual context of cacao, but most joyfully, you'll get your hands dirty making chocolate treats from raw, organic Costa Rican cacao.

CUBA

How to ask for hot chocolate in the local language? Un chocolate caliente por favor? or the more local 'un chorote por favor?'

Signature chocolate flavours? Sweetened 75% cacao

What to order with your chocolate? *Cucurucho* (Mashed coconut, honey, almonds and fruit wrapped in a palm tree leaf cone)

Don't: Expect luxurious foil-wrapped bars; this is raw cacao country

When Christopher Columbus' caravel sailed into the Bay of Baracoa, at the far-flung eastern end of Cuba more than 500 years ago, he noted the 'countless trees... beautiful palms... and greenness of the fields' in the ship's diary. Columbus would have spied Baracoa's mountains, lashed by rain and bathed in tropical sunshine, pregnant with banana, coffee, mango, jackfruit, papaya, coconut and cacao pods. These red, yellow and green Trinitario, Forastero and Criollo oval pods cocooning cacao beans sprout from the trees of Baracoa, the cocoa hub of Cuba.

First cultivated on the island in the 17th century, it was the breakfast drink of choice until the 19th century. Cacao is processed at the Rubén David Suárez Abella Chocolate Factory, nicknamed the Che Guevara Chocolate Factory, as the Argentine guerrilla opened the facility in 1963. Thanks to Catalan confectioner Quim Capdevila, who helped open a chocolate school in Havana in 2001, Cuba's chocolate fame is expanding. European companies began importing beans from Baracoa destined for the boutique chocolate stores of the smart boulevards of European capitals. Belgium's Marcolini was the first to market Cuban bars more than five years ago.

Hurricane Matthew in 2016 devastated Baracoa's plantations; in 2017 the government invested in machinery with European know-how in a bid to double output to 3000 tonnes a year. Baracoa's cacao co-operatives harvest twice a year and, post-Matthew, now sell 100% to the Cuban state. An annual chocolate festival is held in Jamal, near El Güirito, in March, and the annual Baracoa Valentine's Arte Erótico show indulges visitors with an erotic chocolate display.

FINCA LAS MUJERES

Carretera Baracoa-Yumurí, El Güirito, Baracoa;
+53 5479-3717

◆ Tastings   ◆ Classes
◆ Roastery   ◆ Cafe

THINGS TO DO NEARBY

Restaurant Baracoando
In chef Aristides Smith's home, Cuba's only vegan restaurant has fresh juices and cacao *cucurucho*. *www. facebook.com/pages/ category/RestaurantBara coando- 459318957748813*

La Cocina de Ortiz
Trained in the top restaurants in Havana Ineldis Ortiz now serves river shrimp, fresh juices and hot Baracoa chocolate brownies. *Calle Rafael Trejo 15, +53 5800 1237. No web.*

Bike the Atlantic Beaches
Hire bikes to explore the wild, palm-fringed beaches south of Baracoa, drinking piña coladas and devouring delicious BBQ fish en route on a self-powered pedal tour.

River Swims & Waterfalls
Find locals to take you to bathe in the cool waters of the area's River Duaba, splashing about in its waterfalls or at the black sand beach where the river becomes Playa Duaba.

Daisy Pelegrín Cobas, crowned the Queen of Cacao by Baracoa's historian, greets visitors at her family's Finca Las Mujeres buried in the rampant fertile greenery outside Cuba's oldest city. At the pale blue farm house, backing on to a 15-hectare (37-acre) organic cacao plantation, gregarious Daisy drops copious chocolate facts, and never misses a chance to tease her male visitors about the natural Viagra inherent in chocolate! Settling down on hideback chairs around Daisy's table – stacked with unvarnished chocolate bars, silver wrapped baubles, petite bonbons and what appear to be brown tennis balls – Daisy explains how her banana-plant-shaded beans-in-pods make their way to chocolate bars. Visitors tuck in to her hyperlocal cacao treats that echo ancient culinary traditions, sipping *cucurucho*, a thick mix of cacao, coconut milk, cinnamon and

honey, thickened by banana flour, a nourishing drink which has fuelled farmers' lives in eastern Cuba for generations. Then snap off a chunk of her rustic chocolate bar made from Criollo, Forastero and Trinitario beans. Daisy picks up the heavy ball of compacted cacao, a feature in every Baracoa kitchen, and grates it before offering her highlight – her bonbons – a delicious confection of squishy banana and grated plantain encased in a delicate dollop of cacao and sugar.

ECUADOR

How to ask for a cocoa farm in the local language?
Donde hay una granja de cacao?

Signature chocolate flavours? Look for chocolate made from the Arriba Nacional bean.

What to order with your chocolate? In the highlands, the ubiquitous *bizcocho*, a dry, somewhat buttery biscuit, is de rigueur. Also favoured is dunking a white cheese straight into your cup and eating it after, or simply dipping bread.

Do: Make sure to try the local beans.

Romantics couldn't do much better than Ecuador, a world-leading producer of cut roses and high-grade cacao. No wonder: cacao has its origins in the Amazon, and archaeological evidence of it on remnants of pottery more than 5000 years old have been uncovered in southern

parts of Ecuador. Once the world's biggest exporter of cacao, Ecuador is back in the game as a producer of both cacao, and increasingly, chocolate itself. Although it's been surpassed by West Africa and Indonesia in quantity – it's now just seventh in total world production – the quality of the aromatic strain here (the 'arriba' or 'nacional' bean, which varies in flavour depending on where in the country it is grown) is cherished by Europe's top makers.

Pacari, one of the Ecuadorian heavy hitters on the national and global chocolate stages, discovered the world's penchant for their cacao in 2002 and took off running (three gold medals at the International Chocolate Awards), as did Quito's Republica de Cacao. You'll find their chocolates far from the Amazon and as far away as New York City movie theatre concessions.

Elsewhere in the country, Mindo in the Andean cloud forest has become a hub of chocolate makers, and no wonder why. There's hardly anything more satisfying after a long hike than plopping a big hunk of soft white cheese into your chocolate and recovering the remains after you've downed the liquid, or dipping a crispy *bizcocho* into the frothy mixture. Don't knock it till you've tried it.

EL QUETZAL DE MINDO

9 de Octubre, Mindo; www.elquetzaldemindo.com;
+593 862-63805

◆ Tastings   ◆ Classes   ◆ Cafe
◆ Roastery   ◆ Shop

THINGS TO DO NEARBY

Mashpi Lodge
Mashpi is among South America's most luxurious wilderness lodges, with 500 bird species to spot within this 1200-hectare (3000-acre) cloud rainforest reserve.
www.mashpilodge.com

Reserva Maquipucuna Biológica
This privately owned 14000-acre reserve was among Ecuador's ecotourism trailblazers, with guides to show you the forest's highlights.
www.maquipucuna.org

Bellavista Cloud Forest Reserve
If the prospect of glimpsing spectacled bears or giant weasels at this lodge isn't enough, soaring views of peaks might convince you to visit. *www. bellavistacloudforest.com*

Mindo Canopy Adventure
Become like a cloud forest bird (or capuchin monkey), and soar through the jungle canopy on any of ten zip lines at this thrilling activity spot.
www. mindocanopy.com

 In the nation producing the biggest yields of high-quality cacao in the world, El Quetzal de Mindo is the original bean-to-bar chocolate experience, much imitated since its founding in 2009, but generally considered the best. Location alone sets the bar high: up in picturesque cloud forest north of Quito. Whilst they actually source their cacao from several farms hereabouts, this is nevertheless a rare opportunity to see the plants growing, beans being harvested, fermented, roasted and winnowed (separated from the chaff) and chocolate being made (a process you can help out with on a couple of sought-after four-day courses annually) all in one place. What with the knockout mountain views and wondrous restaurant, where everything from the barbecue sauce to the brownies uses El Quetzal de Mindo's own small-batch chocolate, lots of people crave to stay, and they can – in rooms that include a free chocolate tour in the price. Owners Barbara and José also operate as chocolate-makers in Michigan, USA: so their bars marry Ecuadorian beans with flavours either Ecuadorian-grown (such as macadamia) or Michigan-grown (like blueberries). Being in charge of every stage of the process means that this chocolate can delight with from-the-source extras like *miel de cacao*, a syrup derived from cacao fruit.

YUMBO'S CHOCOLATE

Av Quito, Mindo; www.yumboschocolate.com;
+593 98 000 4417

◆ Food ◆ Classes ◆ Cafe
◆ Roastery ◆ Shop ◆ Tours

When Ecuadorian Claudia Ponce and Italian Pierre Molinari joined forces to create Yumbo's in 2016, the reaction was immediate: two national awards in two years, one of them for another potent pairing, their signature coffee-chocolate bar. A debt is owed to the rich Ecuadorian soil and its aromatic Arriba cacao, much sought-after but only accounting for 5% of global production. Yumbo's roots are in the coastal communities, buying from AMATIF, a 100-family Afro-Ecuadorian collective in Esmeraldas prov-ince. Eating this chocolate satisfies, body and soul. Tours begin with a hearty chocolate drink and include various tastings; you'll end up educated and sated in a lush garden, recipe for the beloved house chocolate brownie in hand.

THINGS TO DO NEARBY

Bird of Paradise Tours
Mindo's unique cloud forest is a global birding destination. Let Sandra Patiño show you around, from the must-see Andean cock-of-the-rock to hundreds of other species.

Tarabita and Waterfall Walk
Buzzing over a river on a pulley driven by an old car engine is great, but take time on the other side to explore exhilarating cataracts and pools.

GUSTAVO VÁZQUEZ DE CACAO

Carlos Luis Plaza Dañin/Juan Merino Unamuo, Guayaq-uil; www.facebook.com/decacao.ec; +593 98 338 3076

◆ Tastings ◆ Classes ◆ Transport
◆ Cafe ◆ Shop ◆ Food

Step back in time with Gustavo Vázquez into his 1940s style cafe, all classic wood and iron fixtures, to a time when cacao was king and Guayaquil its global exporting nexus. De Cacao is a throwback to the time bean-laden freighters sallied forth daily from the Malecón. A mural and sepia-toned period photos set the scene, as does a potted cacao plant. Gustavo uses only the best *fin de aroma* product, but there's a nod to his other passion, too – he trained as a chocolatier in Barcelona, and as a barista in Italy. He knows exactly how to prepare a perfect espresso, *ristretto* and *lungo*. On weekends you can get sandwiches, but let's face it, you're here for the sugar-free mousses

THINGS TO DO NEARBY

Faro of Cerro Santa Ana
Scale the conveniently numbered steps to the city's best view. If you're tired or peckish, fret not – plenty of side streets give you a chance to refresh.

Malecón 2000
See and be seen on this pedestrian walkway, amusement park and collection of eateries, which even has a scale model of Guayaquil.

flavoured with fruits like *maracuya* (passion fruit) and choc-olate cigars filled with peanut, almond and salt paste. The Ecuador bonbon represents the three chief national exports: banana, coffee and cacao, all in one mouth-watering bite. 'I wanted to celebrate the culture of chocolate in our country, and especially Guayaquil, which was the main export city of cacao, but never had a chocolaterie', says Vázquez.

PACARI

Julio Zaldumbide N24-703 y Rubio de Arevalo, La
Floresta, Quito; www.pacari.com; +593 2 380 9230

◆ Tastings ◆ Classes ◆ Cafe
◆ Transport ◆ Shop ◆ Food

THINGS TO DO NEARBY

Iglesia de la Compañía de Jesús
One of the finest Baroque churches in South America, every inch of the interior is covered with intricate carvings and lashings of gold leaf.

Zazu
For a contemporary twist on traditional Ecuadorian cuisine made from fresh, local ingredients, try Zazu's ceviches (or even guinea pig). *zazuquito.com*

TelefériQo
Ride the TelefériQo for spectacular views of the Avenue of the Volcanoes. The air gets rarer as the cable cars climb. *teleferico.com.ec*

Ochoymedio
Named after the iconic Fellini film *81/2*, this Floresta indie cinema shows art films alongside its popular bar and cafe. *www.ochoymedio.net*

It's thought that Ecuador's chocolate-making history stretches back more than 5000 years, but it's only since 2002 that this pioneering Ecuadorian brand has been an industry game-changer. Now Pacari's fair trade, biodynamic, organic, multi-award-winning chocolate is for sale in around 30 countries. At its Casa de Experiencias in La Floresta – Quito's coolest barrio – there is no end of treats in store. Free chocolate tastings on Tuesdays and Thursdays mean trying their different ranges, including chocolate with Andean and global flavours, herbs, fruits and their limited edition flavours.

On Wednesdays and Fridays, you can learn to make divine vegan truffles ($10 per person); small groups can even organise an indulgent chocolate and wine or world-class Guatemalan rum pairing. There's also a vegan-friendly cafe serving up everything from *humitas* – steamed corn cakes – to hot chocolate and ice cream. And Pacari's creative chocolate is always available to buy – perhaps flavoured with Andean rose, Peruvian pink salt or even gin. Away from the capital, Pacari works directly with more than 3500 small-scale farmers, who set a fair price for their products. You can discover more about cacao and see their sustainable practices in action on a tour to the Kichwa centre of Archidona, around three hours from Quito.

HONDURAS

How to ask for hot chocolate in the local language? *Un chocolate caliente, por favor.*
Signature chocolate flavours? Dark!
What to order with your chocolate? Nothing. Keep it simple.
Do: Try chocolate tea made from dried cacao beans.

Cacao is native to Honduras and was so important in ancient times that Copán, the southernmost known major Maya city, used the area's exceptionally aromatic variety as currency. Recent DNA tests have confirmed that Copán's modern-day strains are some of the purest known and date back some 1200 years to the Classic Maya period. Chocolate has also been found in archaeological examinations of Copán tombs, making it the earliest known use of cacao in a recipe to make chocolate.

As Honduras' temperatures rise due to climate change, coffee, one of the country's most important exports, has

become less viable and some farmers are turning to cacao. With this shift has come creativity, with the production of chocolate bars of course, but also more unusual products like chocolate liquors and chocolate body scrubs. Tours of chocolate plantations are also on offer in Copán Ruinas and Lago Yojoa, where you can see how cacao is grown, how chocolate is processed and then taste the delicious results. Meanwhile, Honduras is becoming rightfully known for the quality and flavour of its cacao and its crop is gaining popularity with foreign, premium chocolate producers.

Around much of the country you won't find many home-grown chocolate products (yet), but in cities and larger towns Honduran-made chocolate bars are sold in many shops. Some more upscale restaurants and cafes may also serve locally produced hot chocolate or chocolate tea. If you go to a cacao plantation, don't miss trying the wonderfully tart yet sweet cacao fruit.

TEA & CHOCOLATE PLACE

Calle Yaragua, Cópan Ruinas; www.facebook.com/El-LugardelTeyChocolate; +504 2651-4087

◆ Tastings   ◆ Cafe   ◆ Food
◆ Transport   ◆ Shop

THINGS TO DO NEARBY

Copán Archaeological Park
A Unesco World Heritage Site, this ancient Maya city is worth at least two days' exploration. Hire a guide to learn about the importance of chocolate here. *www.ihah.hn*

Macaw Mountains
Take a walk through lush jungle to mingle with native birds, some too domesticated to leave and others that will be set free to restore populations. *www.macawmountain.org*

Hacienda San Lucas
This 100-year-old retreat is an enchanting place to stay or just come for a several course meal and to hike the on-site Maya structures. *www.haciendasanlucas.com*

Luna Jaguar Hot Spring
This Maya-themed spa sits 24 kilometres (15 miles) north of the archaeological site of Copán at a point where natural hot springs meet cool river waters. *www.lunajaguarspa.com*

Chocolate becomes a near-spiritual experience at this shop, tasting room and cafe on a jungle-clad, Honduran hillside. Embracing the Maya passion for cacao, David Sedat, a leading archaeologist at Copán since the 1970s, created this enchanting spot to accompany his Experimental Botanical Station. The station works towards regenerating farmlands and ecosystems – and ultimately to alleviate poverty and raise nutrition standards in the area – via agro-forestry. The bounty, in the form of cacao, teas and a unique array of herbs and medicinal plants, get blended at the Tea and Chocolate Place into delicious and healing treats for a good cause.

Staff meet you as soon as you enter the airy, bright space, offering samples of what's on offer (including local honey and salsas). Delve deeper by asking about the medicinal tea blends for an array of ailments. Then order a pot of hot chocolate or tea, perhaps a brownie, and take a seat on the colourful Maya textile-clad terrace that overlooks the slopes of the botanical station. Sunset in particular is magical. On your way out, stock up on chocolate bars, bulk teas, handmade soaps and more. Warning: if you try the chocolate tea, addiction may ensue; save room in your luggage.

MEXICO

How to ask for hot chocolate in the local language? *Un chocolate* ('choc-oh-lah-tay') *caliente, por favor.*

Signature chocolate flavours? Oaxacan chocolate 'pops' with spicy cinnamon and sugar.

What to order with your chocolate? Hot chocolates are best enjoyed with a sweet bread, such as a *pan de yema*.

Don't: Expect a hot chocolate to always be prepared with milk; it's usually mixed with hot water. If you want it with milk, ask for 'con leche'.

While all kinds of sweet stories do the rounds as to the origins of chocolate, most researchers agree that the *Theobroma cacao* chocolate tree ('food of the gods'), first grew in the regions of Central America and current-day Mexico thousands of years ago. The earliest traces of chocolate compounds have been found at archaeological sites containing ancient Olmec vessels that date from 1500 BC, indicating that the Olmec people imbibed cacao as a

ceremonial drink. The Central American Maya people took chocolate to new heights. They consumed and revered chocolate, in the form of drinks, in both celebrations and as a beverage, mixing cocoa paste with water, combined with a honey sweetener and chilli peppers. Then the Aztecs bumped up the value of chocolate even further. To them, it was gold. They not only venerated it, but also used beans as a currency to buy goods and services. Like the Maya people, they also enjoyed it as a spicy chocolate drink. Montezuma, the Aztec ruler, is said to have consumed litres of chocolate daily for energy...and as an aphrodisiac. He even gave it to his military for a caffeinated pep up.

Not surprisingly, the Spanish colonists introduced chocolate to Europe in the 16th century. While the background is a little hazy, all tales are plausible. One depicts Christopher Columbus coming across a trade ship with a cargo of cacao beans, and returning to Spain with them in the early 1500s. Another belief is that the Aztecs plied Spanish conquistador Hernán Cortés with chocolate after he witnessed Montezuma revelling in his favourite brew. Still another

TOP HOT CHOCOLATES TO LOOK OUT FOR

1. CHILATE (Guerrero)
2. CHAMPURRADO (or atole with chocolate; Oaxaca)
3. BUPU (Juchitán de Zaragoza, Oaxaca)
4. POPO (Veracruz)
5. TEJATE (Oaxaca)

theory is that the local Guatemalan Maya presented cacao beans as a gift to Philip II of Spain in 1544.

One thing is clear: chocolate was a hit in Europe, especially among the elite, who imbibed it as a drink, after blending it with cane sugar and the likes of nuts, cinnamon and other spices. Some of these additions were later adopted by Mexicans, too, when the spices were introduced to them by the Spanish. In current-day Mexico, drinking chocolate has never left the local diet. In many places, it is enjoyed on a daily basis, or at specific festivals. In the region of Oaxaca, one of Mexico's major chocolate producing areas, chocolate is prepared into drinks containing a delicious blend of cinnamon (and other spices), sugar and pure chocolate. Usually the chocolate is blended with water (not milk) by using a *molinillo*, just as their forebears have done for centuries. Thousands of producers grow cacao as well, predominantly in Chiapas and Tabasco, and artisanal chocolatiers (particularly in Mexico City and major cities) sell high-quality, handmade chocolates flavoured with everything from *chapulines* (grasshoppers) to tequila.

JONATHAN MARTÍNEZ REYES,
OWNER XOCOLA-T, GUANAJUATO

'Mexican people usually drink, not eat, chocolate. But eating it is definitely growing in popularity, changing the culture of chocolate consumption in Mexico.'

XOCOLA-T

Baratillo 15, Alameda, Guanajuato; www.facebook.com/
gtogtoxocolat; +52 473-129-0221

◆ Tastings ◆ Classes
◆ Cafe   ◆ Shop

THINGS TO DO NEARBY

Teatro Juárez
This magnificent building, inaugurated in 1903 and festooned with statues of the muses, is one of the city's main landmarks. Be sure to visit its Moorish interior.

Museo de las Momias
Perhaps best visited before (not after) chocolate tastings, this museum houses mummified bodies unearthed from cemeteries in the 1800s. *www.momiasdeguanajuato.gob.mx*

Museo Casa Diego Rivera
Diego Rivera's birthplace is now a fabulous museum that exhibits a fascinating permanent collection of his preliminary sketches and original works.

Jardin de la Unión
Guanajuato's beautiful triangular plaza is filled with laurel trees and is the city's main social hub for locals and visitors – as well as mariachis.

You'll whiff the delightful aromas of Xocola-T (pronounced 'sho-koh-lah-tay') before you see this tiny chocolate store on pretty Plaza Baratillo in Guanajuato. A chocoholic's nirvana, it is on the bucket list of visitors both local and foreign. The owners, Maida and Jonathan Martinez, first started out by selling their chocolates on the local streets and now make their handmade chocolates on-site. We're talking entirely natural ingredients with 100% Mexican fillings: everything from *chapulines* (grasshoppers) and *gusanos* (caterpillars) to *nopales* (cactus) and rich *chicharrón* (fried pork fat). Or you can wrap your tongue around other flavours, such as fruity mango, tamarind or spicy chilli. Purists might prefer to stick to the medallions of chocolate that run from 65% to almost pure cacao.

And, for those of us who know that chocolate is definitely a health food, there's not a trans fat in sight here. Staff will patiently run through the many choices as these change frequently and happily explain the offerings, all made with natural flavourings and pure cocoa. Once you've made your selection – by simply pointing at your preferences one by one – your chocolates will be packaged in boxes. (There's no hurry; this is serious, after all).

If you can't pull yourself away, grab a seat at one of two tables, and linger over a Mexican hot chocolate. Or better still, partake in a pairing session with the local mezcal and handmade chocolate.

CHURRERÍA EL MORO

Eje Central Lázaro Cárdenas 42, Centro Histórico,
CDMX; elmoro.mx; +52 55-5512-0896

◆ Tastings   ◆ Transport   ◆ Food

◆ Shop   ◆ Cafe

Lest you think churros with hot chocolate are purely a Spanish treat, let El Moro correct you. Doughnut-like sweet churros come rolled in cinnamon or azúcar to complement hot chocolate, ranging from gentle Mexicano style to heart-thumpingly syrupy, Español style. The churros are perfect for dipping in your drink, and they come out piping hot from an elaborate mechanism that visitors can watch through windows onto the street. Although the 24-hour Centro Histórico location is the oldest and full of character, with festive outfits for the staff, sparkling new locations decorated in blue and white tile can also be found throughout the city in hip neighbourhoods such as Roma and La Condesa. It makes for a lovely re-fuelling pick-me-up, a can't-miss stop in Mexico's capital city.

THINGS TO DO NEARBY

Zócalo
The heart of central Mexico City is the Plaza de la Constitución, or the zócalo. Measuring 220m (721ft) from north to south, and 240m (787ft) from east to west, it's one of the world's largest city squares.

Diego Rivera Murals at Palacio Nacional
Inside this grandiose colonial palace and government office you'll see Diego Rivera murals (painted between 1929 and 1951) that depict Mexican history over centuries.

CHOCOLATE MAYORDOMO

Francisco Javier Mina 219, Oaxaca; www.chocolate-
mayordomo.com.mx; +52 951-512-0421

◆ Roastery   ◆ Cafe
◆ Shop   ◆ Transport

THINGS TO DO NEARBY

Guelaguetza
Oaxacan citizens spend all year counting down to this dazzling summer dance festival, with troops in regional costumes whirling and stomping as festival goers eat, drink mezcal and make merry.

Monte Albán
The former capital of the Zapotec people, Monte Albán, with its grand ball court and carved sculptures, has a spectacular setting 9 miles west of Oaxaca City.

Templo de Santo Domingo
This magnificent baroque church was finished in 1751. Its intricate façade and painted dome inspired awe in believers and non-believers alike.

Zócalo
Locals still take their evening stroll around Oaxaca's tree-shaded central square, full of ice pop vendors and itinerant guitarists, and surrounded by gracious arcades.

Oaxaca is a city of scents – roasting chili peppers, incense spilling from Colonial churches, many-spiced mole simmering in *cazuela* pots. Entwined through it all is the fragrance of chocolate, a food so sacred to the region it was once used as currency. Near the Mercado 20 de Noviembre is the flagship location of Chocolate Mayordomo, which calls itself, quite fairly, 'el sabór the Oaxaca' – the flavour of Oaxaca. The company has been producing cinnamon- and almond-spiced chocolate since 1956, and its chocolate tablets are sold in supermarkets across the country and beyond. Lean over the worn wooden counter to order a box of the *chocolate clásico*, to be mixed with hot milk and frothed with a wooden whisk called a *molinillo* into hot chocolate, or combined with hominy

flour and spices into a warming drink called *champurrado*. The shop smells, looks and feels much as it could have sixty years ago, with vintage scales and burlap sacks of cacao beans. Buy a tub of chocolate-spiked mole paste in red, black or *coloradito*, a reddish version made sweet with mashed plantain. Or try it at the in-store restaurant, slathered over chicken, along with a chocolate tamale and a glass of hot chocolate.

EL SABOR ZAPOTECO

Av Benito Juárez 30, Teotitlan del Valle; cookingclasse-selsaborzapoteco.blogspot.com; +52 951-516-4202

◆ Tastings   ◆ Cafe
◆ Roastery   ◆ Classes

You'll quickly discover that chocolate Oaxaqueña (the hot chocolate drink particular to Oaxaca) is integral to local daily life and traditions and is famous around Mexico. Chocolate blocks – comprising toasted cacao beans, plus oodles of sugar and cinnamon – are on sale throughout Oaxaca, along with wooden *molinillos* (whisks), carved wooden tools used for creating froth once the chocolate is melted and blended with hot water.

If you want to learn how to make a chocolate Oaxaqueña, you're in good hands with Reyna Mendoza, a chocolate 'specialist' from Teotitlán del Valle, 28km southeast of Oaxaca, where hot chocolate has been imbibed daily for centuries. At her cooking school, El Sabor Zapoteco, Mendoza teaches the art of preparing traditional chocolate.

THINGS TO DO NEARBY

Museo de las Culturas de Oaxaca
This museum, housed in monastery buildings adjoining the Templo de Santo Domingo, covers the history of Oaxaca state and the pre-Hispanic practices that continue today.

Mercado El Merced
A typical neighbourhood market in Oaxaca, the food halls here serve up some of the culinary region's best local delights, from empanadas to hot chocolates.

KI'XOCOLATL

Santa Lucía Park, Calle 60, Mérida;
www.kixocolatl.com; +52 999-923-3384

◆ Shop
◆ Cafe

THINGS TO DO NEARBY

Parque Santa Lucía
The square adjacent to Ki'xocolatl's cafe hosts romantic trova musicians on Thursday nights and a flea market on Sundays, when central Mérida is car-free.

Gran Museo del Mundo Maya
Opened in 2013, this vast exhibit space showcases not just the ancient people of the Yucatán Peninsula, but also the dinosaurs that roamed here long before.

Los Dos
Join a class at this cooking school to learn traditional Yucatecan recipes and tour the central market, where some vendors sell handmade bitter chocolate disks. *los-dos.com*

Choco-Story
Brees' hacienda isn't open to visitors, but this adjacent chocolate museum is. While you're here, visit Uxmal and the smaller Maya ruins of the so-called Ruta Puuc.

 Combining the Yucatec Maya word for 'delicious' with the Aztec Nahuatl word for 'chocolate', Ki'xocolatl reflects cacao's millennia-deep history across Mexico – even though it was founded by a Belgian, Mathieu Brees. Following his chocolate obsession to the New World, Brees now runs one of the world's few fully bean-to-bar operations – and has reintroduced cacao production in the Yucatán Peninsula some eight centuries after it was last practised. On an hacienda south of Mérida, the state's capital, Brees cultivates the rare Criollo varietal much as the ancient Maya did: working purely by hand, shading the fragile plants with taller trees, and tapping into the peninsula's underground river system of freshwater cenotes.

Brees' work is showcased at the Ki'xocolatl cafe in central Mérida (and three other shops around the city).

The products here use the Yucatán cacao as well as more conventionally grown beans from neighbouring Chiapas. Sitting on a scenic small plaza, you can sample drinking chocolate spiced with chili or rich ice cream, and stock up on Xocotherapy cocoa-butter beauty products.

But the real stars are the chocolate bars made from only the Yucatán plantation's Criollo beans. Try one in the shop, and buy more to sample in a few months' time, as the cacao ages and changes, much like wine. On hot days, the chocolate frappe is also a much-needed treat.

NICARAGUA

How to ask for hot chocolate in the local language? *Un chocolate caliente por favour.*

Signature chocolate flavours? Nicaragua is best known for its rare, rich varieties of bean, which are well worth tasting.

What to order with your chocolate? *Tiste* (A cocoa- and corn-based beverage served in a jícaro cup).

Do: Visit a coffee *finca* as well while you're in the country for a complete bean experience.

Visitors to Nicaragua can trace the history of cacao back for centuries, covering the chocolate-making process on route and sampling as they go. Then it's time to don your cap and apron and get hands-on at Granada's Chocomuseo, from grinding the beans in a stone pestle

and mortar to choosing your ingredients – perhaps nuts, nibs, salt or chilli – while the multilingual staff shout encouragement. Best of all, you get to take your bespoke bar home. Those stopping in Granada can also stay at the boutique hotel Mansion de Chocolate, an old colonial house constructed by Nicaragua's president Evaristo Carazo Aranda in the 19th century and expanded by later generations. The on-site spa even offers a 'choco therapy'.

Today, the country exports several thousand tons of fine cocoa a year, mostly to European companies such as Ritter, making it the biggest producer in Central America. Comparatively little is kept for domestic use, but a rising interest in chocolate tourism has been met by increased offerings. With Nicaragua rumoured as the first place Christopher Columbus was exposed to cacao beans, it has a long heritage to draw from.

ARGENCOVE

Primer Calle Sur Xalteva, de la Iglesia 1C al Sur,
Granada; www.argencove.com; +505 8113-1592

◆ Tastings ◆ Shop
◆ Roastery

This artisan, bean-to-bar start-up has spent the last few years sourcing cacao from all over the country and experimenting with fermentation, drying and flavours. And they've kept it local, from their employees to bars named after Nicaragua's natural wonders, including Masaya Volcano and Laguna de Apoyo, and packaging inspired by Granada's Spanish colonial floor tiles, as well as supporting several community projects. On a by-appointment tour of their small Granada factory led by the Australian chocolate maker, you'll learn about the entire process, starting with plucking the pod off the tree. Taste it in all its forms, from cacao fruit to beans to sublime chocolate, discovering flavours shaped by origin, cacao percentage and additions such as cashew, saffron and passion fruit.

THINGS TO DO NEARBY

Masaya Volcano
You can almost drive to the edge of this still-active volcano – take a night tour and peer in to the 'devil's mouth' of bubbling molten lava, which glows when active.

The Garden Cafe
Head to this cool cafe for organic salads, superfruit smoothies, craft beer and a fair trade shop stocking local designers and producers. *www.gardencafegranada.com*

CHOCOLATE MOMOTOMBO

Plaza Altamira Mod.2, Managua; www.momotombo-chocolatefactory.com; + 505 2270-2094

◆ Food ◆ Classes ◆ Cafe
◆ Roastery ◆ Shop

Founded in 2004 by Sonia Moraga and Carlos José Mann to draw upon Nicaragua's rich history of cacao production, these artisanal bean-to-bar chocolate makers create sweet concoctions using Nicaragua's finest cacao. Chocolate beverages, handcrafted chocolates and gift boxes are for sale, and their products have taken gold among the Central American producers in the International Chocolate Awards. Working with local growers to source their beans, they focus on utilising and celebrating the regional cultivars.

THINGS TO DO NEARBY

Museo Arqueológico Huellas de Acahualinca
Discovered by miners in 1874, fossilised tracks here record the passage of perhaps 10 people as well as birds, raccoons, deer and possum from some 6000 to 8000 years ago.

Reserva Natural Volcán Momotombo
The perfect cone of Volcán Momotombo rises red and black 1280m (4255ft) above Lago de Managua. It is a symbol of Nicaragua, and the volcanic country's most beautiful threat.

PERU

How to ask for chocolate in the local language? *¿Se puede probar unos chocolates?* (Can I try some chocolates?)
Signature chocolate flavours? Try bars flecked with local black mint, ginger or artisan salt.
How to order your chocolate? *Chocolate amargo* (bitter chocolate).
Do: Sample single origin bars to take in the distinct flavours of different growing regions.

The home of powerful ancient empires, Peru, in the emerald heart of the Andes, has always been a country that slipped easy definition. Diversity, ranging from its geography and species to cultures, is in its DNA. Just take a walk through the country's thriving markets displaying jungle fruit alongside highland grains and a rainbow array of tubers. Innovation embraces tradition in the novoandina cuisine that has caused a culinary revolution. Enter into this fertile culinary landscape the humble cacao bean.

Cacao first appeared wild in the north of the Amazon, where it was domesticated some 5000 years ago before spreading to Mesoamerica. It's now grown in sixteen of Peru's twenty-four regions, mostly by small-scale farmers. The family plantations of the Cuzco region have been handed down through the generations, with age-old cultivations. Contrast that to newcomers in the central jungle, which turned to cacao growing as an alternative to the illicit coca crops tended by the drug trafficking networks rampant in the late 1990s. In these remote places, chocolate offers social and financial security to struggling farmers.

But it's more than a good cause. Peruvian cacao is known for its dazzling diversity in flavour, thanks to regional variations in soil, geography and cultivation. Piura white beans produce a light, brown-sugar citrusy bar, the northern Amazon produces floral berry flavours while varieties from Cuzco have a deep cinnamon-clove flavour. Peruvian single origin bars are even winning international awards, proof that Peruvian chocolate has the power to thrill every palate out there. Start tasting to find your match.

EL CACAOTAL

Jr Colina 128 A, Barranco, Lima; www.elcacaotal.com;
+51 1 4174988

◆ Tastings   ◆ Classes
◆ Roastery   ◆ Shop

THINGS TO DO NEARBY

Lima Tasty Tours
This is Lima as only locals know it, with fun vendor interactions in the vast markets of the city, little-known culinary treasures and tastings galore. *www. limatastytours.com*

Barra Chalaca
This casual ceviche and seafood bar combines masterful cooking and playful rapport for the win. Come early for lunch, as there's always a wait. *www.barrachalaca.pe*

Museo Amano
Get to know ancient Peru through its most breathtaking textiles and ceramics, via an intimate experience in the former home of a top private collector. *www.museoamano.org*

Museo del Pisco
In a historic 16th-century casona, this wonderful bar educates patrons on Peru's signature drink with outstanding original cocktails rife with local herbs and jungle fruit. *www.museodelpisco.org*

 Every chocolate bar has a story behind it. Especially if you are Amanda Jo Wildey, an anthropologist who first visited cacao farmers in the Amazon who were adopting the crop as an alternative to harvesting coca (leaves used in the manufacture of cocaine). Now she helps get their product to market via El Cacaotal, a sustainable chocolate shop in the happening Lima neighbourhood of Barranco. Providing the perfect opportunity to sample Peru's cacao, the shop offers fair trade compensation for small-scale farmers around Peru with over 200 delicious varieties and connoisseur expertise. Call it an edible library.

Customers can join fun blind tastings, or curate their own box of fair trade selections with tasting notes useful in creating their own chocolate party once back home. Wildey says the flavours depend largely on chocolate origins and handling, which can make it fruity, or nutty, or even like jasmine – all without adding a single ingredient. In addition to award-winning Peruvian bars such as Shattell's 70% Chuncho and Maraná's 70% Cusco, you can try delicious inclusions like hot pepper, pomegranate and salt, or even the quintessentially Peruvian ingredients such as lemongrass and quinoa. Products are arranged by region, and portraits of the cacao farmers themselves grace the walls. An adjacent chocolate lab offers excellent workshops in English.

CHOCOMUSEOS

locations throughout Latin America;
www.chocomuseo.com

◆ Tastings ◆ Classes ◆ Cafe
◆ Roastery ◆ Shop

If ever there was a people-centred model for joyfully, even playfully, celebrating chocolate in all its potency and complexity, it is ChocoMuseo. Take the most laudatory, family-friendly and educational qualities of small-scale museums, cafes, stores and factories, make chocolate the pivot on which they turn, and that's a ChocoMuseo – like a community-based organisation run by and for honorary Oompa Loompas.

At present, approximately two dozen ChocoMuseos are located in seven Latin American countries: Colombia, Costa Rica, Dominican Republic, Guatemala, Mexico, Nicaragua and Peru. Although each one has its own special character, influenced by the country and culture that hosts it, they're all united by a venerable overall mission: to teach about and share the experience of chocolate – where it comes from, how it's made and how it can be enjoyed.

This is accomplished through a combination of welcoming, free-to-access boutiques – museum/cafes with public workshops and gift shops – and paid services, such as classes and tours, treats like bars, fudge, ganache, flavoured truffles and jams, and, in some locations, chocolate-influenced liqueurs, beauty products and spa treatments.

Many visitors turn up first for the hands-on, instructional museums (with explanations in English and Spanish) and demonstrations covering the history of cacao, chocolate and the chocolate-making process. However, they return for the interactive chocolate-making classes, most designed to be family-friendly. Aprons on for a chance to roast, peel, grind, mould, taste and more!

In the midst of this, the production of chocolates and chocolate-based products continues for all to see (and buy), using local, organic ingredients and local staff, the latter actively encouraged to drive ideas and initiatives that are sometimes embraced across the whole network, including selling chocolate to corporate clients like bakeries, restaurants and hotels, and renting machinery to chocolate makers and students.

USA

How to order your hot chocolate? If you're at NYC's famous Serendipity, that'd be a frozen hot chocolate, please.
Signature chocolate flavours? Peanut butter rules the roost.
What to order with your chocolate? Try local spirits as well.
Do: Get beyond the big brands.

Chocolate is ubiquitous in the land of Uncle Sam: walk into any supermarket or pharmacy and you're greeted with a wealth of European and American chocolate bars to tempt buyers. The number of specialty chocolatiers in major cities and even small towns seems ever-expanding as well. Chocolate, once the poster child for bad teeth, acne and obesity, is downright trendy.

It was not always so. Although a robust chocolate culture grew up in the 19th century, especially around Chicago's German immigrants, by the early 20th century the field was dominated by two men: Forrest Mars and Milton Hershey. Opposite in personality, they were the big fish who swallowed the minnows in the cocoa sea. Hershey's company town in Pennsylvania remains worth a visit, host to a theme park, HersheyPark, sports arena, and naturally, the Wonka-esque Hershey's Chocolate World. Things got heated again when Godiva, once a signature Belgian chocolate purchased by the Campbell's Soup company in 1966 (the Lindt you buy in the states, despite the company's origins in the Swiss Alps, is made in a New Hampshire factory), made chocolate chic again with a slick ad campaign in the 1970s; Godiva still produces *Chocolate Notes* magazine to flog its brand. More recently, artisanal chocolatiers have flourished.

Check any major city and you'll stumble into a chocolate shop: New York's Rockefeller Center has two or three on the same block, and if you miss that, there are two in Grand Central Terminal, as well. On the opposite coast, San Francisco's touristy Fisherman's Wharf is dominated by the colossus of Ghirardelli Square and its namesake chocolate firm. Founded by Italian immigrant Dominico Ghirardelli in 1952 after his sweet-shop experiences in Uruguay and Peru, he came to San Francisco with 600 pounds of cacao and a dream; it is the third-oldest chocolatier in the US, though now owned by Switzerland's Lindt and Sprüngli. A must-

TOP 5 CHOCOLATIERS TO VISIT

THORNCREST FARMS AND MILK HOUSE CHOCOLATES, CONNECTICUT

If you want rich milk chocolate from cows that are truly loved (pampered, even), go no further than this farmhouse on a hill in Litchfield County. www.milkhousechocolates.net

GHIRARDELLI CHOCOLATES, SAN FRANCISCO, CA

If it's hot, have a fudge-smothered ice cream sundae. If it's cold and foggy, have a hot chocolate. You can't lose. Most of their beans come from Ghana. www.ghirardelli.com

MADE CHOCOLATE, ATLANTIC CITY, NJ

Dame Judi Dench's character in the film *Chocolat* exclaims, 'Is this a chocolaterie or a confessional?' Made, with its old church pews and full-on cacao-laden drinks, is both. www.madeachocolate.com

INTRIGUE CHOCOLATES, SEATTLE, WA

Aaron Barthel's Pioneer Square shop makes more than 150 varieties of truffles, including some made with anejo tequila and black tea, with a base of 70% Belgian dark chocolate. Juniper berry chocolate? Alder smoked sea salt? There's something for everyone here. www.intriguechocolate.com

THE FUDGE POT, CHICAGO, IL

Chocolate-covered strawberries are still the fave here, but truffles are gaining traction. Jim Datallo apprenticed with the Mars family before striking out on his own in 1963. thefudgepotchicago.com

have at Ghirardelli Square (a national historic landmark) is one of 15 sundaes with their signature fudge topping.

Jacques Torres, aka 'Mr Chocolate', the youngest French pastry chef to win the *Meilleur Ouvrier de France*, funnels bonbons from his production facility in Brooklyn to the Grand Central shop; his chocolate 'museum' is now closed but six NYC shops attest to his success. Meanwhile in Boston, Taza, famous for their discs inspired by Mexican hot chocolate, has a chocolate bar inside the Public Market (think samples!). Smaller towns are in on the action too, making local artisanal chocolate all over, some almost too good-looking to eat, and delicious once you sacrifice them to take a bite. These few examples are but a taste; whether digging into a fudge-swirled ice cream sundae in July or sipping a hot chocolate against December's frost, there's a yummy chocolate-based treat for every season, thoughtfully sourced from regions across the world. Chocolate, whatever the season, is cool again, and boutique chocolate makers everywhere are coming out with their own unique contribution to add to the mix.

DANDELION CHOCOLATE

740 Valencia St, San Francisco; www.dandelionchocolate.com;
+1 415-349-0942

◆ Tastings ◆ Classes ◆ Cafe
◆ Roastery ◆ Shop ◆ Transport

THINGS TO DO NEARBY

Paxton Gate
Unsettling interior decoration is the theme at Paxton Gate, from taxidermied deer heads to anatomical sketches. Enquire ahead for taxidermy classes. *paxtongate.com*

Mission Murals
The Mission District is rich in Latinx culture and awash in street art begging to be toured. Highlights are the MaestraPeace Mural, colourful Balmy Alley and the ever-changing political canvas at Clarion Alley.

Anchor Brewing Company
Through the 1906 earthquake and even the Prohibition era, Anchor Brewing endures, serving IPAs, lagers and mango wheat beer in a beloved taphouse. *www. anchorbrewing.com*

Borderlands
Sci-fi, fantasy, rare books and early editions crowd the shelves of this caffeine-fuelled bookstore. Settle in for cappuccino and ginger cookies after ogling the magazine racks. *www. borderlands-books.com*

This small-batch chocolate factory cultivates an elegant air with its salon dining room, cafe and well-curated bookshop. First, calibrate your taste buds with a few free samples: let a small square of rich, nutty Maya Mountain melt on your tongue, before contrasting it with fudgy, buttery Camino Verde. Palate primed, embark on one of the regular tours of the factory floor, inhaling the scent of cacao beans roasted and ground on-site. True connoisseurs should book the 'bean-to-bar' class, which delves into chocolate history and cacao-growing techniques. The grand finale involves getting delightfully sticky making your own chocolate – you'll leave with bars moulded by your own hands (and too precious to share).

If you're short on time, finish with a drink at the cafe – perhaps a cocoa-nib-sprinkled 'Frozen Hot Chocolate' – before perusing the gift shop's dessert recipe books and whole dried cacao pods. For a more languorous chocolate experience, settle in at the swish dining room, Bloom Salon. Their afternoon tea ($45) is a delectable spread of profiteroles, macarons, chocolate soufflé and other sweet morsels, accompanied by tea or (you guessed it) hot chocolate.

Want to graduate from amateur to all-knowing chocolate savant? Dandelion also runs chocolate-tasting classes enabling you to fine-tune your palate.

RECCHIUTI CONFECTIONS

One Ferry Building, Shop #30, San Francisco;
www.recchiuti.com; +1 415-834-9494

◆ Tastings   ◆ Classes
◆ Transport ◆ Shop

Recchiuti chocolates, flavoured with lemon verbena, Piedmont hazelnut and fleur-de-sel caramel, are so beautifully arranged and glamorously backlit that they almost resemble jewellery on display in a luxury store. Founders Michael and Jacky Recchiuti have poured more than two decades into perfecting these couverture chocolates – that is, chocolate made with at least 32% cocoa butter, for a creamy finish – and ingredients are sourced from local farmers markets wherever possible. The sister store (at 801 22nd St), in up-and-coming industrial neighbourhood Dogpatch, has occasional chocolate and booze pairings on Friday afternoons; check ahead online. Must-trys are lavender and vanilla ganache in dark chocolate, and the signature Peanut Butter Pucks.

THINGS TO DO NEARBY

Coit Tower
Admire the view from this tower; the Social Realism-style murals are equally captivating. Look for Telegraph Hill's parrots nearby. *www.sfrecpark.org/ destination/telegraph-hill-pioneer-park/coit-tower*

Vesuvio Cafe
Former haunt of Jack Kerouac and his Beat buddies, Vesuvio's is an atmospheric spot for stiff drinks and banter with booze hounds and literature buffs. *www.vesuvio.com*

VALERIE CONFECTIONS

3364 W 1st St, Los Angeles; www.valerieconfections.com;
+1 213-739-8149

◆ Tastings ◆ Classes ◆ Food
◆ Transport ◆ Shop ◆ Cafe

Like LA itself, chocolatier Valerie Gordon thinks outside the (chocolate) box. Her self-training left her with a neophyte's passion for asking 'why not?' and a philosophy her business- and life-partner Stan Weightman calls 'not to do something that's been done before, or that someone else is doing exceptionally well'. The result: Valerie's unique truffles filled with jasmine-tea-infused cream ganache; bittersweet chocolates filled with liquid caramel filling that genuinely flows; and the smoke and spice truffle with paprika and hickory-smoked salt. Since debuting her original six flavours of chocolate-dipped toffees in 2004, Valerie has branched out to three cafe-style locations around Los Angeles, serving treats from truffles to petit fours, jams like strawberry-vanilla bean and Blenheim apricot, sweet and savoury galettes and hand pies.

Her 2013 book, *Sweet*, was a James Beard Award finalist and includes favourite dessert recipes from bygone LA restaurants like Blum's Coffee Crunch Cake (with coffee whipped cream frosting studded with candy crunchies), also sold at the shop. And the Food Network featured her supremely elegant rose petal petit fours (vanilla bean cake with rose petal and passion fruit ganache, topped with a candied rose petal). Purist that she is, Valerie won't consider artificial flavours, chemicals, stabilisers or preservatives, or farming practices involving child labour or animal cruelty. Even the packaging is special, thanks to a partnership with Commune, the LA-based design firm. Valerie's chocolates inspire bold graphics with their unique ingredients.

© 2020, Valerie Confections

THINGS TO DO NEARBY

Grand Central Market
Can't make it to one of LA's celebrated weekly farmers markets? Try the circa 1908 (yet still current) food hall at Downtown LA's Grand Central Market. *www. grandcentralmarket.com*

Griffith Observatory
Take a trip to the Griffith Observatory, home to a state-of-the-art planetarium, hiking trails and views of the Hollywood sign and the Pacific. *www. griffithobservatory.org*

KATHERINE ANNE CONFECTIONS

2745 W Armitage Ave, Chicago;
www.katherine-anne.com; +1 773-245-1630

◆ Tastings ◆ Classes ◆ Cafe
◆ Transport ◆ Shop

THINGS TO DO NEARBY

The 606
An elevated train track converted into a 4.3km (2.7-mi) walking and cycling trail, the 606 unfolds overhead and sidles past backyards, art installations and murals.
www.the606.org

Busy Beaver Button Museum
Peruse thousands of oddball badges, including one from George Washington's campaign, on display in an unusual office building.
www.buttonmuseum.org

Rosa's Lounge
Hear Chicago's famed blues music in this authentic club, with an arm's-length-away stage and top local players.
www.rosaslounge.com

Galerie F
A low-key gallery immersed in the street-art scene, it puts on fresh exhibitions and sells cool prints and band posters.
www.galeriefchicago.com

The image that pops to mind when you think 'cozy chocolate nook' – ie a hideaway with fresh-flower-topped tables under shabby-chic chandeliers, and piles of chocolate truffles to pair with mugs of fresh drinking chocolates – is spot on for Katherine Anne Confections. The wee storefront tucked amid condo buildings has a display case that'll bulge your eyeballs.

Go ahead, try to decide between the mocha caramel or goat cheese walnut truffles, the raspberry champagne or coconut rum beauties. The cherry ricotta truffles tempt, then there's the apricot feta one, and on and on. Owner Katherine Duncan and her staff make 175 flavours throughout the year

using local, seasonal ingredients. Watch the rich, gooey treats emerge from the open kitchen right behind the counter and plot your course. The shop creates decadent drinking chocolate, too, so your next decision is which of the 12 flavours to sip alongside your truffles. Staff provide guidance on the various types, but if you can't commit to one your best bet is to order a flight of three mini cups. The salted caramel, chilli-spiked Mexican chocolate, and bourbon and hazelnut pours – all bobbing with enormous house-made marshmallows – never fail to please.

© 2020 Katherine Anne Confections

VOSGES HAUT-CHOCOLAT

951 W Armitage Ave, Chicago;
www.vosgeschocolate.com; +1 773-296-9866

◆ Tastings ◆ Classes
◆ Transport ◆ Shop

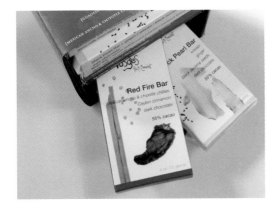

Vosges founder Katrina Markoff seems to delight in playing with expectations. At the glam chocolatier's Lincoln Park boutique, trays of healing crystals mingle among truffles clad in sumptuous purple packaging, generating a boho-luxe vibe that might suggest style over substance. And yet on closer inspection, it's a wildly creative culinary backbone that truly defines Markoff's creations, revealing her days training under innovative chefs like Ferran Adria of el Bulli. Markoff excels at marrying single-origin chocolate with ingredients typically found in savory dishes, creating surprising combinations that shouldn't work, but do. See, for instance, her reishi mushroom-studded bar, or the Rap, a dark chocolate praline truffle infused with horseradish.

The largest of her four Chicago shops is the place to stock up on fan faves like dark chocolate bacon bars, plus limited edition items like hibiscus and peppercorn truffles enrobed in petal pink 'ruby cacao'. A cafe also serves up warming drinking chocolate as well as elixirs, potent brews of pure cacao said to boost energy levels without the letdown that follows a caffeine buzz. To get inside Markoff's creative process, try the Naga, a mellow confection of curry-spiked coconut cream; it's the truffle that inspired her to launch her company in 1998.

THINGS TO DO NEARBY

Art Effect
Hit this long-running corner shop for all the quirky little treasures you never knew you needed, like Dolly Parton-embossed serving trays and illuminated globes. *www.shoparteffect.com*

Steppenwolf Theater
Founded by teenagers in 1974, this once-scrappy theatre is today a national gem showcasing the talents of ensemble members like John Malkovich and Tracy Letts. *www.steppenwolf.org*

Summer House Santa Monica
With its fresh interior, upbeat tunes and roving rosé cart, this SoCal-inspired restaurant feels sunny even as Chicago's brutal winters rage. *www.summerhousesm.com*

The Mousetrap
Off Colour Brewing bucks the trend for hoppy IPAs to spotlight funky yeasts. The brewery's welcoming taproom pours stars like tart Troublesome next to experimental brews. *www.offcolourbrewing.com*

LA BURDICK

220 Clarendon St, Back Bay, Boston; www.burdick-chocolate.com; +1 617-303-0113

◆ Roastery   ◆ Transport
◆ Shop   ◆ Cafe

THINGS TO DO NEARBY

New Old South Church
This magnificent Venetian Gothic church on Copley Square is the 'new' Old South because up until 1875 the congregation worshipped in what is now Boston's Old South Meeting House). *www.oldsouth.org*

Boston Public Library
Founded in 1852, this esteemed library lends credence to Boston's reputation as the 'Athens of America.' The old McKim building has a magnificent facade and exquisite interior art. *www.bpl.org*

Gibson House Museum
Catherine Hammond Gibson's Italian Renaissance row house remains virtually unchanged since 1860, preserving a piece of Victorian-era Boston complete with furnishings. *www.thegibsonhouse.org*

Saltie Girl
This seafood bar is a delightful place to feast on tantalising dishes that blow away all preconceived notions about seafood. from classic lobster roll to the torched salmon belly. *www.saltiegirl.com*

Whether in Chicago, Boston, Cambridge or New York City, once you step inside an LA Burdick store you can't possibly come out empty-handed. Its location in Boston's Back Bay carries the classic white chocolate mice, as well as tasty beverage options to consume on-site in the cozy cafe. As founder Larry Burdick defines them, his chocolates are the encounter of 'Swiss know-how, French gastronomic thoughtfulness and American imagination'. Each bonbon is hand-shaped, hand-decorated and hand-packed, representing the quintessence of crafts-manship combined with fresh and selected ingredients. Almond chamomile, cashew sesame and honey caramel are only some of the mouth-watering flavours part of the assortment. If you wish to enjoy a moment of pure chocolate bliss, sit at the tables inside the store and enjoy the acclaimed Dark Hot Chocolate together with a slice of decadent Chocolate Raspberry Cake. If bringing home an LA Burdick signature treat, there is nothing better than the chocolate mice and penguins: smooth flavoured ganaches handcrafted through 12 steps over 3 days. Larry learned to make these treats when he trained in Switzerland in the late 1970s, and they have remained his most popular creations.

DANCING LION CHOCOLATE

917 Elm St, Manchester;
www.dancinglion.us/cacao; +1 603-625-4043

◆ Tastings   ◆ Classes   ◆ Cafe
◆ Transport ◆ Shop   ◆ Food

Equal parts adventurer, scientist and artist, Richard Tango-Lowy travels to exotic destinations to purchase high-quality chocolate from small cacao farms and artisan chocolate makers, chocolate developed from heirloom cacao beans. At his compact, inviting shop and cafe, his team experiments with every new arrival, blending the chocolate with various ingredients, from chillis to blood oranges, until it tastes spectacular. A master-chocolatier, Tango-Lowy's passion is evident the moment he dives into the origin story of whatever gorgeous bonbon has caught your eye. He has never repeated a recipe, so nibbling a confection here is truly a once-in-a-lifetime experience. Developed using ancient Mesoamerican techniques, the frothy Olmec drinking chocolate is a spicy link to the past.

THINGS TO DO NEARBY

Currier Museum of Art
Home to works by John Singer Sargent, Georgia O'Keeffe, Monet, Matisse and Picasso (among many others), this fine-arts museum is Manchester's greatest cultural gem. *www.currier.org*

White Mountains
It's a 130km (80-mi) drive north from Manchester to New Hampshire's White Mountains, a striking region of soaring peaks and lush valleys where hiking trails abound. *www.visitwhitemountains.com*

MADE CHOCOLATE

121 S Tennessee St, Atlantic City;
www.madeacchocolate.com; +1 609-289-2888

◆ Tastings   ◆ Transport   ◆ Cafe
◆ Roastery   ◆ Shop

It's fitting that a decadent chocolatier sprang up in America's original Sin City. When Vegas was a mere dream, AC was serving up illicit hooch and countless other earthly pleasures. Now, blocks from a legal distillery, the husband-and-wife Pellegrinos have opened a Church of Chocolate here, complete with repurposed pews. Unique to many chocolate cafes, Made actually has its own bar, with well-considered wine pairings and cocktails featuring – what else? – chocolate. Adult chocolate milk is spiked with vodka and whipped cream and chocolate martinis tickle the taste buds, but the *pièce de résistance* is the cheeky Confession Manhattan. Drinkers of the Confession unburden themselves on index cards, with messages ranging from raunch to rhyming couplets (sometimes both).

THINGS TO DO NEARBY

Little Water Distillery
Dip into the Gantner brother's small-batch spirits (whiskey, light and dark rum, gin and vodka) in a converted warehouse, complete with live music, near Gardner's Cove. *www. littlewaterdistillery.com*

Kim and Kelsey's Cafe
You'll forget you're north of the Mason-Dixon line when you dive into plates of fried whiting, chicken and sides of grits and collard greens. Healthy? Probably not. Delicious? Most definitely. *www.kelseysac.com*

KAKAWA CHOCOLATE HOUSE

1050 Paseo De Peralta, Santa Fe;
www.kakawachocolates.com; +1 505-982-0388

◆ Tastings   ◆ Shop
◆ Cafe

THINGS TO DO NEARBY

Canyon Road

Maybe the longest strip of galleries in the United States, this pretty little adobe-lined street is the centre of Santa Fe's major art scene. Friday-night openings are busy.

Meow Wolf

A collective of young Santa Fe artists turned a bowling alley into an alternate universe of art, tech, music and story. *meowwolf.com*

State Capitol

An excellent selection of work by New Mexican artists adorns the hallways of this distinctive building, laid out like the Pueblo *zia* symbol that adorns the state flag.

Joseph's Culinary Pub

Green-chile cheeseburgers are a New Mexico staple, and this elegant restaurant serves one of the best, with plenty of chile. *www. josephsofsantafe.com*

Step into this typical old Santa Fe adobe house, with its thick walls and creaky wooden floor, and of course you first smell chocolate. Then you pick up other tantalising scents: spicy cinnamon, soft vanilla, resinous pine nuts – all ingredients in the shop's dozen-plus varieties of hot chocolate – or, as they're called here, 'elixirs'. These drinks are based on rigorously researched historical recipes, from ancient Mesoamerica's water-based brew to the decadent orange-blossom-scented version Marie Antoinette is thought to have favoured. If you find yourself unable to decide, the staff is quick to offer samples, or can offer a guided tasting.

Then again, there's another decision dilemma in the glass case full of dense, delectable truffles, which incorporate seasonal Southwestern flavours such as smoke-laced mescal and desert-grown lavender. These can be packed to go – and you can pick up bags of elixir mixes, to prep at home. A second branch in Santa Fe, as well as a shop in Salem, MA, also stock these treats.

Regardless, be sure to sample at least one option from the 'Americas' side of the elixirs menu. The chocolate *atole*, corn-based, chile-spiced and barely sweetened with honey, will put you back in touch with chocolate's roots as a drink that was considered not just delicious, but also medicinal and sacred.

RAAKA CHOCOLATE

64 Seabring St, Red Hook, Brooklyn, NYC;
www.raakachocolate.com; +1 855-255-3354

◆ Tastings ◆ Classes ◆ Transport
◆ Roastery ◆ Shop ◆ Tours

A dedication to flavour pervades everything – even the air – in Raaka's bustling, utilitarian, bean-to-bar chocolate factory-warehouse in Red Hook, Brooklyn. Not just any flavour, but chocolate made from single-origin, unroasted beans, which is to mainstream cacao confections what wine is to grape juice.

Like grapes, cacao beans acquire special character from the place in which they grow, different from that of other beans in other places. This uniqueness is largely lost when cacao is roasted, but nurtured when beans are naturally fermented, dried and shipped to Raaka's taste masters who, from scratch, combine and process them with other ingredients to craft distinctive, playful and often idiosyncratic chocolate treats. Such as Green Tea Crunch bars, using Zorzal beans from the Dominican Republic, Bourbon Cask Aged bars from Tanzanian Kokoa Kamili beans, and dozens more.

THINGS TO DO NEARBY

Pioneer Works
A nonprofit cultural centre and art gallery, the cavernous hall (with lots of creative side studios) is a space for performances, workshops and more. *www.pioneerworks.org*

Steve's Authentic Key Lime Pies
One thing's certain: the key lime juice is fresh squeezed. That's why this outpost of delicious tartness has been a pie lover's delight for 20-plus years. *www.keylime.com*

Fort Defiance
A full three-meals-a-day kitchen and active bar keep locals and visitors happy from early until late at this modest but vibrant social heart of Red Hook. *www. fortdefiancebrooklyn.com*

Van Brunt Stillhouse
Locally produced whiskeys are devotedly produced in small batches and served in the tasting room of this hidden distillery. It's stillhouse-style taken very seriously. *www. vanbruntstillhouse.com*

Also fundamental to Raaka is its commercial relationships with trusted, high-quality cacao growers. Printed inside every colourful Raaka wrapper is an overview of their 'transparent trade' practices, a 'values-driven sourcing model' based on clear, stable pricing and supply chains that benefit everyone from growers to chocolate-lovers.

Raaka offers factory tours, chocolate-making classes and a spread of free-to-taste samples that's nearly impossible to pull away from.

STICK WITH ME

202A Mott St, Nolita, NYC;
www.swmsweets.com; +1 646-918-6336

◆ Tastings ◆ Classes ◆ Cafe
◆ Roastery ◆ Shop ◆ Transport

THINGS TO DO NEARBY

Tenement Museum
Events, exhibits and preserved apartments give visitors a close encounter with the American immigrant and migrant experience from the 19th century to the present. *www.tenement.org*

Museum of Chinese in America
This immersive and interactive museum brings to vivid life 160 years of the evolving history and culture of the country's Chinese Americans. *www.mocanyc.org*

New Museum
Manhattan's contemporary art museum fills a modern, aluminium-clad building with talk-of-the-town curated shows and programs. *www.newmuseum.org*

Elizabeth Street Garden
Community gardens are socio-cultural rallying points in NYC. This popular green retreat full of sitting areas is much beloved and fiercely defended. *www. elizabethstreetgarden.com*

The bright display case at Stick With Me is alive with artful, orderly ranks of polished chocolate bonbons. The kaleidoscopic arrangement instantly sets the taste buds atingle. Does it hint at equally striking flavours? Yes indeed it does.

And well it should. Stick With Me, an artisanal confectioner specialising in the bold flavours of big desserts wrapped in small chocolate moulds, was launched in 2014 by Susanna Yoon, who had trained as a pastry chef at Cafe Boulud and Per Se, two of NYC's top Michelin-starred restaurants. This background guided her passion for all flavours – and textures too – not just those of different chocolates. Thus were born gorgeous, complex, chocolate-swaddled, bite-sized taste explosions like macadamia rice puff, bourbon maple pecan and speculoos s'more.

Yoon's focus on flavour is enhanced by her devotion to freshness. Besides the Valrhona chocolate she imports from France, only quality US ingredients are used to produce small batches at her compact, Nolita-based shop, where Yoon and her staff are visible in the kitchen hand-piping ganache, pralines and much more into varicoloured chocolate shells. One Willy Wonka fantasy made real: the kalamansi (Philippine lime) meringue pie bonbon. The delightful packaging is an extra treat, and you may want to pick up some caramels as well.

TOP NYC CHOCOLATE-THEMED RESTAURANTS

Left and right: © 2020, Chocolate Room; photo credit Paul Takeuchi

© Hemis / Alamy Stock Photo

JACQUES TORRES CHOCOLATE

350 Hudson Street, Manhattan and 6 other NYC locations; www.mrchocolate.com

◆ Transport ◆ Classes ◆ Cafe
◆ Food   ◆ Shop

Also known as Mr Chocolate, Jacques Torres is a world-recognized top chocolatier and bean-to-bar pioneer. His seven retail stores (plus 40,000-square-foot chocolate factory) in NYC anchor his growing brand. All the shops have comfy seating areas for sipping thick hot chocolate and savouring the sweets, including bonbons, bars, bark, brittle, truffles, chocolate-covered treats and much more, especially his famous chocolate chip cookies. For a hands-on adventure, the Hudson Street shop has a Chocolate Making Experience.

THE CHOCOLATE ROOM

269 Court St and 51 Fifth Ave, Brooklyn, NYC; www.thechocolateroombrooklyn.com

◆ Tastings ◆ Transport ◆ Food
◆ Cafe   ◆ Shop

This family-friendly, restaurant-style dessert cafe/store with two Brooklyn, liquor-licensed locations is a leading go-to for a quality chocolate fix. Two standout extravagances are the brownie sundae and much-celebrated chocolate layer cake (about as close to a Brooklyn Blackout as one can get), though the staff also fashions bonbons, confections, ice creams, hot fudge, shakes, floats, drinks, mousses and lots more. The owners are Brooklynites who donate extensively to the community and support local bean-to-bar producers.

MARIEBELLE

384 Broome St, Soho, NYC;
mariebelle.com; +1 212-925-6999

◆ Transport   ◆ Classes   ◆ Cafe
◆ Food   ◆ Shop

That the decorated confections look and are displayed like jewellery is no mistake at MarieBelle, where the beauty of the bonbon is (almost) as important as the taste. For anyone impatient to sample the ganache beneath the artisanal designs, there's a cosy, Parisian-style Cacao Bar at the back of the Soho-based store that also serves an acclaimed 'Aztec' hot chocolate made from 65% single-origin South American chocolate, not cocoa powder, as well as a fancy, chocolatey high tea. There are sister shops in Japan too.

AYZA WINE & CHOCOLATE BAR

11 W 31st St, Manhattan, NYC;
www.ayzanyc.com; +1 212-714-2992

◆ Tastings   ◆ Transport
◆ Cafe   ◆ Food

Ayza is a modern and elegant Midtown Manhattan retreat known for its full French-Mediterranean meal menu and devotion to pairing fine wine with top-notch chocolate. Arguably NYC's only full wine and chocolate bar, Ayza sources its desserts from quality chocolatiers like Jacques Torres, Michel Cluizel and Cioccolada, the latter dairy-free, gluten-free, soy-free and kosher to ensure a fit with the restaurant's vegan-friendly approach. Adding to the appeal are the innovative chocolate martinis, served in six flavours.

ESCAZÚ CHOCOLATES

936 N Blount St, Raleigh; www.escazuchocolates.com; +1 919-832-3433

◆ Tastings　◆ Classes　◆ Cafe
◆ Roastery　◆ Shop

Your eyes may say you're in 21st-century Raleigh, North Carolina, but your tongue has been transported to 16th-century Spain. That's the magic trick of Escazú's historic drinking chocolates, based on antique recipes. The Spain hot chocolate is sweetened with unrefined sugar and scented with star anise, cinnamon, almond and chillis, while an 18th-century Italian version is fragrant with jasmine and orange blossom. Chocolate is not just a taste experience but an intellectual one as well at this bean-to-bar shop. Cacao is sourced in Venezuela and other Latin American countries and roasted in a vintage 1920s Spanish ball roaster before being crushed in antique stone grinders. The delectable results include truffles flavoured with home-grown herbs, and a popular goat milk chocolate bar.

THINGS TO DO NEARBY

North Carolina Museum of Art
There are few better ways to spend an afternoon than at this excellent (and free) art museum, with a wide-ranging collection and an outdoor sculpture trail.
ncartmuseum.org

Pullen Park
Founded in 1887, this family attraction still has a sweet turn-of-the-century vibe, with a kiddie train, an antique carousel and a pond full of paddle boats.
www.raleighnc.gov/parks

FRENCH BROAD CHOCOLATE FACTORY

821 Riverside Drive, Suite 199, Asheville;
www.frenchbroadchocolates.com; +1 828-348-5169

◆ Tastings　◆ Classes　◆ Cafe
◆ Roastery　◆ Shop　◆ Tours

THINGS TO DO NEARBY

Biltmore Estate
See how Gilded Era gentry lived at America's largest private home, built in 1895 by a Vanderbilt heir to look like a French chateau. It's one-of-a-kind.
www.biltmore.com

Blue Ridge Parkway
Heaven is autumn on the Blue Ridge Parkway, when the gorges and mountaintops explode in scarlet and amber. The 755km (469-mi) parkway passes just by Asheville.

Burial Brewery
If you like it dark and hoppy, this industrial-cool microbrewery is your spot, with beer bearing gothic names like 'Hellstar' and 'Death and the Miser'.
burialbeer.com

Pisgah National Forest
Hike, swim and climb in this half-million-acre (more than 800 sq km) paradise, its piney slopes blooming with mountain laurel, the sound of tinkling waterfalls echoing through its gorges.

Jael and Dan Rattigan could have been a corporate executive and a lawyer, respectively. But instead the couple dropped out of graduate school, bought a vegetable oil-fuelled school bus to live in, and headed to Costa Rica to learn about artisanal chocolate making. A year and a half later, the two pointed their bus north towards the Blue Ridge mountain town of Asheville, North Carolina, where they opened the French Broad Chocolate Lounge. The lounge was an instant hit for bonbons flavoured with everything from lemongrass to local honey, towering chocolate-stout layer cakes and 'liquid truffle' sipping chocolates. The pair soon expanded into the bean-to-bar game, opening a factory on the banks of the river for which their company is named.

Tour the factory to learn how cacao becomes grapefruit-olive-oil-fennel truffles or chocolate-covered caramels infused with local whiskey. Smell the earthy unroasted cacao and see the grinders gnash the beans into brown silk. Are there tastings? But of course. There's a fully loaded chocolate cafe too. Half-hour tours are every day at 2pm and 4pm, while hour-long tours are Saturdays at 10am and 11:30am. Book ahead, though fifteen-minute walk-throughs are daily from 1pm to 6pm and don't require reservations.

CACAO

414 SW 13th Ave, Portland;
cacaodrinkchocolate.com; +1 503-241-0656

◆ Tastings   ◆ Classes   ◆ Cafe
◆ Roastery   ◆ Shop   ◆ Transport

Quintessentially Portland (an internet search of Cacao + Portland turns up a *Portlandia* sketch in which a couple use the shop's name as their bedroom safe-word), Cacao carries a wide selection of the world's finest bean-to-bar chocolate made by small local and international producers. But what makes Cacao a must-visit are their single-origin drinking chocolates, which come in three varieties (classic dark French-style, a lighter Venezuelan milk with cinnamon and a spicy dark drinking chocolate infused with ginger, coconut milk and other spices). You can order each individually by the mug or go for the flight, which includes a demitasse serving of all three. No wonder Stumptown has the reputation for being one of the country's best foodie destinations.

THINGS TO DO NEARBY

Powell's City of Books
The world's biggest brick-and-mortar bookshop and a must-visit for bibliophiles. Powell's travel section alone dwarfs most airport book stores.
www.powells.com

Blue Star Donuts
Not over-indulged yet? Chocolate donuts are just the start of the offerings here at this fancy coffee and donut shop right downtown. Expect a wait.
www.bluestardonuts

HERSHEY'S CHOCOLATE WORLD AND HERSHEYPARK

Chocolate World Way, Hershey;
www.hersheys.com/chocolateworld; +1 717-534-4900

◆ Tastings ◆ Classes ◆ Cafe
◆ Roastery ◆ Shop ◆ Food

© Thanida Sinfan / Shutterstock

THINGS TO DO NEARBY

Hershey Gardens
Another Milton Hershey production (it was a gift for his wife), this lovely garden blooms with roses in spring. The butterfly atrium is a highlight.

The Hershey Story
This museum tells the tale of how Milton Hershey went from Mennonite farm boy to candy magnate, making this patch of rural farmland a factory town.

Harrisburg
Pennsylvania's state capital, 20 minutes from Hershey, has the gracious state capital complex, a pretty riverfront, a dinosaur-bone-filled museum, and several Revolutionary War sites.

Amish Country
This part of Pennsylvania is home to America's largest community of modernity-shunning Amish people, whose farm tours, buggy rides and homemade jams and quilts are a major tourist draw.

In 1903, confectioner Milton Hershey began construction on an enormous chocolate factory in his rural hometown of Derry Township, Pennsylvania. Hershey had developed a method for making milk chocolate more shelf stable, a trade secret he called 'the Hershey Process'. The rest is history – sweet, sweet history. Today the town – now called Hershey – is home to Hershey's Chocolate World. Families ride trams on a Disnified 'factory' tour involving singing animatronic characters, don glasses for the 4D *Chocolate Movie*, and take a turn at making their own candy bars. The hangar-sized gift shop will sell you a 5lb (2.3kg), $60 'world's largest' Hershey bar if you so desire. Next door, Hersheypark was founded in 1906 as a leisure spot for Hershey's army of workers and their families. Today

it's a classic American amusement park, with candy-themed kiddie rides, roller coasters, a water park and, of course, ice cream galore.

Note the Hershey Process produces butyric acid, which gives Hershey's chocolate its characteristic tang; other US chocolate manufacturers now imitate it. To Americans, it's the taste of childhood. But those used to British or Swiss milk chocolate sometimes say it has an unpleasant whiff of parmesan cheese, which also contains butyric acid.

OLIVE & SINCLAIR

1628 Fatherland St, Nashville;
www.oliveandsinclair.com; +1 615-262-3007

◆ Roastery   ◆ Tours
◆ Shop

THINGS TO DO NEARBY

High Garden Tea
This magical tea shop feels like an apothecary of old. Loose-leaf teas line the walls and a welcoming tea room and kombucha bar can entertain for hours.
www.highgardentea.com

Five Points Pizza
This unpretentious eatery serves up simple, perfect pies with crunchy-soft crusts that will leave you swooning. Sit down for a pie or get a slice to go.
www.fivepointspizza.com

The 5 Spot
Venues like this are what make Nashville 'Music City'. Small, dark and intimate, the stage hosts a wide range of local acts. The Sunday Night Soul event is especially wonderful.
www.the5spot.club

Shelby Bottoms Greenway
A slice of nature in the city, Shelby Bottoms has 5 miles of paved, accessibility-friendly trails as well as 5 miles of easy off-road trails. Explore the riverside landscape and see if you can spot any local wildlife.

Nashville, Tennessee, has become a veritable boom town of culinary delights – while hot chicken may be its most famous dish, you'll need a little something sweet to balance out all that spice, and that's where Olive & Sinclair (O&S) comes in. This small chocolatier is one of the most prolific candymakers in town; you'll see these bars in many a gift shop, and for good reason.

O&S does things the no-frills, old-fashioned way from their cozy location in the heart of leafy East Nashville; fair trade beans are roasted and shelled, and then the chocolate is ground in two beautiful stone melangers dating back to early 1900s Spain and France. The results are a smooth dark chocolate (usually 67–75% cacao) and a creamy white chocolate that serve as the basis for the maker's many creative bars: sea salt, cinnamon chili, cherry cordials, bourbon brittle and more. And O&S' impact on Nashville's food scene doesn't end there – they work closely with local breweries, distilleries and tea shops, providing cocoa nibs for creative, tasty brews.

While the majority of their products are chocolate-based, we'd be remiss not to mention their decadent duck fat caramels, not-too-sticky confections with a perfect hint of savoury richness. Balance that with a taste of the bourbon brittle, and you'll be in Nashville candy heaven.

© 2020 Olive and Sinclair; photos by Greg Roos

CACAO & CARDAMOM

5000 Westheimer Rd Suite 602, Houston;
www.cacaoandcardamom.com; +1 281-501-3567

◆ Tastings   ◆ Classes
◆ Cafe   ◆ Shop

THINGS TO DO NEARBY

The Menil Collection
See surrealist and modern European paintings and sculptures at this museum and campus formed from John and Dominique de Menil's private collection. *www.menil.org*

Hugo's
This modern Mexican restaurant by award-winning chef Hugo Ortega knows how to do every meal, but don't miss the staggering buffet brunch. *www.hugosrestaurant.net*

Gerald D Hines Waterwall Park
Formerly called Williams Waterwall, this fountain is 12m (64ft) tall and surrounded by 118 live oaks. It's the most photographed landmark in Houston.

Galleria
Shop till you drop Texas-style at this mixed-use shopping mall, with 339 stores as well as restaurants and even hotels. *www.simon.com/mall/the-galleria*

Owner Annie Rupani's chocolate might be the most stylish you've ever seen: In addition to chocolate bonbons, dragees and mendiants, her chic uptown store specialises in chocolate high heels. That's right: shoes you don't wear but rather eat. Think high heels, ballet flats, and even men's dress shoes, all made out of rich chocolate. And if that isn't enough for you, she also makes chocolate ganache 'lipsticks' that will delight any makeup lover.

While Rupani was studying for her law school admissions exams, she started making chocolate confections. After taking the test, she realised she loved chocolate, not law. In 2014 she started Cacao & Cardamom, named for chocolate's central ingredient and an important spice in her South Asian culture.

Situated in a nondescript Houston strip mall, her shop beckons gourmands with its dramatic dark-wood interior. Chocolate confections are displayed like jewels in a glass case that runs the length of the store, with more goodies on the adjacent shelves. There are also one or two tables up front where you can enjoy gelato and a bonbon or two. If you have to choose just one treat to take home, go with the Louboutin-inspired chocolate high heel with red soles.

KATE WEISER CHOCOLATE

3011 Gulden Ln, Suite 115, Dallas;
www.kateweiserchocolate.com; +1 469-619-4929

◆ Tastings   ◆ Classes
◆ Cafe   ◆ Shop

After coming up as a pastry chef at well-known restaurants in Kansas City and Dallas, Kate Weiser decided she wanted to focus exclusively on chocolate. She opened her first location in 2014, and now she has three shops total — two in Dallas and one in Fort Worth. Think clean, modern design, mouthwatering ice cream and macarons and gorgeous bonbons that look more like jewels than dessert. Each bonbon takes four days to create, starting with shining the moulds and ending with painting the bonbons with coloured cocoa butter. Flavours range from 63%

dark chocolate to buttery popcorn. If you visit around the holidays, don't miss Carl the Snowman, a festive chocolate snowman with drinking chocolate mix in his belly and a head of marshmallows.

THINGS TO DO NEARBY

Sixth Floor Museum at Dealey Plaza
Time travel back to November 1963, when JFK was assassinated on this spot. The museum honours his legacy and documents that day.
www.jfk.org

Dallas Museum of Art
This major museum offers a high-caliber world tour of ancient and contemporary art. Treasures range from Greek, Roman and Etruscan masterpieces to A+ work from the Mimbres pueblos of New Mexico. *dma.org*

TEJAS CHOCOLATE + BARBECUE

200 N Elm St, Tomball;
www.tejaschocolate.com; +1 832-761-0670

◆ Tastings ◆ Classes ◆ Cafe
◆ Roastery ◆ Shop ◆ Food

Chocolate and barbecue aren't obvious bedfellows, but when Scott Moore Jr first started making bean-to-bar chocolate in 2010, he saw some similarities: He cooked both his cacao beans and his meat 'low and slow', the Texan way. His single-origin bars began gaining notoriety for their smoked flavours, and when an old home in Tomball came on the market, he realised he could open a barbecue joint and a chocolate factory. The result? A welcoming house with rustic, neon signs and some of the best brisket in Texas (Tejas is even on *Texas Monthly*'s prestigious list of top 10 BBQ joints in the state) — plus fire-roasted cacao beans that turn into single-origin bars and house-made truffles in flavours like salted caramel.

THINGS TO DO NEARBY

Matt Family Orchard
Pick your own blackberries, blueberries and pumpkins, at this 40-acre farm. Or hit up the farm store for already-picked fruit, honey and more. *www. mattfamilyorchard.com*

Gleannloch Pines Golf Club
Tomball boasts more than 30 golf courses, and at this unique destination, the courses are designed to look like those in Ireland and Scotland. *golfgleannlochpines.com*

© 2020, Tejas Chocolate

CAPUTO'S

314 W Broadway, Salt Lake City;
www.caputos.com; +1 801-531-8669

◆ Tastings   ◆ Classes
◆ Shop

This circa 1997 family-run business has been a major supporter of Utah's artisan chocolate industry since its early days, not only selling their products but also providing shoppers with an introductory taste. Caputo's also promotes these 'made in Utah' confectioneries and other treats through chocolate tasting 101 classes held at three of their locations. Every shop keeps chocolates on hand for sampling via what's called 'a chocolate file,' alphabetised by maker. Another chocolatey promotion by Caputo's is its annual festival, highlighting a specific country of origin; proceeds benefit the Heirloom Cacao Preservation Initiative. Caputo's four locations stock some of the world's best chocolate, many organic and fair trade certified, in milk, dark or white, sourced from across the US and all over the globe.

THINGS TO DO NEARBY

Temple Square
Tour the extensive complex owned by the Church of Jesus Christ of Latter-day Saints, whose Tabernacle building is where the Tabernacle Choir meets for its weekly rehearsals.
www.templesquare.com

Mount Olympus Hike
Go on an epic journey with this easy-to-follow but strenuous trail that leads to the summit of this peak on the east side of the Salt Lake Valley.
www.utah.com/hiking/mt-olympus-trail

© Alison J. Hann / Shutterstock

THEO CHOCOLATE

3400 Phinney Ave N, Seattle;
www.theochocolate.com; +1 206-632-5100

◆ Tastings ◆ Classes ◆ Cafe
◆ Roastery ◆ Shop ◆ Transport

It's no coincidence that the USA's first certified organic, fair trade, bean-to-bar chocolate company is here in Seattle: the clean-and-green Emerald City has a long-standing community of organic farmers and markets. Theo fits right in with beans sourced from individual farmers in South America and Africa, and hits the mark with its salted almond bar, a 70% dark chocolate blend; and the Big Daddy, a bite-sized version of the campfire standard s'more (graham cracker, caramel and marshmallow) covered in dark chocolate and milk chocolate drizzle. The Theo Classic Library box comes stacked with 10 tempting treats. Theo's popular factory tour walks you through the process, from an actual cacao tree to observing chocolates being made, with tasting options throughout.

THINGS TO DO NEARBY

Pike Place Market
Indulge farmstand fantasies at Pike Place Market. Since 1907, its multiple floors have been Seattle's source for produce, seafood and more. *pikeplacemarket.org*

Chihuly Garden & Glass
Let your eyes pop at the outlandish contemporary glass art at Chihuly Garden & Glass, in both indoor galleries and a landscaped garden. *www. chihulygardenandglass.com*

TABAL CHOCOLATE

7515 Harwood Ave, Wauwatosa;
tabalchocolate.com; +1 414-585-9996

◆ Tastings ◆ Classes ◆ Cafe
◆ Roastery ◆ Shop ◆ Tours

© 2020, Tabal Chocolate

THINGS TO DO NEARBY

Harley-Davidson Museum
Hundreds of motorcycles show the styles through the decades, including the flashy rides of Elvis and Evel Knievel, plus interactive exhibits.
www.harley-davidson.com

Milwaukee Art Museum
This lakeside cultural institution features a stunning winglike addition by Santiago Calatrava as well as an excellent art collection.
mam.org

Lakefront Brewery
Lakefront Brewery, across the river from Brady St, has afternoon tours, but the swellest time to visit is on Friday night when there's a fish fry, 16 beers to try and a polka band letting loose.
www.lakefrontbrewery.com

Madison
College town Madison reaps a lot of kudos – most walkable city, best road-biking city, most vegetarian-friendly, gay-friendly; just plain all-round friendliest city.
www.cityofmadison.com

One step inside the charming historic storefront home of Tabal Chocolate and you're enveloped in a very sensory experience. The aroma of roasted cacao beans floods the shop where sampling and asking questions are more than encouraged. They're expected. Chocolate bars in the Tabal family (infused with everything from chilli pepper to blueberry rooibos tea) are lined up on a table along with abundant samples of each one. It's matriculation by tasting, but there's also a larger, societal motive for learning about Tabal's chocolate. 'It's social justice – from bean to packaging,' says chocolate maker Dan Bieser, who started the business in a rented commercial kitchen in 2012. Named after the Mayan word that means 'relationship', Tabal focuses on building direct, long-term connections with cacao bean farmers in Central and South America to create pure, high-quality chocolate. This process controls environ-mental impact and helps the farmers support themselves. Bieser's bean-to-bar shop, which also offers chocolate- and truffle-making classes, is the only one like it in Milwaukee. The shop is a working factory, staffed by devotees who are just as eager to share the process. To start, the cacao pods are picked, fermented and dried. Once the beans are shipped to Tabal, they're sorted and roasted, cracked and winnowed. Left are the crunchy, toasty edible nibs which are then ground and melted, cooled and moulded into bars.

TOP CHOC FEST

CHOCOA CHOCOLATE FESTIVAL
AMSTERDAM, NETHERLANDS

Amsterdam's winter festival, held each February, has a special focus on sustainable cocoa production, with an emphasis on encouraging supply chain practices that help farmers thrive. It's one of the best festivals for aspiring chocolatiers interested in the business side of this tasty enterprise, though classes and talks are open to the general public.

CHOCOLATE SHOW
NEW YORK CITY, USA

This annual chocolate festival takes place in New York City each fall and features classes and workshops as well as opportunities to sample the wares of exhibitors and see cacao pods up close.

SALON DU CHOCOLATE
PARIS, FRANCE

Chocaholics won't want to miss this five-day chocolate festival's tastings, workshops, demonstrations and more at Paris Expo Porte de Versailles. There are special activities for kids, and if you miss the annual event in Paris, Salon du Chocolate holds offshoots throughout the calendar year in other locations. The annual fashion show is mind-boggling.

OLATE VALS

CHOCOLART
TÜBINGEN, GERMANY
It's all about *schokolade* (chocolate) at this irresistible six-day festival, with programme highlights including tastings, praline-making courses, cocoa painting, workshops and cookery courses. The event takes place in the streets of Tübingen's beautifully illuminated Altstadt, and the timing in December means you can visit local Christmas markets too.

CHOCOLATE FEST
ST GEORGE'S, GRENADA
A celebration of the island's organic chocolate production, this annual festival (held each May) features a number of chocolate-centric activities that serve to educate participants on the history of cocoa in the country, illustrate how local cocoa goes from 'tree to bar,' and explore the food's current role in the culinary scene.

EUROCHOCOLATE
PERUGIA, ITALY
Now in its 23rd year, Umbria's annual Eurochocolate event (each October) pulls in 900,000 people, every one of them obsessed with all things cocoa-based. There are tastings, chocolate cooking classes and even edible sculptures on show. Trawl the stalls to stock up on bars and liqueurs from Europe's best chocolatiers and then lose the crowds in Perugia's spectacular cobbled alleys and gorgeous piazzas.

AS

IA

DAVAO CITY, *PHILIPPINES*

Over 80% of the chocolate production in the Philippines comes from the Davao region, and award-winning Filipino chocolatiers Theo & Philo, Malagos and Auro Chocolate all source from Davao farmers to create their unique bars. Factory visits and even a chocolate bar crawl make chocoholics here say 'yum'.

HO CHI MINH CITY, *VIETNAM*

HCMC is base to Vietnam's first artisan chocolate producer, Marou. Watch their skilled team tempering and moulding chocolate crafted from local fair trade cacao, and enjoy the result in Marou's cafe. It's not the only game in town, either; Belvie Chocolate Cafe, Cyrus Chocolaterie and more are in the mix as well.

UBUD, *INDONESIA*

Bali's Pod Chocolate Factory is based here, and visitors can see Indonesian cacao be fermented, dried, roasted, ground and turned into a range of delicious gourmet sweets. And why not: cocoa is one of Indonesia's top agricultural exports, and Balinese chocolatiers have a rich resource in Indonesian smallholders.

INDIA

How to ask for hot chocolate in the local language? India has 24 official languages, but in Hindi, you might ask *Ek garam chocolate doodh milega?* Hot chocolate isn't very big in India, however, for obvious reasons.

Signature chocolate flavours? Plain milk chocolate, unadulterated by any flavouring is the popular pick.

What to order with your chocolate? Whipped cream!

Do: Try chocolate *paan* street food if you dare (it includes betel leaf).

Despite a rather serious sweet tooth, India hasn't forayed too deep into the chocolate world; Indians are traditionalists, mostly seeming to prefer the inexpensive and sugary charms of bars of chocolate from Cadbury (now distributed as Mondēlez India), Nestlé or local brand Amul. Canny marketing has helped push the big brands into homes to such an extent that the word 'Cadbury' was often seen as synonymous with chocolate. And although each brand offers a dark, milk, and white, the plain milk chocolate bar remains by far, an Indian favourite. That is, until now – a fledgling artisanal chocolate industry has been reaching its fingers across the country, working with small-time cacao

farmers (mostly from states in the south of India), pouring far more cacao and far less sugar into their creations. These homegrown brands are infusing their chocolates with all kinds of flavours. Certainly, the time-tested coffee, nuts and dried fruit, but also more intriguing ones such as peppercorn, custard apple, *bhut jolokia* (ghost pepper) chilli, Alphonso mango and red pepper.

This is still a niche market though, not least because of its upmarket pricing, and these aren't the type of chocolates you'd pick up at your local grocery store. Indeed, the bad news is that there's certainly no danger of the Indian market overtaking that of major producers, whether in growing or chocolate manufacturing, anytime soon. In 2015-16, for instance, Indian cacao production measured only about 1% of that of Côte d'Ivoire. The good news? There's plenty more room to grow!

CHITRA'M

No.7, Sathyamurthy Rd, Coimbatore, Tamil Nadu;
chitramcraftchocolates.com; +91 98438-06006

◆ Tastings ◆ Cafe ◆ Workshops
◆ Roastery ◆ Shop ◆ Food

 Several things set Chitra'm Chocolates apart from the rest. Chocolatier Arun Viswanathan, who trained in Brussels, eschews all synthetic flavourings like vanillin, lecithin, preservatives and vegetable fats in his chocolate, and uses only unrefined sugar for a healthier piece of chocolate. Each bar uses distinctive Indian flavours: dark chocolate comes flecked with turmeric and palm sugar, white chocolate is spiked with rose and saffron, *ragi* and coconut is stirred into milk chocolate bars, white chocolate spiked with moringa and lemon, dark chocolate with the lash of green chilli and raw mango, plus vegan chocolate.

As a result of all this innovation, Chitra'm has won medals at the International Chocolate Awards. Stop by their 35-seat cafe, Infusions, located by the chocolate factory, to sample their goods (including Chitra'm hot chocolate).

THINGS TO DO NEARBY

Kasthuri Sreenivasan Art Gallery & Textile Museum
A pitstop at this museum provides an excellent view into India's handloom industry. *www. kasthurisreenivasan artgallery.com*

Gass Forest Museum & Insect Museum
This colonial-era museum, established in 1903 by British forest officer HA Gass, houses a thicket of natural history exhibits, from taxidermied animals to slivers of mica.

ENTISI

Krishna Villa, Santacruz West, Mumbai, Maharashtra;
entisi.com; +91 80805-54554

◆ Classes
◆ Shop

 Entisi's small, sleek chocolate salon is rather succinct in size with no seating, but it is heaving with toothsome chocolates: espresso and fruit bonbons cloaked in kaleidoscopic colours, fruit and nut dragées, but also cool outliers such as matcha apricot and *til chikki* (a sticky sesame confection) chocolate.

Nikki Thakker, Entisi's owner, orders her chocolate from abroad; it arrives semi-finished, and is shaped into the finished product at her Willy Wonka–esque chocolate lab, where large machines work in tandem with adroit-fingered chocolate artists who craft each piece just so. Bestsellers are the Daily Dose box of bonbons (one for each day of the week), 54% dark chocolate cubes and Entisi's Nutella-esque hazelnut spread.

THINGS TO DO NEARBY

Granth Book Store
A short rickshaw ride away is this little bookstore. What Granth lacks in square footage, it makes up for in the density and variety of its stock. *Granth.com*

Chapel Lane
The area of Santacruz is named after a cross, originally built of wood in the 1850s, that sits on this 300m (984ft) lane; nowadays, you'll find three distinctive crosses here.

INDONESIA

How to ask for hot chocolate in the local language? *Boleh saya mau es krim cokelat?*

Signature chocolate flavours? Get your Central Javan *serabi* (coconut-milk pancakes) topped with chocolate.

What to order with your chocolate? Bars incorporating chilli, ginger, cinnamon and coffee pay homage to Indonesia's role in the spice trade.

Do: Try avocado juice blended with ice and chocolate syrup.

Cacao grown in Indonesia typically produces chocolate with a lighter colour and distinctive flavour. The crop was introduced by Europeans and its cultivation went in fits and starts until efforts by the government and private farmers in the second half of the 20th century led to the country becoming the third largest producer in the world. Most has been for export, but internal consumption is slowly rising and more companies are setting up base here

to produce local chocolate products from the harvest.

Visits to cacao farms and processing factories let visitors experience the country's cocoa industry. At Big Tree Farms in Abiansemal, a factory processes coconut-palm sugar and cocoa in a facility notable for its architecture – it's one of the world's largest commercial buildings constructed from bamboo, and has been designed to be a showcase of sustainable building practice. Pod Chocolate Factory runs tours as well, and Indonesian-based chocolatiers are gaining steam at a rapid pace. In Yogyakarta on Java, Chocolate Monggo was established in 2015 by a Belgian expat, and the chocolaterie has since expanded into a factory with cafes across the island. Meanwhile, award-winning Indonesian chocolate producer Krakakoa has created a farmer-to-bar model that trains local farmers to grow organically.

POD CHOCOLATE FACTORY

29 Jalan Denpasar-Singaraja, Mengwi, Bali;
www.podchocolate.com; +62 361-2091011

- ◆ Roastery ◆ Shop ◆ Workshops
- ◆ Cafe ◆ Tours ◆ Food

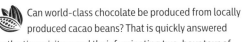 Can world-class chocolate be produced from locally produced cacao beans? That is quickly answered by the time visitors end their fascinating two-hour tour of Bali's Pod Chocolate Factory, where they witness firsthand through a huge glass window how modern European machinery roasts and tempers beans that were produced here on the island of Bali by local farmers. And the real proof of the pudding? That comes when tasting the work of Pod's master-chocolatiers in the colourful bamboo cafe, from The Purist, 99% dark chocolate, to Nectar, flavoured with sea salt, chilli or cinnamon. Although there are no formal classes, everyone gets a chance to try the messy task of 'fresh chocolate making', moulding your own chocolate bar to take home afterwards.

THINGS TO DO NEARBY

Jatiluwih Rice Fields
At Jatiluwih, which means 'truly marvellous', visitors are rewarded with gorgeous vistas of centuries-old rice terraces, which have received Unesco status.

Warung Babi Guling Tabanan
No one can visit Bali without trying *babi guling*, succulent roasted suckling pig, perfectly prepared at Ibu Dayu's cafe just down the road from the factory.

SORGA CHOCOLATE

Jalan Pura Mastima, Jasri, Karangasem, Bali;
www.sorgachocolate.com; +62 363-21687

- ◆ Roastery ◆ Shop ◆ Classes
- ◆ Cafe ◆ Tour

Located on the wild east coast of Bali, this bamboo garage-style factory offers visitors a unique opportunity to witness the making of organic sustainable chocolate: from fermenting and sun-drying of the beans during harvest season, through roasting, grinding, tempering and pouring, plus the possibility of joining a workshop on making chocolate bars and truffles. The owner of Sorga Chocolate – it means Heavenly Chocolate – is American Emerald Starr, known as the 'Chocolate man of Bali', who began educating local farmers on correct cacao cultivation methods after arriving here in the 1990s, before opening this production facility in 2014. Today Sorga has a 'Made with Love, Tastes like Heaven' mantra; to test it just bite into a Ginger Crunch or Rambutan bar.

THINGS TO DO NEARBY

Jasri Bay Hideaway
In the same village as Sorga (nay, the same street), spend a relaxing night in a traditional wooden cottage right by the ocean.
www.jasribay.com

Taman Soekasada Ujung
Ten minutes drive up the coast, discover this idyllic Balinese water palace surrounded by pools, floating pavilions and verdant tiered gardens.
+62 363-4301870

JAPAN

How to ask for hot chocolate in the local language?
Hottochokore kudasai.
Signature chocolate flavour? Matcha green tea.
What to order with your chocolate? A plate of trendy
'souffle pancakes'.
Don't: Don't eat or drink on the street; it's considered rude.

If it's new and cool, Japan is on it, and chocolate is
no exception. This love of novelty makes for some
wild flavours – hello, wasabi Kit Kats! Adorableness is
another Japanese obsession, which means convenience
stores filled with tiny chocolate panda cookies and itty-bitty
chocolate mushrooms.

But Japan is also serious about craft and precision. The
top European chocolatiers all have outposts in Tokyo and
other major cities, often sitting side-by-side in *depachika*
(high-end department store food halls) with homegrown

brands like Royce' and Meiji. Luxury chocolates are a
common gift for hosts or business associates. On Valentine's
Day, women are expected to buy fancy *honmei choco* (love
chocolate) for their spouses and partners; male friends and
coworkers receive cheaper *giri choco* (obligation chocolate).
A week or two before the holiday, Tokyo hosts the massive
Salon du Chocolat, a festival showcasing the finest brands
and hottest new products.

The Japanese bean-to-bar movement is growing, with
artisans producing truffles and bars in regionally inspired
flavours like matcha, black sesame, yuzu and shiso (a
leafy herb). Though the country currently relies entirely
on imported beans, that may be changing – one chocolate company is attempting to grow cacao on the remote
subtropical Ogasawara islands.

CACAOKEN

17-79 Higashitokuzen, Iizuka-shi, Fukuoka Prefecture; cacaoken.com; +81 94 821 1533

◆ Tastings   ◆ Classes   ◆ Transport
◆ Roastery   ◆ Shop

 Cacaoken got its name by fusing the Japanese words for 'cacao' and 'laboratory,' as the family business started in 2012 as a space to experiment with unique cacaos. The entire operation takes place in a bright red trailer parked just next to their home. Stepping inside the space, the scent of roasted cacao and melted chocolate is concentrated, while dozens of products provide a feast for the eyes. Capping the counter is a chocolate fountain for preparing frothed chocolate drinks and fruit dips. In Cacaoken's ever-expanding menu, consumers see the result of their constant experimentation with products highlighting native Japanese plants and dishes, including seasonal specialties sold only in their physical shop. Local favourites include the cacao nib honey, shiso milk chocolate and black sugar bonbons.

THINGS TO DO NEARBY

Patisserie Saison
Locally praised for their personal pastries and fresh French flavours, Saison beautifully represents Japan's creative interpretations of classic European sweets.

Katsumori Park
Drenched in cherry blossoms every spring, during the rest of the year the park is a family-friendly haven for locals seeking to rest amongst nature.

GREEN BEAN TO BAR

Nishitetsu Tenjin Class, 1-19-22 Imaizumi, Chuo-ku, Fukuoka City; greenchocolate.jp; +81 92 406 7880

◆ Food   ◆ Shop   ◆ Transport
◆ Roastery ◆ Cafe

Japanese chocolate makers rarely venture into pastry, but Green Bean to Bar has managed to master both. Entering their cafe puts you face-to-table with an array of single-origin and flavoured chocolate bars, freshly opened for sampling each morning. From Japanese citrus to cherry blossoms, their specialty bars are only available in Japan and rotate out on a monthly basis. Just below the counter is the selection of bonbons, made with their own bean-to-bar chocolate and select regional fruits. Green Bean to Bar's pastries are also notoriously well-crafted; you can't miss their cocoa-nib-studded double chocolate cookies and layered chocolate mousse. For those short on time, order a seasonal hot chocolate to go and explore their glassed-in chocolate factory while you wait.

THINGS TO DO NEARBY

Fukuoka Castle
The historic grounds of this castle were constructed during the Edo period; a quick hike to the highest point offers a 360-degree view of downtown Fukuoka.

Fukuoka City Zoological Garden
This botanical garden showcases over 1000 species of plants, beautifully arranged for visitors to explore on their own, as well as a small zoo on-site.

SHIROI KOBITO PARK

Miyanosawa 2-jo 2-chome, Nishi-ku, Sapporo, Hokkaido; www.shiroikobitopark.jp/english; +81 11-666-1481

◆ Tastings ◆ Classes ◆ Cafe
◆ Transport ◆ Shop

You can only rarely get a delicate Shiroi Kobito cookie outside Hokkaido, which makes them a sought-after souvenir, packaged in blue-and-white boxes featuring Mount Rishiri. It helps that the cookies themselves – dainty sandwiches of *langue du chat* wafers and white chocolate – are delectable. Indulge in Shiroi Kobito and other chocolate delicacies from the Ishiya company at this sweet little Sapporo theme park. It's meant to look European, which means half-timbered Tyrolean chalets next to Victorian brick clock towers. Watch cookies being made in the factory or sign up to make your own at the Cookiecraft Studio. Then dig into chocolate fondue and Shiroi Kobito parfaits at the cafe. Kids love the pony rides and the miniature steam train (and the chocolate, too).

THINGS TO DO NEARBY

Sapporo Beer Museum
Tour the handsome ivy-covered brick building of Japan's oldest brewery, founded in 1876, then move on to the Tasting Salon for an only-in-Hokkaido Sapporo Classic.
www.sapporobeer.jp

Odori Park
This narrow rectangular green space flows for 13 blocks through central Sapporo. Watch kids play on *Black Slide Mantra*, a sculpture/slide by famed Japanese-American sculptor Isamu Noguchi.

KIT KAT CHOCOLATORY GINZA

3-7-2 Ginza, Chuo-ku; nestle.jp/brand/kit/chocolatory;
+81 3-6228-6285

- ◆ Tastings
- ◆ Cafe
- ◆ Shop
- ◆ Transport

Introduced to Japan in 1973, this humble British wafer-based chocolate bar was a quick success, perhaps because its name sounds similar to the Japanese phrase *kitto katsu*, 'you will surely win'. But the brand truly exploded in the early 2000s when Nestlé Japan began experimenting with new flavours. At first they were relatively tame – strawberry, green tea. But soon locals were scooping up bars in flavours like miso soup, soy sauce, green bean and even cough drop. Today, Kit Kat Chocolatory shops sell limited-edition luxury versions created by the master-chocolatier Yasumasa Takagi. At the main branch in Tokyo's wealthy Ginza neighbourhood, crowds line up for naturally pink 'ruby chocolate' Kit Kats and elaborate Kit Kat parfaits, many impossible to find elsewhere.

THINGS TO DO NEARBY

Hama-rikyū Gardens
This Edo-period garden is the grounds of a long-gone shogunate palace. Today you can sip matcha in a traditional teahouse and wander beneath centuries-old black pines.

Tsukiji Outer Market
The famous fish auctions have moved to a new location, but this sprawling market is still an excellent spot for sashimi breakfasts and browsing kitchen knives and crockery.
www.tsukiji.or.jp/english

MALAYSIA

How to ask for hot chocolate in the local language? *Teh tarik* (pulled tea) is the national drink, but if you're craving chocolate, order a *Satu Milo sila*.

Signature chocolate flavour? Durian-filled chocolates may tempt the adventurous.

What to order with your chocolate? Durian pastries.

Do: Add a stop in Malaysian Borneo to your itinerary.

Most of Malaysia's cocoa production happens on the island of Borneo (also shared by Indonesia and Brunei). The states of Sarawak and Sabah both have strong agricultural sectors, with Cocoa Kingdom in Tanjung Aru one of the easier-to-visit sites. For those unable to visit a cacao farm or stop at Teck Guan Cocoa Museum in Tawau, Kuala Lumpur boasts Harriston Boutique; brave the tour groups being pushed through this chocolate emporium and small-scale production line to sample unusual local variations such as durian-filled chocolates. Similarly to other cacao-producing countries that export their cocoa, there is a recent move to increase the number of local factories and bean-to-bar companies while continuing to grow Malaysia's export numbers.

CASA LATINA & CACAO LAB

20 Persiaran Ampang, Kuala Lumpur;
www.casalatinacacaolabkl.com; +60 3-42652332

◆ Tastings   ◆ Classes   ◆ Cafe
◆ Roastery   ◆ Shop   ◆ Transport

Bubbly Venezuelan celebrity chef Tamara Rodríguez Sanchez settled in Malaysia a couple of years ago, and swiftly set about creating an authentic corner of South America in her funky Cafe and Cacao Lab. Importing fermented beans from her homeland, as well as using local produce from a plantation in Malaysia's state of Pahang, she roasts on-site and creates an ever-changing selection of pralines and truffles. Her chocolate workshop is a hands-on course, covering everything from bean-to-bar to creating your own truffles, while other classes cover Latin cuisine and even salsa lessons! Tamara explains that 'our handmade chocolates use mainly Latin American flavours, including pisco, but when we make pralines with the local durian fruit, it always sells out quickly'.

THINGS TO DO NEARBY

Hari Hari Datang
Almost next door is this popular food court, packed with inexpensive stalls showcasing Malaysia's dazzling street food cuisine, with Malay, Chinese and Indian dishes.

Ampang Point
Head for some serious retail therapy at one of KL's ubiquitous modern shopping malls, packed with locals, fashion boutiques, bars and bistros. *www. ampangpoint.com.my*

SENIMAN KAKAO

29 Jalan Pudu Lama, Kuala Lumpur;
www.senimankakao.com; +60 3-74907788

◆ Food   ◆ Classes   ◆ Cafe
◆ Roastery   ◆ Shop   ◆ Transport

The owners of this cool new locale are on an impassioned mission to promote sustainable, locally grown Malaysian cacao that produces high-quality bean-to-bar chocolate. They have toured smallholder plantations across the nation, reward growers with prices exceeding the market rate and use an artisan roaster to produce a pure, healthy cocoa powder. They creatively transform this base into a divine range of pralines and truffles as well as delicious drinking chocolate that can be mixed with coffee, coconut or soy milk. All this is presented in a lovingly-restored colonial shop-house in downtown KL. Chocolate classes and tastings are coming soon, while food is served throughout the day, and who can resist banana fritters served with a chocolate shot?

THINGS TO DO NEARBY

Central Market
The city's landmark art deco food market was saved from demolition and is now a lively space filled with craft souvenirs and tasty local food stalls. *www.centralmarket.com. my*

Mr Chew's Chino-Latino Bar
In KL's vibrant nightlife quarter around Bukit Bintang, this hip locale with a patisserie bar serves mean martinis and tasty tapas, plus a late-night DJ. *www.mr-chew.com*

PHILIPPINES

How to ask for hot chocolate in the local language?
Request *sikwate*, made of *tablea* (ground cacao beans) and
hot water.

Signature chocolate flavour? Theo & Philo has a green
mango dark chocolate bar.

What to order with your chocolate? How about making
your chocolate part of a healthy breakfast by ordering
champorado, chocolate rice pudding?

Do or Don't: Make your *sikwate* from unfermented tablea;
the flavour is less rich.

Make a beeline for the Davao region on Mindanao
island if you're a chocolate lover visiting the
Philippines; this area to the south, firmly in the globe's
'cacao belt', produces about 80% of the entire country's
cacao crop of roughly 10,000 metric tons annually, bringing
in $6 million. Cacao production was brought by Spanish
colonists, though for a long time it was more commonly
found in people's backyards than on large farms, where
it was easily in reach for preparing the chocolate drink
sikwate. Now cultivation is on the rise again, though it still
has a long way to go before catching up to regional heavy-
weight Indonesia.

Davao is also home to Malagos (profiled opposite), which
won a bevy of awards at the 2019 Academy of Chocolate
awards. Planning to be in the north instead? Outside of
Manila, Tigre y Oliva make single-origin bars from Davao
beans, and in Manila proper, Theo & Philo manufactures
their single-origin bars using Davao beans and sugar from
Bacolod on Negros island. Hiraya Chocolate (also on Luzon
island) makes their Filipino-flavoured bars from Barangay
Malabog's beans, grown on Mindanao.

MALAGOS CHOCOLATE GARDEN

Malagos, Baguio District, Davao;
malagoschocolate.com; +63 82-221-8220

◆ Tastings   ◆ Classes   ◆ Cafe
◆ Rooms   ◆ Shop   ◆ Food

Located on a family-run farm in Davao, Malagos Chocolate Garden has become a must-visit destination for all chocolate lovers. Visitors come to the Malagos Gardens to enjoy family-friendly activities, such as the obstacle course, butterfly garden and human chessboard, often staying for lunch at the on-site restaurant. Luxury-seekers also gravitate to the hotel and spa, located near the back of the gardens by the chocolate museum. But if you can't book a chocolate massage or bath, it's still worth stopping in at the gift shop after a long day of exploring. There you can pick up dark chocolate bars and cocoa nibs, as well as truffles and chocolate-covered guyabano (aka soursop) or mango. The family's cacao was recently recognised for its excellent flavour by the Heirloom Cacao Preservation Fund.

THINGS TO DO NEARBY

Cacao City
This cacao- and chocolate-centric shop in Davao City is perfect for visitors looking to grab a cup of cocoa or pick up locally made products using Philippine cacao. *cacaocity.com*

Philippine Eagle Center
Home to a few dozen massive Philippine eagles, the centre cares for the critically endangered animals, and educates tourists through daily tours. *philippineeaglefoundation. org*

SINGAPORE

How to ask for hot chocolate in the local language? Most residents speak English, so that's your best bet!

Signature chocolate flavour? Milk chocolate is the most common here.

What to order with your chocolate? Coffee and tea always make good partners.

Do: Look for local ingredients in chocolate bars and desserts.

Asia doesn't have a longstanding chocolate tradition, and until recently the region hasn't been a hotbed of chocolate activity. Traditional Singaporean desserts are full of flavours like pandan leaf, red bean and durian. Ask the average Singaporean for chocolate and you might get an ice cream sandwich or a green tea Kit Kat. However, in the past few years, Asia's appetite for chocolate has exploded, making it the fastest-growing market in the world. The average consumption in Asia is still only about a pound (0.45kg) of chocolate per year, but in Singapore it's much higher at 4.5lbs (2kg) per year (compare that to about

9.5lbs, or 4.3kg, per capita in the United States).

In other words, Singapore isn't quite like the rest of Asia. The country is known for its international culture, with Chinese and Southeast Asian influences as well as European ones. It's a special place where East meets West, and its chocolate reflects that. Chocolate is often seen as a luxury and a perfect gift, and big brands that make Belgian- and Swiss-style confections dominate the landscape: you'll probably see names you're familiar with, from Godiva to Lindt. Yet you'll also find a variety of outstanding local chocolatiers, bean-to-bar makers, and pastry chefs. Many make traditional European-style truffles and bonbons, but more and more, makers like Fossa and others are using distinctly Asian flavours in confections and desserts. Think black sesame, yuzu and even lychee, reinforcing the unique multicultural heritage of this part of the world.

FOSSA CHOCOLATE

Several locations; www.fossachocolate.com; +65 9679-8088

◆ Tastings   ◆ Classes

This award-winning bean-to-bar chocolate maker is one of the first in Singapore and boasts snazzy packaging as well as interesting flavours, from single-origin Indonesian bars to shrimp-and-bonito dark chocolate. Though the factory isn't open to the public, Fossa hosts regular meetings of its Chocolate Tasting Club, where you'll sample products created across the globe as well as learn how the stuff is made. It also offers private, customisable bookings for a bespoke experience. Fossa was started by a trio of twentysomethings who wanted to make chocolate from scratch. After trying a fruity single-origin Madagascar bar, they realised cacao beans have a variety of flavours. They named the company Fossa after a catlike animal native to Madagascar, and the rest is history.

THINGS TO DO NEARBY

Chomp Chomp Food Centre at Serangoon Garden
Hawker cuisine is at its finest at this collection of food stalls. Find *hokkien mee*, *sambal* stingray and satay for dinner or a late-night snack.

Bishan-Ang Mo Kio Park
At one of the largest parks in Singapore, find large grassy areas for picnics, jogging and cycling paths and an impressive playground.
www.nparks.gov.sg

TAIWAN

How to ask for hot chocolate in the local language? *Rêkêkě*, pronounced with rhyming syllables like 'rococo' but 'ɜ' (as in the British 'her') instead of 'əʊ'.

Signature chocolate flavours? Tea-flavoured chocolate pays homage to one of Taiwan's other traditional crops.

What to order with your chocolate? Taiwan's own Kavalan whisky.

Do: Taiwan spans the subtropical and tropical zones; do put your bonbons in the fridge in summer.

Within the last decade, Taiwanese chocolatiers and chocolate makers have dazzled adjudicators at top international contests, and had Taipei's Michelin-star restaurants serving their products to eager customers. Despite being latecomers to the scene, the island's chocolate landscape is full of promise and unfolding as we speak. In 2018, the International Chocolate Awards invited the country to host its inaugural Asia-Pacific competition. A growing number of local brands are crafting top-notch truffles and bonbons with imported beans, but the most unique chocolate experience one can have in Taiwan is by visiting a cacao farm.

If you venture into the sun-drenched cacao-growing heartland in the southernmost county of Pingtung, you will be greeted by a rare sight – glossy-leafed cacao trees with their white flowers and multicoloured fruits, basking in the shade of betel nut palms twice their height. And what strange bedfellows they seem at first. Not too long ago, the highly lucrative betel nut was every farmer's pet crop. But 'Green Gold', as it was called, was found to be damaging to health, so farmers were encouraged to diversify. Cacao was the result. Cacao trees love sunny, humid weather, but can't take too much wind or direct sunlight. The betel nut trees act like umbrellas, shading the cacao trees with their fronds. During typhoon season, farmers tie the chocolate trees to their taller neighbours to keep them from toppling. Only in Taiwan would you see a stimulative fruit chewed by indigenous peoples for thousands of years offering protection to the Maya 'Food of the Gods'.

Chiu Ming-song of Choose Chius is a betel-nut-turned-cacao farmer who launched the first made-in-Taiwan chocolate in October 2010. He says, 'Cacao does not turn into chocolate overnight. We were seen as fools. But after years of experimentation, we drew a starting line for Taiwan's

TOP 5 CHOCOLATE-LACED DELIGHTS

CHOCOLATE STOUT
by Taiwan Head Brewers
www.facebook.com/taiwanheadbrewers

CEMAS KAKANEN CHOCOLATE PINEAPPLE CAKE
from Chiayi *www.facebook.com/CemasKakanen*

MIYAHARA ICE CREAM
from Taichung *www.miyahara.com.tw/en*

SOYPRESSO CHOCOLATE-FLAVOURED SOY MILK
Taipei *www.soypresso.com.tw*

BREAKFAST OF TOAST WITH CHOCOLATE SAUCE AND FRIED CHICKEN CUTLET
Tainan *various*

cacao industry.' Taiwan's cacao is of a very good quality, a high-end product in high demand that some believe is on its way to becoming 'Brown Gold'. There are 300 hectares (741 acres) of farmland devoted to cacao cultivation and most of it is in the Wanluan and Neipu districts in Pingtung. All three varieties of beans are grown: aromatic Criollo; strong-tasting Forastero; and Trinitario, a crossbreed between the two. The papaya-sized fruits are green, red and yellow; if you break open the pods, you'll see white pulpy flesh wrapped around the beans. The pulp is edible – it is sweet and delicious, similar to mangosteen. The main growing seasons are March to June, and September to November. Most of the farms have both cacao processing and chocolate-making facilities, often mere steps from each other. You can tour the premises and learn how to make your own confectionery. You can also enjoy tree-to-bar chocolates and refreshing cacao derivatives like ice cream and soda. Taiwanese chocolate is strong-tasting and well-balanced, with notes of caramel and berry. But what make it stand out are the local ingredients such as high-mountain teas and lychees used to infuse the chocolate, making it wonderfully and unmistakably Taiwanese.

CHOOSE CHIUS

328, Fufeng Rd, Neipu, Pingtung;
www.facebook.com/taiwancocoa; +886 8-778-5070

◆ Tastings   ◆ Classes   ◆ Cafe
◆ Roastery   ◆ Shop   ◆ Food

THINGS TO DO NEARBY

Neiwei Flea Market
This weekend flea market offers everything under the sun: cut-and-paste shard figurines, swords and marionettes, plus a view of daily Kaohsiung life.

Pier-2 Art Center
An attractive sprawl of old warehouses right by Kaohsiung Harbour now makes for fabulous shopping, art browsing and eating. *pier-2.khcc.gov.tw*

Cijin Island
You can spend half a day on this narrow island visiting old military sites and temples, cycling by the coast and feasting on fresh seafood.

One Bar
Enjoy southern Taiwanese dishes with a modern twist in a retro-futuristic setting, then head to the bar upstairs for cocktails. *www.facebook.com/ONEBARRR*

In the leafy town of Neipu, along a quiet road flanked by fields and ponds growing everything from coffee to turtles, is the farm of the charismatic Chiu Mingsong, Taiwan's first bean-to-bar chocolate maker. Choose Chius is one of very few on the island that uses 100% local cacao in their creations. If you join the two-and-a-half-hour tour (up to 5 people, book at least a week in advance) run by the knowledgeable Mr Chiu and his son Chiu Yu-guang, you'll learn about the history of cacao in Taiwan firsthand from the family that started it all; you'll see the colourful fruits growing in their orchard, and get to make bonbons and drinking chocolate from scratch at a workshop. Chiu Senior, who spent the last 15 years cultivating cacao and the last 20 growing coffee, is an inspiring host with a contagious passion for his crops, but he doesn't speak English. The younger Chiu speaks a little and manages the rest with Google Translate. The Chius also have a factory, a restaurant and a shop on the premises. Their chocolates are known for their high cocoa butter content which makes them velvety and sumptuous. Their signature confectionery is 'Nama Chocolate': ridiculously indulgent squares of silken solidified ganache made of top-notch cocoa and cream, and dusted with cocoa powder. The cocoa liquor used to make their sublime drinking chocolate is also for sale; just add milk and stir. There's also cacao juice, a drink you'll only see at a cacao plantation. Poetically named 'Tears of the Moon', it's sweet, refreshing and a good source of antioxidants. Chocolate ice cream and chocolate smoothies are served at the restaurant, as is an array of classic Taiwanese dishes, including hotpot. The area is quite remote, but worth a trip.

COCOSUN

No.2-55 Fuxing Rd, Wanluan, Pingtung;
www.cocosun.com.tw; +886 8-781-0569

◆ Tastings   ◆ Classes   ◆ Cafe
◆ Roastery   ◆ Shop   ◆ Tours

Self-styled 'tourist chocolate factory' Cocosun is a child-friendly chocolate farm with cute cacao-themed decorations on the premises and an attractive orchard; the restaurant serves chocolatey delights and brick oven pizzas; and there's an eclectic selection of fruit, confectionery and other paraphernalia in the shop, including a cocoa butter moisturiser. Cocosun is also one of very few farms in Taiwan that runs tours in English (book two weeks in advance). Participants visit their chocolate-making facility – well known in the industry for being advanced – and see cacao beans turn into something that tantalises the taste buds. Want to be more hands-on? Join a 40-minute bonbon-making workshop (book a week in advance). Try their fermented pulp slushy with citrus and chocolate notes.

THINGS TO DO NEARBY

Wan Tai Pork Knuckles
The town of Wanluan is best known for braised pork knuckles and this small, old restaurant in an area full of similar shops makes them tender and boldly seasoned.

Wugoushui Village
A still-inhabited village founded in the Qing dynasty, Wugoushui has three dozen beautiful courtyard residences, ancestral halls and temples.

FU WAN CHOCOLATE

100 Dapeng Rd, Donggang, Pingtung;
www.facebook.com/FuWanCacao; +886 8-835-1555

◆ Cafe ◆ Classes ◆ Lodging
◆ Roastery ◆ Shop ◆ Tours

THINGS TO DO NEARBY

Donglong Temple
Originally built in the Qing
dynasty, this resplendent
temple is a centre of Wang
Yeh worship in Pingtung,
with an archway covered in
gleaming gold foil.

Kao Wei Xian
Everything at this
Donggang barbecue joint,
from chicken wings and
pork belly to rice cakes and
asparagus, is skewered and
grilled –good for a snack
for one or a feast for many.

Huaqiao Seafood Market
A t this massive seafood
market right by the harbour
and ferry in Donggang,
you can buy fresh fish and
shrimp, get dried cuttlefish
and eat fresh sashimi.

Little Liuchiu Island
From Donggang, hop on a
boat to Taiwan's largest
coral island for days of
snorkelling, sea turtle-
spotting, temple visiting
and fresh seafood.

Fu Wan, owned by Warren Hsu, an internationally certified chocolate taster, is cacao farm, factory and holiday resort rolled into one. When you step into their shop and cafe, you're almost transported to downtown Taipei: a cool white space accented with yellows and greens echoes the palette of the product packaging and the hues of the cacao fruit. On a green feature wall hang laurels from the prestigious International Chocolate Award. Fu Wan chocolates have incredibly nuanced flavours; what's more, some of them feature unique ingredients like pink shrimp, a specialty of Donggang fishing port nearby; *magao* or mountain peppercorn, a spice used by Taiwan's indigenous peoples; and fruity Iron Goddess tea from the mountains of northern Taiwan. The delectable drinking chocolate comes spiced, sweetened with black sugar or laced with Cointreau. You can also buy cacao mocktails made with amber–hued cacao syrup, chocolate stout beer, truffles and mendiants, and chocolate-swirled loaves. Fu Wan uses local cacao for their tree-to-bar confectionery, but also imports Papua New Guinean and Ecuadorian beans.

Fu Wan runs tours of the premises and a DIY workshop. You'll pass racks of cacao beans drying in the sun, see barrels covered by banana leaves and smell sourdough and alcohol in the air; a farmer sitting in the shade with a sprawl of cacao fruits in front of him may offer you a taste of fresh cacao pulp. The helpful and well trained staff speak little English, but there is a gallery with bilingual infographics.

FEELING 18 CHOCOLATIER

Puli Township, Nantou County;
feeling18c.com; +886 4-9298-4863

◆ Transport ◆ Shop
◆ Cafe

 Feeling 18 began in 2006 as one man's dream to bring quality chocolate to the mountain town where he grew up. The name itself references the degrees Celsius at which chocolate is optimally stored, as in their temperature-controlled chocolate vault. Over the last decade-plus, the shop became so popular that the owner expanded his brand to include a cafe & tea room, pastry boutique and gelateria. If you find yourself waiting in a queue, pop next door for a triple scoop of local flavours; we recommend

Assam Milk Tea, Lychee Rose and Makau Fleur De Sel. If you visit between April and October, you'll also see local vendors selling fresh passion fruit, as the surrounding town of Puli is famous for them.

THINGS TO DO NEARBY

Sun Moon Lake
This turquoise lake in Nantou County was an important site for the island's aboriginal peoples, and has become famous for its ropeway, cable car and sunset boat rides.

Formosan Aboriginal Culture Village
In the country's geographic centre, amusement park Formosan is dedicated to celebrating and teaching about the many native cultures on Taiwan.

VANILLA KNIGHT

No 241-2, Section 1, Zhongshan Rd, Puli Township,
Nantou County; vanillaknight.com; +886 4-9299-2276

◆ Tastings ◆ Classes ◆ Cafe
◆ Roastery ◆ Shop ◆ Transport

Nantou County is thousands of miles west of vanilla's native Mexico, yet the plant thrives in central Taiwan's tropical climate, and Vanilla Knight takes full advantage. Farmer & Chef Zhenglin Wei first planted his vanilla orchids back in 2012, in a greenhouse just blocks from the cafe. Those orchids now supply all the vanilla used in his shop's pastries, chocolates and drinks. Mimicking the openness of the vanilla garden, the cafe is full of natural light, its high ceilings prominently showcasing images of the vanilla-harvesting process. Guided farm tours in basic

English can be arranged with advanced notice. Visitors can't miss the stunning galaxy-inspired bonbons, and the vanilla pudding and bourbon vanilla ice cream are worth the trek.

THINGS TO DO NEARBY

Hohocha Tea Farm & Tastery
Opened in 2019, Hohocha is dedicated to teaching the public about production of the many varieties of black tea for which central Taiwan is famous.

Puli Winery
Home to both a winery and whisky distillery, this complex houses a museum, tasting area and local food pavilion, all located right in downtown Puli.

YU CHOCOLATIER

No 10, Alley 3, Lane 112, Section 4, Ren'ai Rd, Da'an
District, Taipei; www.yuchocolatier.com;
+886 2-2701-0792

◆ Tastings   ◆ Classes   ◆ Cafe
◆ Roastery   ◆ Shop   ◆ Transport

This chic spot in Taipei has won over connoisseurs from all across the world with its complex chocolates. Chef Yu Hsuan-cheng, Kaohsiung native and a former English literature major, fell in love with chocolate making and went on to attend Ferrandi Paris, a leading institution of culinary arts. This was followed by stints at Michelin three-star Pavillon Ledoyen and chocolatier Jacques Génin. Within two years of its founding, Yu Chocolatier bagged seven medals at the International Chocolate Awards.

Yu's bonbons, pralines and truffles sit elegantly under glass. Expect to find flavours like passion fruit, oolong tea and ginger. But don't be surprised if you also spot items from a Taiwanese grandma's larder: fermented sticky rice, marinated plum, even soy sauce and sesame oil. It is with these unlikely but brilliant ingredients from his country that Chef Yu has created his showpieces for the Salon du Chocolat, a Paris-based trade fair for the chocolate industry.

THINGS TO DO NEARBY

Bao'an Temple
Recipient of a Unesco Heritage Award for its restoration and revived temple rites, this exquisite complex is full of prime examples of traditional decorative arts. *www.baoan.org.tw/english*

Da Dao Cheng
Taipei's oldest district is known for its traditional Chinese medicine shops, dried goods stores, fabric market and Lunar New Year sundries market.

Da'an Forest Park
Taipei's Central Park is where the city comes to play; and play it does, from kids rollerblading to picnicking families to old men playing chess.

Shida Night Market
A small but lively place for a cheap meal of traditional Taiwanese snacks like oyster omelets and pork buns, washed down by fruit juices and boba tea.

You can sip liquor with your candy in a confectionery and spirits pairing, provided you are lucky enough to land a table at the cozy shop. Bottles of cognac, rum, grappa and even Taiwan's very own award-winning Kavalan cherry-cask whisky (which also appears in a chocolate alongside smoked longan) stand gleaming behind the counter. If you are not sure what to order, the pleasant English-speaking staff can help. Yu also has a daily selection of sumptuous French-style cakes and tarts.

VIETNAM

How to ask for hot chocolate in the local language? Let's be honest, you should be drinking iced coffee here–; fortunately, it tastes almost chocolatey. Ask for *nâu dá* or *cà phê sữa dá*.

Signature chocolate flavour? It's the locally grown Trinitario beans that are the star here.

What to order with your chocolate? An egg chocolate or egg coffee drink.

Do: Visit a cacao farm while you're in Vietnam.

French missionaries first brought cacao to Vietnam in the late 19th century, but the crop sputtered along and subsidies to cacao farmers ended in 1907, with little more done until the late 20th century. Today Vietnam has a growing crop of cacao beans being produced each year, including from a hybrid Trinitario strain made from a

Forastero-Criollo cross. Vietnam's first artisanal chocolate brand Marou (profiled opposite) is leading the way in the country's nascent chocolate industry with their Ho Chi Minh City cafe, but with increased cacao beans yields anticipated from Vietnam, even more are sure to follow.

Not too far behind already is Azzan Chocolates in Buon Ma Thuot, which offers appointment-only tours of their cocoa plantation. Also in Ho Chi Minh City, Belvie Chocolate uses Belgian chocolate techniques on Vietnam's Trinitario beans, and Pheva makes single-origin bean-to-bar chocolate from Trinitario beans harvested in Ben Tre. In the Mekong Delta, visitors learning about the region's agriculture can enjoy a homestay at Lam The Cuong's cocoa farm (Mien Tay Homestay); tours on the farm explain the production process and how the beans become the chocolate products you love to eat.

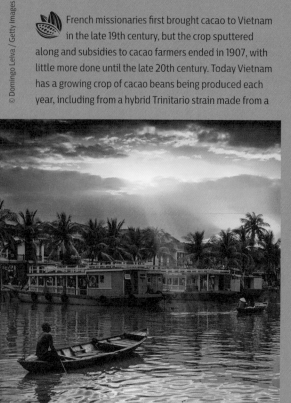

MAISON MAROU SAIGON

167–169, Calmette, Phường Nguyễn Thái Bình, Quận 1, HCMC; marouchocolate.com; +84 28-3729-2753

◆ Tastings   ◆ Classes   ◆ Cafe
◆ Roastery   ◆ Shop   ◆ Transport

Since it was established in 2011, Marou co-founders and French expats Samuel Maruta and Vincent Mourou have built a thriving single-origin chocolate business in southern Vietnam. Marou Chocolat Cafe pays homage to their accomplishments, as well as the founders' French heritage, with their wide selection of bonbons, pastries, and drinking chocolates. The company uses only Vietnamese cacao, and in their cafe you'll find treats high-lighting the six distinct Vietnamese regions from which they source, plus a rotating schedule of on-site events. Go for an *egg chocolat* drink if you've got a few minutes to spare; it's a decadent play off of northern Vietnam's egg coffee. Before you leave, grab some shop-exclusive filled bars and bonbons for a taste of Vietnam even after your return home.

THINGS TO DO NEARBY

Ho Chi Minh City Museum
Telling the storied tale of the Vietnamese capital, this museum brings together war-worn artefacts and traditional antiquities from the many ethnic tribes of Vietnam.
hcmc-museum.edu.vn

Ben Thanh Market
The go-to spot for local street food, Ben Thanh has become a symbol of Saigon, open daily to sell local crafts, souvenirs, and southern Vietnamese dishes and drinks.
ben-thanh-market.com

© James Pham / Lonely Planet

TOP CHOCO TREATS

CHOCOLATE MOONCAKES
CHINA

Eaten during the Mid-Autumn Festival, mooncakes are round pastries traditionally filled with lotus paste and salted egg yolks. But these days, luxe chocolate versions with nuts or gooey caramel make chic gifts.

EGGETTES
HONG KONG

Hot ball-shaped waffles known as eggettes or *gai daan zai*, are a favourite Hong Kong street snack. Chocoholics adore versions stuffed with chocolate chips or Nutella.

CHAMPORADO
PHILIPPINES

This thick chocolate porridge is the ultimate Filipino comfort food. Made with glutinous rice and concentrated cacao tablets, it's served with a swirl of condensed milk for breakfast or as an afternoon snack.

TSOKOLATE DE BATIROL
PHILIPPINES

Spanish colonists brought chocolate from Mexico to the Philippines in the 18th century, spawning the beloved *tsokolate*, a thick hot chocolate made with round cacao tablets called *tablea* and whisked with a wooden stick called a *batirol*.

POCKY
JAPAN

These chocolate-covered cookie sticks are the quintessential Japanese convenience store treat, in flavours like hazelnut, matcha, blueberry, choco-coconut and the classic 'men's' (dark chocolate).

OLATE of ASIA

TAIYAKI
JAPAN
Find these fish-shaped waffles fresh off the iron in Japan's *depachika* (department store food halls). They're traditionally stuffed with red bean paste, but chocolate, cheese and custard fillings are almost as popular.

DURIAN CHOCOLATE
MALAYSIA
With a smell likened to rotten onions – or rotting flesh – the durian fruit inspires both devotion and disgust. Same goes for chocolates flavoured with its vanilla-garlic-turpentine tang.

MILO DINOSAUR
SINGAPORE
Milo, an Australian chocolate malt powder, is wildly popular in Singapore. In the outdoor food courts known as hawker centres, a Milo Dinosaur is an iced Milo drink with a small hill of crunchy undissolved Milo powder on top.

CHOCO PIE
KOREA
Cake rounds sandwiched with marshmallow and swathed in chocolate, the Choco Pie is South Korea's most beloved nostalgic snack – and a hot black market item in North Korea.

SNOW ICE
TAIWAN
Sample popular chocolate versions of this ultra-fine shaved ice dessert, served with lashings of chocolate syrup and topped with strawberries and mochi.

EUR

TOP 5 CHOCOLATE CITIES

OPE

PARIS, FRANCE

Try chocolates from Pralus and L'Etoile, the 44 flavours at Alain Ducasse's La Manufacture de Chocolat or artisan sculptures made by Patrick Roger. The city is also home to the annual Salon du Chocolat festival.

BRUSSELS, BELGIUM

In the contest for who makes the world's best chocolate, Belgium is a main contender. From decadent chocolate fountains to legends like Pierre Marcolini and Frederic Blondeel, Brussels delivers.

ZÜRICH, SWITZERLAND

Swiss chocolate may be best recognised in the Toblerone and Lindt chocolates readily found abroad, but Zürich abounds in boutique chocolates on a whole other level from Taucherli and many others.

YORK, UK

Well-preserved medieval York also holds the remains of industrial Britain's chocolate boom, when major players in confectionery built their chocolate businesses here, now nostalgically remembered across town.

MODICA, ITALY

Perugia has the annual Eurochocolate festival (and is home to Baci Perugina), but this small Sicilian village is rightly famous for chocolate, made the same way as the ancient Aztecs did.

AUSTRIA

How to ask for hot chocolate in the local language? *Eine Tasse heisse Schokolade, bitte.*

Signature chocolate flavour? *Mozartkugel* (pistachio marzipan coated in praline cream and dark chocolate).

What to order with your chocolate? A Wiener Melange coffee (an espresso shot topped with steamed milk and foam).

Don't: Don't just focus on the classics: many contemporary Austrian chocolatiers are remarkable innovators.

Austria's obsession with chocolate? Blame it on the Habsburgs. These sweet-toothed monarchs were the early patrons of confectioners and chocolatiers, many of which survive to this day in Vienna, such as Demel, founded in 1786 and once purveyor to the royal court. In years to come, this triggered something of one-upmanship among coffeehouse confectioners, aiming to outdo each other with cakes fit for an emperor. Along came Sacher with its dark, glossily iced, apricot jam-laced Sachertorte; Cafe Central with its marzipan-filled, orange-infused milk-chocolate

torte; and Demel with the *Annatorte*, a lavish chocolate-nougat torte with ganache layers. Such rich tortes still nod to the Austrian love of decadence today, intertwined with the atmosphere of *Gemütlichkeit* (nostalgic comfort) prevalent in the capital's traditional coffeehouses.

But it's not all just desserts here. Many towns and cities have excellent confiseries that make their own pralines, truffles, ganaches and bars, often beautifully wrapped. One classic is the iconic *Mozartkugel* – a bite-sized, dark-chocolate ball filled with pistachio marzipan and nougat, first created by Paul Fürst in Salzburg in 1890. Over in Vienna, meanwhile, locals go crazy for the pink-wrapped Manner wafer, layered with chocolate-hazelnut cream.

Austria has never rested on its chocolate-making laurels, however. Times are changing when it comes to cacao, as craft chocolatiers are not shy of experimentation. Take bean-to-bar, fair trade Zotter, for instance, with single-origin bars and wonderfully weird flavours from cheese and walnuts to wild gorse, and tequila with salt and lemon. Or Schokov, where bars are pepped up with the likes of lavender, blueberry and hot masala spice. Whatever would the Habsburgs have said...?

CAFÉ SACHER

Philharmonikerstrasse 4; www.sacher.com;
+43 (0)1 51-456-1053

◆ Tastings ◆ Classes ◆ Cafe
◆ Roastery ◆ Shop ◆ Transport

THINGS TO DO NEARBY

Burggarten
Mozart is raised high on a
pedestal in this attractive
park behind the Hofburg,
presided over by the
Jugendstil Palmenhaus
cafe and adjacent
butterfly house. *www.
schmetterlinghaus.at*

Staatsoper
Dress up for a performance
at the lavish gold-and-
crystal State Opera,
Vienna's premier opera and
classical-music venue. Be
sure to book tickets well in
advance. *www.wiener-
staatsoper.at*

Albertina
In former Hapsburg
imperial apartments, the
Albertina showcases one
of the world's greatest
graphic art collections,
alongside paintings from
the likes of Picasso and
Monet. *www.albertina.at*

Haus der Musik
Delve into a world of sound
and music at this hands-on
museum, where highlights
include composing your
own waltz and (virtually)
conducting the Vienna
Philharmonic Orchestra.
www.hausdermusik.com

What could be more Viennese than forking a
decadent slice of Sachertorte in the chandelier-lit,
ruby-red confines of opulent Café Sacher, where portraits
of Hapsburg royalty glower on the walls and pinafored
waitresses waltz in symphony from table to marble-topped
table. If it feels rather regal, it is. Back in 1832, the most
famous of chocolate tortes was created for Prince Wenzel
von Metternich by none other than 16-year-old apprentice
chef Franz Sacher. It was an instant hit, and later became
the sweet hallmark of the ritzy hotel of the same name when
it opened in 1876 before its fame spread across the world.

This is no ordinary chocolate cake: the original is baked
here to a secret recipe, which, we can divulge, contains light,
moist chocolate sponge, and a layer of tangy apricot jam
underlying the rich icing made with, word has it, three kinds
of dark, bittersweet, high-quality chocolate sourced from
Germany and Belgium. Then it's given a final, edible chocolate seal of approval, and served with the requisite swirl of
unsweetened *Schlagobers* (whipped cream).

Want to take one home? No problem: they'll wrap and
box yours beautifully for a lingering taste of Vienna long
after you've left, though it's partly the plush environment
that makes this treat so special.

DEMEL

Kohlmarkt 14, 1010; www.demel.com;
+43 (1) 535-1717

◆ Transport   ◆ Shop
◆ Cafe   ◆ Food

Whipping up divine cakes, confectionery, chocolate and all manner of dainty fancies since 1786, Demel was once the purveyor to sweet-toothed Hapsburg royalty. Even Empress Sisi, famous for her waspish 48cm (19-inch) waist, was partial to the delicacies here. The coffee house is fairy-tale Vienna at its finest, replete with gilt-edged mirrors, coffered ceilings and rococo salons alight with chandeliers. But it has substance as well as grand style: the Viennese still flock here today for properly thick hot choco-late, homemade truffles and bars of melting chocolate, all in beautiful retro wrappings.

But let's be honest, you likely came for the cake, and you won't be disappointed: Demel's selection is legendary. After peeking into the glass-walled open kitchen to see bakers skilfully mixing and glazing, snag a marble-topped table and order a sumptuous slice of Demeltorte: walnut-choco-late torte with a thin layer of apricot jam and milk chocolate glaze, sprinkled with candied violets. Or maybe Annatorte, an indulgent chocolate, orange liqueur-infused torte, with dark ganache layers and an elaborate hazelnut nougat swirl on top, said to resemble former proprietor Anna Demel's bun. For double indulgence, pair it with an 'Anna Demel' coffee laced with orange liqueur and whipped cream.

THINGS TO DO NEARBY

Hofburg
Set aside at least a couple of hours for a spin of Vienna's fine romance of an imperial palace, home base of the Habsburgs from 1273 to 1918.
www.hofburg-wien.at

Kunsthistorisches Museum
A vast repository of fine arts in a stately neoclassical building, the Kunsthistorisches Museum wings you from Classical Rome to Egypt and the Renaissance to superb Old Masters. *www.khm.at*

Volksgarten
A peaceful escape sidling up to the Hofburg, these landscaped gardens have leafy avenues, rose-trimmed gardens and the neoclassical Temple of Theseus to explore.

Peterskirche
Topped by a bulbous copper dome, this is one of Vienna's most impressive baroque edifices, with a striking dome fresco painted by JM Rottmayr. Regular organ recitals happen here.
www.peterskirche.at

BELGIUM

How to ask for hot chocolate in the local language? In Dutch, *Voor mij een kopje warme chocolademelk.*
Signature chocolate flavours? Buttercream truffle.
What to order with your chocolate? A spicy speculoos biscuit.
Do: Be aware that many famous name Belgian chocolates like Godiva, Côte d'Or and Galler are now foreign-owned.

Belgium is a cosmopolitan nation, with its vibrant city of Brussels recognised internationally as the de jure capital of Europe, but is most credible as the world's chocolate capital. This tiny independent kingdom was founded in 1830, in a union between the diverse people of Dutch-speaking Flanders and francophone Wallonia. Several things unite these unreservedly friendly, welcoming, fun-loving people: beer, frites, their beloved Red

Devils football team and above all, a passion for chocolate. Brussels has over 300 chocolate boutiques, chocolatiers, museums and hands-on workshops where passionate amateurs can get their hands deliciously sticky creating their own chocolates. With some 2000 artisan chocolate makers dotted around the country, you can discover tantalising chocolate on the high street of every Belgian town and village, with the choice of reasonably priced but high quality industrially manufactured big name bars and bonbons, handmade chocolates bought in the atelier where they're produced and avant-garde truffles and pralines for choco-connoisseurs created by maître-chocolatiers, celebrities in Belgium just like fashion designers and film stars.

The term 'Belgian Chocolate' really does have a significance for global consumers in these days of fakes and copies, as there are firm rules and regulations ensuring that the chocolate really is produced in Belgium itself. Even if a famed Belgium brand is actually owned by an international company, the chocolate is still produced here before being exported around the world. So what makes Belgian chocolate so unique? Many Belgian chocolatiers keep their reci-

TOP 5 ARTISAN CHOCOLATIERS IN BRUSSELS

LAURENT GERBAUD

Creative bonbons using exotic ingredients like Turkish figs and Chinese ginger. *chocolatsgerbaud.be*

WITTAMER

Chocolate-maker to the Belgian royal family, best tasted in their old-world *salon de thé* on the Grand Sablons square. *wittamer.com*

ZAABÄR

Top atelier for creative chocolate-making workshops. *zaabar.be*

MARY

Founded in 1919 by Mary Delluc, boutique small batch chocolates best eaten fresh. *mary.be*

BELVAS

The place for not just fair trade, organic chocolates, but also selections of vegan and gluten-free creations. *belvas.be*

PIERRE MARCOLINI, CHOCOLATE MAKER

'Belgium is blessed today with having some of the world's most talented and exciting artisan choco-latiers, and between strengths and reality, the only force that separates them is courage.'

pes top secret, and the august Royal Belgian Association of Chocolate states, 'it is Belgium's heritage, the knowledge, the expertise. The blending and selection of the cocoa beans'. Traditionally there are no added low-quality fats in Belgium's signature creamy chocolate, and the concept of bean-to-bar has always been entrenched here.

Belgium's place in chocolate history was enshrined in 1912, when Jean Neuhaus invented the soft fondant-filled praline, but cocoa was first introduced here in the 17th century on the arrival of these magical beans from Mexico; at the time, both were part of the Spanish Hapsburg empire. Things got serious when the newly independent nation founded its colonial empire in Africa, wealthy not just in minerals and diamonds but vast cacao plantations in the then-Belgian Congo. There are excellent museums devoted to chocolate and its history in every major city here, though while they go to great efforts to highlight how Belgian chocolate makers are committed to ethical fair trade of cocoa today, there is a regrettable amnesia when it comes to documenting the exploitation and utilisation of slave labour during the nation's inglorious colonial era.

CHOCOLATE NATION

7 Koningen Astridplein, Antwerp;
www.chocolatenation.be; +32 3 2070808

◆ Tastings   ◆ Classes   ◆ Cafe
◆ Transport   ◆ Shop

Belgium's first-ever chocolate factory was opened on this site in Antwerp in 1831, making it the perfect venue for this new museum devoted to Belgian chocolate. The port here was always a major entry site for cacao beans coming from Belgium's colonies, and even today, Antwerp is the largest storage site of cacao beans in the world. A visit lasts over an hour, passing through 14 themed spaces, with tastings all along the way!

The highlight for kids is undoubtedly the giant fantasy machine demonstrating how chocolate is made, while for adults there are more epicurean pleasures like the chance to pair chocolate with beer, wine and whisky. As the museum crafts its own chocolate, don't leave without taking home their Octave bean-to-bar.

THINGS TO DO NEARBY

Antwerp Zoo
Located in a vast zoological park, Antwerp's historic zoo dates back to 1843, but is thoroughly modern in the way it respects and protects its 1160 species.
www.zooantwerpen.be

Le Royal Cafe
Antwerp Central is one of Europe's most awesome train stations, and its grandiose cafe is a riot of opulent art nouveau marble, wood panelling and mirrors.
www.brasserieroyal.be

CHOCO-STORY

41 Rue de l'Etuve, Brussels;
www.choco-story-brussels.be; +32 2 5142048

◆ Tastings   ◆ Classes   ◆ Cafe
◆ Roastery   ◆ Shop   ◆ Transport

THINGS TO DO NEARBY

Manneken Pis

Belgium's most famous monument, the diminutive Mannekin Pis statue, is forever surrounded by crowds (he has a wardrobe of 900 costumes, changed every few days). *www.mannekenpis.brussels*

Fritland

Brussels without frites is unthinkable, and the queues outside this stall just off the Grand Place testify to the quality of their fresh frites, always fried twice.
www.fritlandbrussels.be

Episode Belgium

The Belgium capital is shopping heaven for vintage fashion fans. Episode is an institution, stacked with Hawaiian shirts, sneakers, kitschy cravats and baseball caps.
www.episode.eu

Maison Dandoy

After marvelling at the spectacular Grand Place, walk across to this venerable bakery specialising in a Belgian tradition: irresistible speculoos biscuits.
www.maisondandoy.com

Brussels boasts two very different chocolate museums. Out in the suburbs, the quaint Belgian Chocolate Village offers a spectacular location – a 19th-century chocolate biscuit factory– with a tropical greenhouse growing cacao trees. But the buzz right now is in the centre of the city where Choco-Story has recently reopened in a new venue. This museum originally began life 20 years ago as the Brussels Museum of Cocoa and Chocolate, created by the family behind Godiva, and was then transformed into a more interactive concept alongside the creators of modern chocolate museums in Bruges, Paris, Prague and Mexico.

Housed in a labyrinthine 17th-century house, visitors embark today on a comprehensive, fun and epicurean chocolate journey, beginning with cocoa's origins during the Maya and Aztec reigns in Mexico up to chocolate's arrival in Europe in the 17th-century, from the Swiss creating solid chocolate in 1802, forerunner of our beloved chocolate bar, to Nestlé's invention of milk chocolate in 1875, up to Belgium's invention of the praline in 1912. All the technical transformation stages, from bean to bar, are explained, and then the best part begins when a master-chocolatier demonstrates how to make a praline and the serious business of tasting can begin.

FREDERIC BLONDEEL

39 Rue de Ganshoren, Koekelberg, Brussels;
www.frederic-blondeel.be; +32 468 315080

◆ Transport ◆ Classes ◆ Cafe
◆ Roastery ◆ Shop

Frederic Blondeel is Belgium's modest under-the-radar chocolatier, despite being voted the best chocolate maker in Brussels. He has recently closed down his city centre boutiques to launch his own Chocolate Factory out in the boondocks of the Belgian capital in Koekelberg. Here visitors come face to face with an impassioned craftsman, rushing around his new atelier, which incorporates a chocolate showroom, his beloved ancient Santos Palace *torrefacteur* (bean roaster), a modern laboratory and a tearoom. Frederic started out working in his papa's coffee roastery, and the link with coffee remains strong for him: 'I am a roaster first then a chocolatier, so the chocolate that symbolises me is Praline Cafe blending hazelnut with cacao and coffee beans roasted together'.

THINGS TO DO NEARBY

Bar Eliza
The neighbourhood is mainly an industrial area, but the exotic art deco Koekelberg Basilica has a huge park with this lively cafe with a huge terrace, pizzas and games for kids.
www.bareliza.be

Tour & Taxis
Alongside the Brussels Canal, this huge complex of warehouses and an old train station hosts events and concerts, with bars, restaurants and microbrewery En Stoemelings.
www.tour-taxis.com

MARCOLINI

1 Rue des Minimes, Brussels;
www.eu.marcolini.com; +32 2 5141206

◆ Tastings   ◆ Classes   ◆ Cafe
◆ Roastery   ◆ Shop   ◆ Transport

THINGS TO DO NEARBY

Sablon Antiques Market
Marcolini looks out over grandiose Sablon square, which each weekend becomes an antiques market, specialising in African and Asian art and furniture. *www.sablon-antiques-market.com*

Les Brigittines
The nearby Marolles neighbourhood is famous for historic Jeu de Balle flea market and this temple to traditional Bruxellois cuisine, like beef cheeks braised in cherry beer. *www.lesbrigittines.com*

Bozar
The Magritte Museum may be more famous, but the eclectic art deco Bozar offers everything from concerts and cinema to temporary blockbuster exhibitions of avant-garde art. *www.bozar.be*

Crosly Bowling
Crosly is a wonderfully kitsch Americana bowling alley with panoramic rooftop bar and a host of futurist Virtual Reality rooms where you can battle dinosaurs and zombies. *www.crosly.be*

Chocophiles are close to unanimous that Pierre Marcolini is the greatest chocolatier today. There are Marcolini stores all over the world, but everything begins here in Brussels overlooking the affluent Grand Sablon square. The august 19th-century mansion housing his flagship store and manufacturing atelier has seen its facade extravagantly decorated with giant raspberry hearts, red pralines, flowers, flags and macarons, enticing visitors to enter. The interior is surprisingly minimalist and sober, as Marcolini takes his chocolate very seriously. Everywhere there is Marcolini's logo, a giant cocoa husk, giving a clue to what separates his haute chocolate from others. Everything begins for him with the plantation growing the husk that covers the magical unprocessed cocoa bean. 'Tasting great chocolate is like tasting wine', he enthuses, 'so my signature chocolates, taken from a single estate, can be compared to

Grand Cru vintage from Burgundy or Bordeaux'. Each bar even resembles a wine label, detailing country and plantation name, type of bean and percentage of cocoa.

Once you start tasting his creations, the quality of ingredients screams out, be it vanilla from Madagascar, Piedmont hazelnuts, pistachios imported straight from Iran, pink peppercorns from Morocco or zesty Sicilian lemons. Look out for the chocolate-coated vanilla marshmallow.

NEUHAUS

25–27 Galerie de la Reine, Brussels;
www.neuhauschocolates.com; +32 2 5126359

◆ Tastings ◆ Classes ◆ Cafe
◆ Roastery ◆ Shop ◆ Transport

It's hardly surprising that chocolate lovers feel like visiting royalty at Neuhaus, maybe the world's most magical chocolate shop, which is located in the majestic Galerie de la Reine (the Queen's Gallery) built to celebrate the Belgian monarchy. In 1857, Jean Neuhaus, a Swiss emigré, opened not a chocolate shop here but a pharmacy. This was no normal apothecary though, as Monsieur Neuhaus was renowned for his 'confiseries pharmaceutiques', enrobing his medicinal remedies in chocolate to make them more palatable. Eventually the medicinal side was entirely replaced by chocolates, until Jean's grandson created the first ever creamy ganache-filled bonbon in 1905, the birth of the praline. Since then, the name Neuhaus has become synonymous with Belgian chocolate around the word, and it remains a locally owned company, unlike many famous Belgian chocolates now run by multinationals.

THINGS TO DO NEARBY

Delvaux
Along the Queen's Gallery lies the splendid showroom of the royal family's official luggage maker, this Belgian Louis Vuitton officially invented the handbag in 1908.
www.delvaux.com

L'Archiduc
Founded in 1939, this cool art deco club is great for late night cocktails and Belgian specialty beers, an art gallery upstairs and live jazz at weekends.
www.archiduc.net

Brusel
Brussels in the world's comic book capital (just think Tintin or the Smurfs) so plunge into the fantasy world of comic strips in this enthralling bookshop.
www.brusel.com

Theatre Royal de Toone
The Toone is an estaminet, a traditional bar with over 200 ales, and a tiny theatre where the 'actors' are marionettes, ornate historical puppets performing every day.
www.toone.be

Walk into their Galerie de la Reine flagship and it is as if nothing has changed; from the marble and glass facade to the ornate art nouveau display cases. Bite into an iconic Praline Caprice, a nougatine biscuit hand-filled with vanilla cream then covered with intense dark chocolate, and you can be assured that it was entirely crafted in Belgium, quite likely using sustainable cacao beans from Neuhaus' own plantations.

YUZU

11/A Walpoorstraat, Ghent; visit.gent.be/en/see-do/
yuzu-nicolas-vanaise-c; +32 473 965733

◆ Transport ◆ Shop ◆ Cafe

The centre of Ghent is awash with Belgium's rightly famous name chocolate houses: Leonidas, Godiva, Côte d'Or. But for artisan creations, track down the back-street atelier of local-born chocolatier (and former archaeologist) Nicolas Vanaise. Zen is the word to describe both his minimalist tasting room, where customers watch him working through a glass window, and the major influence on his chocolates, as Nicolas is a committed Japanophile, travelling regularly there for inspiration. His pralines are wondrous to look at, resembling calligraphy artworks. From over 200 creations, 30 are on rotating display, an arresting blend of flavours and aromas ranging from hazelnut and yuzu peel to sesame paste and wasabi. 'My favourite', says Nicolas, 'is always the one I am working on – roasted buckwheat and Jura whisky right now'.

THINGS TO DO NEARBY

Opera Ghent
Ghent has a grand 19th-century opera house, where you may well catch the likes of *Don Carlos*, *Cosi Fan Tutte* or the *Goldberg Variations*.
www.operaballet.be

Sioux
Historic home of techno, Ghent has a host of dance clubs. Sioux is a student favourite, with theme nights dedicated to rock & roll, 70s and soul. *www.facebook.com/sioux.gent*

EASTERN EUROPE

How to ask for hot chocolate in the local language?
Czech *Horká čokoláda/kakao*
Ukrainian *какао*
Polish *Kakao*

Signature chocolate flavour? Coffee is a good bet.
What to order with your chocolate? A slice of strudel.
Don't: Expect hot cocoa to be made with water – it's almost always made using milk across Eastern Europe.

Europe's East may not exactly be synonymous with chocolate, but that doesn't mean you won't find some amazing options here. The Czech Republic, Poland and Ukraine all have chocolate producers and traditions to rival their Western counterparts.

Ukraine in particular is the chocolate superpower of the former Soviet bloc, with the capital Kyiv and second city Lviv vying for top chocolate spot. The most famous brand of chocolate in Eastern Europe belongs to Petro Poroshenko, until recently Ukraine's president. His company, Roshen (the middle six letters of his surname), has unusual, *Charlie and the Chocolate Factory*-esque stores with mechanical window displays and confectionery heaped high. Lviv has Eastern Europe's top chocolate festival in late September. Brands to look out for elsewhere are Orion in the Czech Republic, who make the country's favourite Studentská pečeť bars containing nuts and jellied fruit; and E Wendel and Wawel in Poland, who traditionally fill supermarket shelves with myriad flavours.

Hot chocolate is less of a phenomenon in Eastern Europe, the beverage invariably associated with (post) communist-era school dining rooms and cheap self-service cafeterias. However, in major cities where tourists gather you will find western-style hot chocolate, some of it pretty good, despite the absence of an established tradition.

GHRAOUI

Andrássy út 31, Budapest, Hungary;
www.ghraouichocolate.com; +36 1-398 8791

◆ Tastings   ◆ Shop
◆ Transport

In Syria, the Ghraoui name has been synonymous with fine chocolate since 1930, and its luxurious sweets have been considered a prize luxury treat ever since. In 2015, however, after Syria's civil war destroyed Ghraoui's production facility outside of Damascus, patriarch Bassam Ghraoui relocated his family and business to Budapest. The shop on prestigious Andrássy út, designed by the architect of Cartier's shops, presents the handpainted bonbons like fine jewels. New, only-in-Hungary confections, such as the Papillon (walnut cream in milk chocolate), have joined Ghraoui's traditional recipes with almonds and apricots, still imported from Syria. Bassam was opening a Paris shop when he passed away in 2018. His wife Rania continues the business. In his memory, savour a chocolate candied orange.

THINGS TO DO NEARBY

Andrássy út
This 2.5km-long (1.5 mi) avenue, granted Unesco World Heritage status in 2002, is a stunning parade of late-19th-century neo-Renaissance architecture, leading to the grand Heroes' Sq.

Great Synagogue
Built in 1859 in a romantic Moorish style, this enormous house of worship anchors Budapest's old Jewish quarter. A memorial stands to those lost in the Holocaust. *www.dohany-zsinagoga.hu*

LVIV CHOCOLATE FACTORY

Serbska 3, Lviv, Ukraine; www.chocolate.lviv.ua;
+38 (050) 430 60 33

◆ Tastings ◆ Classes ◆ Cafe
◆ Transport ◆ Shop ◆ Tours

THINGS TO DO NEARBY

Ploscha Rynok
Lviv's epicentre is its grand market square, a parade of proud townhouses that gather around a large cobbled space with the city's famous town hall centre stage.

Lvivska Kopalnya Kavy
This zany theme cafe is all about coffee and the fact that the beans that go into Lviv's dark brews are mined underneath the central square! Really!
www.fest.lviv.ua

Latin Cathedral
Lviv has more churches than any other Ukrainian city, and arguably the finest of the bunch is this Gothic affair that dominates the historical core.

Arts & Crafts Market
Lviv's daily arts and crafts market on Teatralna Street is a lively bazaar where you can pick up Carpathian souvenirs, Soviet junk and Putin-embossed toilet paper.

Ukraine's second city Lviv is locally synonymous with many things – strong coffee, Gothic architecture and the country's best beer, to name but a few. Chocolate was always traditionally the preserve of the capital Kyiv – former president Poroshenko's Roshen brand is the best known and has themed stores across this vast country. But in recent years, grand old Lviv has stolen Kyiv's thunder with its delightful Lviv Chocolate Factory. To find out what all the chocolatey fuss is about, head to Serbska Street No 3 in the historical heart of the city where this chocolate extravaganza is stacked through a tall, rickety townhouse like a towering gateau. Inside you'll discover aromatic cafes on almost every level, where you can sip hot chocolate topped with whipped cream, plus counters where staff chip chunks off gigantic slabs of handmade, exclusively organic chocolate for takeaway.

If you want to get under the skin of this Slavic choco-experience, 30-minute tours run between 10am and 5pm, during which visitors can sample various kinds of artisan chocolate. If you want to get your hands sticky, there are masterclasses led by professional chocolate makers. But don't worry if you can't make it to Lviv – the Lviv Chocolate Factory has branches across Ukraine, including seven in the capital of Kyiv alone.

© 2020, Lviv Chocolate Factory

FRANCE

How to ask for hot chocolate in the local language? *Un chocolat chaud s'il vous plaît.*
Signature chocolate flavour? *Noisette* (hazelnut praline).
What to order with your chocolate? *A chocolate macaron is the perfect accompaniment to a cup of chocolat chaud.*
Do: *Dunk your pain au chocolat in the café au lait.*

While Swiss and Belgian chocolates may be the best known around the world, France can make a strong claim to being the most exciting place today for creative bean-to-bar chocolate. Every tiny town boasts an artisan chocolatier, whose specialities may range between reinterpreting traditional favourites like pain au chocolat, éclairs and macarons, to creating revolutionary textures and flavours for pralines and truffles. From simple bistros to gastronomic restaurants, the 'chef pâtissier' has an increasingly important role, and the favourite ingredient is invariably chocolate, be it a quintessential mousse au chocolat, profiteroles smothered with melted chocolate, an impeccable chocolate soufflé or the cult Poire Belle Hélène, poached pear enrobed in chocolate sauce, invented by the legendary Auguste Escoffier in 1864.

French school kids grow up eating homemade 'pain au chocolat', a hollowed-out baguette filled with a chocolate bar, and are told the history of chocolate in France began in 1615 as a priceless gift for the 14-year-old King Louis XIII from his bride-to-be, Anne of Austria. Chocolate then was exclusively consumed as a liquid beverage, a luxury in France enjoyed mostly by the rich aristocracy, most famously Louis XIV, the Sun King of Versailles, who loved his hot chocolate prepared in grand ceremony with exotic flavourings like sugar cane, cloves, chilli and vanilla, which added supposed aphrodisiac qualities while sweetening the bitter cocoa taste. It's likely that chocolate was brought even earlier to France through the port of Bayonne in the south-west by Sephardic Jewish immigrants fleeing persecution in Spain and Portugal, bringing with them cacao beans from far away colonies in Mexico and South America, and more importantly the *savoir faire* to transform beans into not bars but drinking chocolate; the birth of *chocolat chaud*.

France quickly went crazy for this astonishing, addictive drink, and in 1761, Catholic chocolate makers formed an exclusive guild to protect the secrets of production – the Jewish community was systematically excluded from membership. Up until the end of the 19th-century, chocolate was definitely not for the masses in France, but rather an

exclusive pastime or sold in pharmacies as a medicinal product. Meanwhile, the rest of Europe was racing ahead to democratise chocolate during the Industrial Revolution, with van Houten inventing chocolate pressing in Holland, Joseph Fry developing the chocolate bar in England, and Nestlé commercialising the first milk chocolate in Switzerland. France caught up belatedly, with the affordable flavoured chocolate and powders of Chocolat Poulain. Monsieur Poulain went on to invent the instant 'breakfast chocolate with vanilla cream' in 1884, an immediate sensation, as you just needed to add boiling water. When the 20th century arrived, chocolate shops opened up in every French town, stocked with the favourite luxury gift to bring to a dinner party, for Christmas and birthday celebrations, or just as a small delicacy.

For professional chocolatiers and chefs, passionate chocoholics and curious foodies, Paris is the home of the world's most important chocolate festival, Le Salon du Chocolat. For five days at the end of October, you can check out the latest chocolate trends and taste the best cocoa vintages, with 200 chefs, maître chocolatiers and pâtissiers conducting workshops, alongside chocolate products from 60 countries across the globe. Bon appétit!

TOP 5 CHOCOLATE BONBONS

L'Instinct, Patrick Roger in Paris, a white or dark chocolate praline.
www.patrickroger.com

NHK, Jean-Paul Hévin in Paris, a crunchy almond hazelnut praline.
www.jeanpaulhevin.com

Couleur de Bourgogne, Fabrice Gillotte in Dijon, fruit jelly sandwiched between ganache.
www.fabricegillotte.com

Le Fresh Green, Quentin Bailly in Lille, milky lime ganache.
www.questinbailly.com

Les Liqueurs de Richard Sève from Lyons, crystallised sugar shell wrapped in black chocolate filled with a liqueur shot.
www.chocolatseve.com

ANNE AND CAROLINE DEBBASCH,
TOP FRENCH CHOCOLATE BLOGGERS,
WWW.LECHOCOLATDANSTOUSNOSETATS.COM

'France is going bean-to-bar, inspiring artisan chocolatiers to create their own chocolate style. A genuine cacao revolution has started, offering a myriad of flavours and aromas.'

HIRSINGER

38 Place de la Liberté, Arbois;
www.chocolat-hirsinger.com; +33 3 84660697

- ◆ Tastings ◆ Classes ◆ Cafe
- ◆ Roastery ◆ Shop ◆ Transport

Edouard Hirsinger resembles an impassioned poet when discussing his 'chocolat vivant', a term he has even patented. Down in the cellar museum, a treasure trove of ancient baking equipment, vintage cookie moulds and a family recipe book dated 1892, he waxes lyrical about 'the freshness of my chocolates, which are not made to be stored but rather eaten quickly to fully appreciate seasonal fruits and spices; gingery speculoos biscuits enrobed in rich dark chocolate, made from organic South American beans, pralines flavoured with locally distilled absinthe'. The

Hirsinger family have made chocolates for four generations here in Arbois, the Jura's wine-making capital, and Edouard recommends that gourmands taste his passion fruit ganache perfectly paired with the fruity Vin de Paille.

THINGS TO DO NEARBY

Fruitière Vinicole d'Arbois
Housed in a grand château, the wine-making cooperative of Arbois offers tastings to discover the unique wines made in the Jura region.
www.chateau-bethanie.fr

Jura Cycle Tour
Arbois is surrounded by vineclad hills, woods and lakes, with a cycle route mapped out by the local tourism office. *www.jura-tourism.com/itineraire/le-circuit-des-vignes*

CAZENAVE

16 Rue Port Neuf, Bayonne;
www.chocolats-bayonne-cazenave.fr; +33 5 59590316

◆ Tastings ◆ Classes ◆ Cafe
◆ Roastery ◆ Shop ◆ Transport

 Artisan chocolate has been made on the premises of this venerable boutique and cafe since 1854, when Bayonne could claim to be chocolate capital of Europe, as this was where the secret of chocolate making first arrived in France, brought by Sephardic Jews driven from Spain and Portugal by the Inquisition. Sitting in Cazenave's lustrous 19th-century Salon de Thé, with its perfectly preserved art nouveau stained-glass windows, it is clear that most loyal customers come here for their famous Chocolat Mousseux, hot chocolate made from organic South American beans,

topped off with a hand-whipped, bobbing head of Chantilly cream mousse. Locals will also always order the traditional plate of buttered demi-brioche toast, served here since the day they opened over a century and a half ago.

THINGS TO DO NEARBY

Cathédrale Sainte-Marie de Bayonne
This Unesco World Heritage site with 13th-century cloisters is a famed stop for pilgrims following the Camino de Santiago. *www.cathedraledebayonne.com*

L'Atelier Pierre Ibaialde
The other great Bayonne foodie tradition is its famous *jambon*, and this famous artisan charcutier offers tastings and tours of his unforgettable ageing atelier.
www.pierre-ibaialde.com

VALRHONA CITE DU CHOCOLAT

12 Avenue du Président Roosevelt, Tain l'Hermitage;
www.citeduchocolat; +33 4 75092727

◆ Tastings ◆ Classes ◆ Cafe
◆ Roastery ◆ Shop

THINGS TO DO NEARBY

Cave de Tain l'Hermitage
France's highest quality
wine-making cooperative
includes 300 smallholder
vignerons. Taste the wines
then tour the futuristic
cellars.
www.cavedetain.com

Palais Idéal du Facteur Cheval
This surreal temple-like
palace was built over 33
years by a humble village
postman, an incredible
achievement.
www.facteurcheval.com

Train d'Ardèche
Leaving from across the
Rhône at Tournon, this
romantic steam train chugs
its way through narrow
gorges, across an ancient
viaduct, past vineyards and
chestnut orchards.
www.trainardeche.fr

Le Bateau Ivre
Rhône wines are some
of France's greatest -
Côte-Rôtie, Saint-Joseph,
Condrieu – and this cosy
wine bar is the perfect
place to crack open a few
bottles. *www.bateau-ivre-hermitage.com*

Welcome to the Valhalla of chocolate. France's ultimate chocolate factory dominates the small Rhône town of Tain l'Hermitage, with almost 1000 local people employed producing superlative chocolate that is sold worldwide. Valrhona opened their Cité du Chocolat in 2013, and since then over a quarter of a million visitors have made a pilgrimage to this modern, interactive and multisensory museum. The historic factory is next door, and out-of-bounds, but a carbon copy of their production line has been created to give a behind-the-scenes snapshot, as well as workshops, hands-on kitchen courses, a fun space for kids and lots of tastings. While the Cité illustrates the global journey of the cacao bean to chocolate, it also recounts Valrhona's history: founded here in 1922 by a local pastry chef, it has grown to become the gastronomic chocolate of choice for the world's artisan chocolatiers, from 3-star

Michelin restaurants to the neighbourhood patisserie. If this whets your taste buds, then why not inquire about professional training at Valrhona's Ecole du Grand Chocolat, which attracts not just aspiring chocolatiers but pastry chefs, bakers and ice cream makers? Stay for lunch at the Comptoir Porcelana, whose dishes include vegetable casserole with cocoa nibs and slow-cooked duck smothered with Xocolipli chocolate sauce.

BERNACHON

42 Cours Franklin Roosevelt, Lyon;
www.bernachon.com; +33 4 78243798

◆ Tastings ◆ Cafe
◆ Roastery ◆ Shop

THINGS TO DO NEARBY

Halles de Lyon Paul Bocuse
Honouring Lyon's most
famous chef, this gourmet
extravaganza offers not
just a cornucopia of foie
gras, oysters and cheese
stalls but a dozen bistros
and bars. *www.halles-de-lyon-paulbocuse.com*

Musée des Beaux-Arts de Lyon
Housed in a 17th-century
Benedictine abbey, one of
the most important French
art museums outside Paris,
with a major permanent
collection and temporary
shows. *www.mba-lyon.fr*

Le Bouchon des Filles
A Lyonnais *bouchon* is
a traditional bistro. Les
Filles' female chefs serve
specialties like creamy
quenelles de brochet
(pike dumplings). *www.lebouchondesfilles.com*

Le Parc de la Tête d'Or
Created in the same year
as Central Park, this green
oasis in the heart of the city
features botanical glass
houses, a boating lake,
carousels and a zoo.
www.parcdelatetedor.com

Lyon is France's gastronomic capital, and while
the larger-than-life Paul Bocuse was a global
personality, his great contemporary and friend Maurice
Bernachon was the icon for chocolate lovers. Opening a tiny
boutique and workshop in 1952, Bernachon made a name
for himself as a discreet, purist artisan, one of the first bean-
to-bar exponents, never interested in fads, fashions or
strange flavourings. The Maison has remained at the same
address, never opening other outlets, even in Paris, though
that didn't stop Monsieur Maurice working seven days a
week till his retirement at the age of 80. His son married
Bocuse's daughter, and today, grandson Philippe continues
the Bernachon tradition of making chocolate. Philippe is a
gentle giant of a man, stalking around his cluttered laboratory, another world from the adjoining bustling boutique
and salon de thé. Here he personally supervises the initial
roasting of the beans from a secret selection from plantations around the world, then comes the grinding, mixing and
conching to produce his own couverture chocolate block,
the chocolatier's raw sculpting material. The boutique
displays a fragrant selection of pralines, truffles tablettes,
but pride of place is taken by their emblematic President, a
magnificent hazelnut praline genoise with candied cherries.

© Hemis / Alamy Stock Photo

ANGELINA

226 Rue de Rivoli, 75001 Paris;
www.angelina-paris.fr; +33 1 42608200

◆ Tastings ◆ Transport ◆ Cafe
◆ Roastery ◆ Shop

Is this the world's most famous hot chocolate? Well, sipping and gently spooning the wonderfully dense, rich Chocolate African in Angelina's sumptuous belle époque salon is certainly a once-in-a-lifetime experience. Although the clientele has changed since the days of Coco Chanel and Proust, Angelina remains the place for fashionable Parisian ladies to be seen, though it is a firm tourist favourite too. Of course, expect a long queue before you enter the hallowed premises, but all is soon forgotten as you taste the heavenly *chocolat chaud*, made from a secret blend of freshly roasted beans from Ghana, Nigeria and Côte d'Ivoire, and the only question is whether to order a sinful Mont Blanc or virtuous sugar- and butter-free brioche aux fruits rouges.

THINGS TO DO NEARBY

L'Olympia
A legendary concert venue since 1893, where everyone from Édith Piaf and Johnny Hallyday to the Beatles and Madonna has performed live. An unforgettable experience.
www.en.olympiahall.com

Jardin du Palais Royal
Haven of peace in the heart of the city, these 17th-century royal gardens offer fountains, flower gardens and distinctive contemporary sculpture.
www.domaine-palais-royal.fr

A L'ETOILE D'OR

30 Rue Pierre Fontaine, 75009 Paris; no web;
+33 1 48745955

◆ Shop   ◆ Cafe   ◆ Transport

Just down the road from Le Moulin Rouge lies an altar dedicated to chocolate, drawing chocophile pilgrims from across the globe since it opened 48 years ago. Behind the counter, animatedly chatting with customers, is 83-year-young Denise Acabo, an eternal gamine with her trademark tartan skirt and pigtails, a mine of information. All her selections are accompanied by handwritten notes like love letters for her choices – not just chocolate, but rare specialty sweets sourced from across France; nougat noir, bergamotes de Nancy, violettes, fruit jellies, kalouga caramels, caramelised almonds. When it comes to chocolat, Denise firmly insists 'absolutely nothing compares with the master chocolatier Bernachon in Lyon. Just taste their exquisite Tablette au Chocolat Noir, 100% pate de cacao!'

THINGS TO DO NEARBY

Dirty Dick
The Pigalle area is Paris' hip new centre for cocktail bars, and this kitsch tikki hangout was once a sleazy strip club.
www.facebook.com/ dirtydickparis

Marché Saint-Pierre
Want to discover where French fashion designers get inspiration? Just wander past the thousands of textiles displayed in this historic rag trade market.
www.marchesaintpierre. com

MANUFACTURE DU CHOCOLAT ALAIN DUCASSE

40 Rue de la Roquette, 75011 Paris;
www.lechocolat-alainducasse.com; +33 1 48058286

◆ Roastery ◆ Transport
◆ Shop ◆ Cafe

© Perry van Munster / Alamy Stock Photo

THINGS TO DO NEARBY

Musée Carnavalet
Discover the hidden secrets of the City of Light in this fascinating museum dedicated to the history of Paris, housed in a 16th-century palace. *www.carnavalet.paris.fr*

Canauxrama
Romantic cruise along the sleepy Canal Saint-Martin from the Bastille to Parc de la Villette, past picturesque locks and a spooky underground tunnel. *www.canauxrama.com*

Ground Control
Urban renewal made these vast railway warehouses into a community project offering craft beer and natural wine bars, organic bistros and weekend dance parties. *www.groundcontrolparis.com*

Le Viaduc des Arts
Red-brick arches below a long-abandoned train viaduct are now artisan ateliers, while up above, the 'promenade plantée' is a magical green elevated walk. *www.leviaducdesarts.com*

When the world's most famous chef, Alain Ducasse, with a staggering 21 Michelin stars to his name, decides to make his own chocolate you can be sure it will be a serious business. Entitled La Manufacture, the first chocolate factory opened here in 2013, followed by Tokyo, and boutiques in London. Ducasse has certainly found a gem of a location for the first-ever bean-to-bar operation in Paris. Hidden among historic artisan ateliers around the Bastille, the pavement window gives passers-by a peek of the vintage Heath Robinson–like roasters and winnowers, surrounded by bags of cacao beans from faraway Venezuela and Madagascar. Visitors then walk into a sunny courtyard where an old car-repair garage has been transformed into a state-of-the-art chocolate atelier, what Ducasse describes

as 'the realisation of a childhood dream'. Once inside, the aroma of chocolate is so overpowering, it is difficult to know where to look first: the antique glass display case packed with tempting truffles and pralines, what Ducasse terms bonbons, or through the long glass wall separating the boutique from the production area, where melted chocolate is churned and kneaded and poured into moulds. While Ducasse's hot chocolate is intense, his creamy Nutella-like *pâte a tartiner* is simply from another planet.

PATRICK ROGER

108 Boulevard Saint-Germain, Paris;
www.patrickroger.com; +33 1 43293842

- ◆ Cafe
- ◆ Transport
- ◆ Roastery
- ◆ Shop

Walking along Boulevard Saint-Germain, no one misses the chocolate shop of Patrick Roger, which could easily be an avant-garde art gallery, with eye-catching seasonal window displays featuring his incredible life-size chocolate sculptures. The man who describes himself as a 'chocolate artist', and others dub an alchemist or the 'enfant terrible of ganache', painstakingly handcrafts chocolate into beautiful works of art: giant orangutans and yawning hippos, Greek gods, even Rodin's *The Thinker*. When not sculpting away in his private laboratory in the Parisian suburbs, Roger travels the world, visiting cacao plantations and searching for novel tastes. Some of his most delicious creations are the simplest: raisin-filled chocolate nuggets, lemongrass ganache bonbons, iconic lime and caramel demispheres.

THINGS TO DO NEARBY

L'Avant-Comptoir de la Terre
King of Parisian bistros Yves Cambeborde owns this buzzy Saint-Germain tapas bar with over 50 wines by the glass. *www. hotel-paris-relais-saint-germain.com*

Shakespeare & Company
Across from Notre-Dame, this historic English-language bookshop remains an obligatory site of literary pilgrimage. *www. shakespeareandcompany. com*

PRALUS

35 Rue Rambuteau, Paris;
www.chocolats-pralus.com; +33 1 57408455

◆ Bakery
◆ Shop

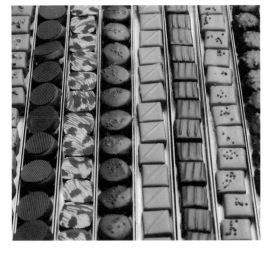

THINGS TO DO NEARBY

Centre Pompidou
This iconic modern art museum offers a lot more than exhibitions, with cinema screens, performance space and kid's activities. *www.centrepompidou.fr*

Paris Prizoners
The global escape game craze has firmly arrived in the French capital, and this escape room offers 60 minutes of fantasy time travel. *www.prizoners.com*

La Bovida
The ultimate emporium for professional chefs searching for state-of-the-art kitchen equipment but open to the public; Japanese knives, Le Creuset pans, crystal wine glasses. *www.labovida.com*

Le Potager du Marais
Parisians are discovering tasty possibilities of vegan cuisine, and this charming bistro creatively readapts classic dishes like bourguignon de seitan, a hearty vegan red wine stew. *www.lepotagerdumarais.fr*

One of the most innovative figures on the French chocolate scene, François Pralus has 15 boutiques dotted across the country, with production centred in the sleepy town of Roanne, near Lyon. But like many of these secretive maîtres de chocolate, the roasting and manufacturing centre is off limits for the public, so his flagship Parisian showroom is the best address to discover the world of Pralus. Monsieur François takes bean-to-bar to the limits, not just importing dried cacao beans from twenty tropical regions across the globe, but planting his own organic plantation in Madagascar. 'You can talk about cocoa vintages just as you can for great wines. The Venezuela grade-up has a slight smoky taste, the Trinitario grade-up is woody, powerful and slightly sharp. Madagascar cocoa is fine and acidic and tastes of red fruit'. To discover this myriad of flavours and nuances, ask for the ten-bar Pyramide des Tropiques, each tablette coming from a different cocoa-producing country; Ghana, Ecuador, Papua New Guinea, São Tomé islands. Remember, though, it is also difficult to resist the signature Praluline, a wickedly delicious praline-filled brioche, invented 65 years ago using a still-secret recipe of François's father, Auguste.

GERMANY

How to ask for hot chocolate in the local language? *Eine Tasse heisse Schokolade, bitte.*

Signature chocolate flavours? Milk, dark and everything in between.

What to order with your chocolate? Black Forest gateau (Schwarzwälder Kirschtorte) for a double whammy chocolate kick.

Do: Try to time your visit with chocolART, Germany's biggest chocolate festival, with tastings, demos, courses and more. It's held in the lovely town of Tübingen in December. *www.chocolart.de.*

Chocolate arrived in Germany in the 17th century, as medicine sold in pharmacies – who would've thought that today it would become such a common, yet impactful taste in the local eating culture?

Germany is Europe's leader in chocolate consumption, with yearly sales of around 213 million kg (470 million lbs) of chocolate bars. But in the beginning, it was an expensive status product enjoyed only by aristocracy. With industrialisation raging into the 19th-century, chocolate became much more affordable thanks to new factories, a lift on cocoa taxes and local beet sugar replacing the costly imported stuff. The famous *Schwarzwaelder Kirschtorte* (Black Forest cake) was also supposedly invented at this time.

But during World War II and the post-war period, everything changed. Chocolate rationing meant German chocolate companies were forced to halt production; and it became unattainable for everyday citizens – although it was given to German soldiers in a performance-enhancer called 'Scho-Ka-Kola' designed to keep them awake.

Lack of access gave chocolate an exalted status. In 1949, during the Berlin Blockade, American pilot Gail Halvorsen dropped candy and chocolate bars by parachute on unauthorized flights over Berlin. Over the weeks, German children picked up over 23 tonnes of sweets from the 'Candy Bomber'. Afterwards, many would talk about the significance of receiving those treats amid war-stricken poverty. 'It wasn't the sweets that impressed me', Mercedes Wild, a little girl in Berlin at the time, told the news agency AFP. 'I grew up fatherless, like a lot of (German) children at that time, so knowing that someone outside of Berlin was thinking of me gave me hope'. Chocolate came to represent something much bigger: freedom and the end of hard times.

When the rationing ended in West Germany in the 1950s, the demand for sweets was insatiable. Germany's juggernaut post-war industrial period saw that the need was met. Two pre-war companies, Ritter Sport and Milka, picked up again and are today Germany's two most popular brands – you can see them in any supermarket lined by the row.

Chocolate also became an important part of German eating habits: whether a slice of German chocolate cake

TOP 5 BLACK FOREST CAKES IN THE BLACK FOREST

CAFE SCHÄFER

In the charming village of Triberg, Cafe Schäfer makes Schwarzwälder Kirschtorte (Black Forest gateau) according to the original 1915 recipe from its creator Josef Keller. *www.cafe-schaefer-triberg.de*

BECKESEPP

With several locations, Beckesepp's modern take on the cake is sold in a takeaway tin. Despite the compact size, it's still big enough to share. *www.beckesepp.de*

CAFE KOENIG

For over 250 years, Cafe Koenig has served Baden-Baden's dreamiest cakes, tortes and pralines. The Black Forest cake has huge cream dollops, true to form. *www.chocolatier.de*

BLACK FOREST GATEAU FESTIVAL

The annual festival held every spring in Todtnauberg celebrates the region's famous export with baking contests, classes, lederhosen and oompah bands. Brace for sugar shock. *www.kirschtorte.de*

GASTHAUS BISCHENBERG

This alpine hotel's homemade Black Forest cake features black and vanilla cake, and cherry and vanilla cream. A short drive from Baden-Baden in quaint Bischenberg. *www.gasthaus-bischenberg.de*

or Black Forest gateau during *kaffee und kuchenzeit* (coffee and cake time) in the afternoon, or Eisschokolade (iced chocolate) served on a hot summer's day. Yet more expensive bean-to-bar chocolate is a trend that is only now slowly catching on. Germans, already known as organic food consumers and top recyclers, are starting to see the value in bean-to-bar as part of the sustainability movement. They increasingly want to know where their products come from, especially when it comes to ethical sourcing and the transparency of ingredients.

Chocolatier Kevin Kugel in southern Germany is opening an even bigger shop in 2020 due to demand for his pretty pralines made with homegrown ingredients, and Berlin lays claim to the award-winning Coda, Germany's first desserts-only restaurant, which also makes its pralines and chocolate from roasted cacao beans. Thomas and Lyudmyla Michel in Brandenburg, just outside of Berlin, started making chocolate for themselves in 2008 when all they could find were mass-produced brands. Their company Edelmond Chocolatiers has been operating since 2010, and sales have grown a steady 15% every year, says Thomas, noting that 'with wine, consumers know that quality and taste isn't cheap, and cacao is the same'.

BELYZIUM

Lottumstraße 15, Berlin; www.belyzium.com/en;
+49 (0)30 4404 6484

◆ Tastings ◆ Classes ◆ Transport
◆ Roastery ◆ Shop ◆ Food

THINGS TO DO NEARBY

Kaschk
Cosy cafe meets craft beer bar. Chill out beneath fairy lights on the back patio or reserve the tables for a game of beer pong.
www.kaschk.de

8mm
This dive bar is beloved by artists of all kinds. Catch a live band or DJ spinning underground rock from punk to garage.
www.8mm.de

Yafo
A tiny eatery à la Tel Aviv, energetic evenings here are fuelled by top-notch hummus, electronic DJs and servers happily downing shooters with guests.
www.yafoberlin.com

Standard
Handmade pizzas made according to Neapolitan tradition. The dough is made fresh daily and many products, like the mozzarella and tomatoes, come straight from Italy.
www.standard-berlin.de

Belyzium is a chocolate shop that takes bean-to-bar one step further. Their organic beans are grown on the same plantation in Belize, and fermented and sun-dried there before being delivered to the vegan-friendly Berlin shop. In a small production facility on-site, the beans are roasted and refined, made into chocolate and packaged – you can watch every step happen behind the glass.

Products in soft, stylish packaging are propped between wood furniture and handmade decorations that make Belyzium feel like a Berlin artist's living room. Besides chocolate bars with varying cocoa percentages, you'll find truffles, cacao beans, cacao husk tea, hot chocolate and ice cream for sale. The owners, Florian Schülke and Klaus Boels, are keen to explain their craft and show off experiments like spirits made with cacao husks.

Some bars are piqued with natural ingredients like salt, pepper and smoked chilli. Otherwise, they are made from just cocoa and small amounts of raw sugar, so vegans can also indulge. Sit in an armchair and have a snack, or better yet, take part in Belyzium's weekly Saturday workshops where you make your own bar to take home. Book ahead on the website, as they tend to fill up a couple of weeks in advance (no wonder why).

CAFE SCHÄFER

Hauptstrasse 33, Triberg, Baden-Württemberg;
www.cafe-schaefer-triberg.de; +49 (0) 7722 4465

◆ Shop   ◆ Transport
◆ Cafe

Think of Black Forest gateau, or Schwarzwälder Kirschtorte, and you might well imagine the boozy, gooey, sickly sweet calorie bomb of 1970s dessert trolleys. But surely the real deal is better? Darned right it is. Locals often sing the praises of Oma (grandma), whose fabulous chocolate-cherry creation, smothered in clouds of whipped cream, was devoured after a brisk, hungry hike in the woods.

As deep, dark and delicious as the fir-clad Schwarzwald itself, Black Forest gateau is found the world over, but only Cafe Schäfer in the quaint cuckoo-clock town of Triberg has Josef Keller's original 1915 recipe, dog-eared with more than a century of sticky thumbprints. Here Claus Schäfer bakes just one or two gateaux fresh every morning. His is a multi-layered masterpiece of springy chocolate sponge, silk-smooth cream with a kirsch liqueur kick, and tart morello cherries, all resting majestically upon a marzi-pan-infused shortcrust base.

'Baking Black Forest gateau isn't rocket science, but it involves time, patience and the freshest ingredients. Mine is light enough to eat a second slice', says Claus. 'The finishing touches are important, too: the piping, chocolate shavings and ring of cherries'. Speaking of the latter, you can't squeeze a gateau in your suitcase, but by all means take home some of his hand-dipped dark-chocolate cherries – they're *wunderbar*.

THINGS TO DO NEARBY

Tribeger Wasserfälle
A walking trail affords misty perspectives of this seven-tiered cascade spilling down through forest in Triberg. It's Germany's highest waterfall.
www.triberg.de

Eble Uhren-Park
A whopping 4.5m (15ft) cuckoo pops out hourly at this giant clock shop on Triberg's fringes. The cuckoo clock is listed as the world's largest by Guinness World Records.
www.uhren-park.de

Panoramaweg
Want to walk off all that gateau indulgence? The panorama trail that leads into the spruce forest above Triberg is beautiful – whether sun-dappled or snow-clad. *www.triberg.de*

Stöcklewaldturm
A hike through forest and pastures from Triberg's waterfall brings you to this 19th-century lookout tower, where views stretch to the Alps on clear days.
www.stoecklewaldturm.de

EDELMOND

Zöllmersdorfer Dorfstraße 4, Luckau;
www.edelmond.de; +49 (0)354 4558 9104

◆ Tastings ◆ Classes
◆ Roastery ◆ Shop

Edelmond Chocolatiers is a family-run business in Germany's scenic Spreewald region, about 1.5 hours from Berlin on public transport. Its creations are delivered around Germany, but between lush green farmland and Venice-like canals, you can visit its small shop at the production facility. Edelmond is the only German chocolate company certified as organic and fair trade, and the owners travel to countries like Haiti and Colombia themselves to source the cocoa and verify their supply chain. The in-house bean-to-bar process is long and painstaking. After roasting, the beans undergo conching for 50 hours or more. Bars are mixed with dried fruits, nuts and spices. But don't miss trying the raw chocolate with tomatoes, strawberries and cucumber – local produce grown in Spreewald's famous soil.

THINGS TO DO NEARBY

Freilandmuseum Lehde
In Lehde, a charming protected village in Spreewald, you can visit historical Sorb farm buildings showing what rural life in the region was like a century ago. *www. museums-entdecker.de*

Museum Schloss Lübben
A little castle and a regional history museum. Check out the Schlossinsel, an artificial archipelago with gardens and a harbour where boat tours are offered. *www.luebben.de*

KEVIN KUGEL CHOCOLATIER

Hauptstraße 37, Nufringen; www.kevinkugel.de;
+49 (0)70 3278 4402 4

◆ Tastings   ◆ Classes   ◆ Cafe
◆ Roastery   ◆ Shop   ◆ Transport

THINGS TO DO NEARBY

Schoenbuch Nature Park
Schoenbuch is known
for pretty hiking trails
and attractions like a
Cistercian monastery and
an observation deck with
360-degree views. *www.
naturpark-schoenbuch.de*

Hasen Restaurant
This restaurant in nearby
Herrenberg serves hearty
Swabian cuisine, and good
vegetarian options are
available.
*www.hasen.de/restaurant/
restaurants-im-hasen*

Collegiate Church
This attractive Protestant
church in Herrenberg has
highlights including a
baroque dome, stone pulpit
and choir stalls. *www.
stuttgart-tourist.de/en/a-
herrenberg-collegiate-
church*

Schlosskeller Herrenberg
This hilltop beer garden has
great views of Herrenberg's
medieval downtown. Sit
under an umbrella and
savour beer, prosecco and
local delicacies. *www.
schlosskeller-herrenberg.
com*

Kevin Kugel is one of Germany's youngest and most philosophy-driven chocolatiers, making his headquarters an excellent stop in southern Germany. It's located in Nufringen, Kevin's hometown, about 30 km (18 mi) from Stuttgart.

The 33-year-old chocolatier and his team hand-make over 3000 pralines daily in the workshop. In the adjoining shop, sleek black wooden shelves showcase chocolate baubles behind glass. A small cafe next door serves pralines and truffles with coffee.

Sustainability and transparency are at the core of the chocolatier's philosophy. Kevin personally visits farms in Ecuador, Mexico and the Dominican Republic to source his cacao beans, and the final bean-to-bar bites feature the highest-quality ingredients he can get.

Some fruits and herbs, like the mint in the mojito truffles and the rosemary, thyme and woodruff, are grown by the chocolatier himself. Plums and pears plucked from his family's garden are brought to a regional distillery and made into spirits for ganache fillings.

During summer, enjoy pralines, truffles and seasonal specialties, like artisanal ice cream, in the cafe's cosy outdoor seating area. There are only 15 spots, but that's changing: in late summer 2020, the business moves to a much larger space in Sindelfingen even closer to Stuttgart.

ICELAND

How to ask for hot chocolate in the local language? *Ég ætla að fá heitt súkkulaði.*

Signature chocolate flavours? Unexpectedly, it's liquorice.

What to order with your chocolate? Icelanders love their coffee, which is eased down nicely with a chocolate treat, since it's typically bitter.

Do: Try the liquorice flavour!

You might be surprised to know that the 358,780 people that live in Iceland have a big sweet tooth. So much that every Saturday is for them 'Candy Day', as on this day of the week supermarkets in the country apply a 50% discount on all self-serve candies and chocolates. As import taxes are particularly high in Iceland, the most popular chocolates on the island are made by national companies. They don't make the chocolate themselves, but buy chocolate from big manufacturers and remelt it into bars, candies and treats that can be found in supermarkets. Icelandic chocoholics love flavours like milk, caramel, coconut and toffee, but the queen of all chocolate inclusions is undoubtedly liquorice. This Nordic country has made a name for itself for combining liquorice ('lakkris' in Icelandic) and chocolate: every single chocolate brand at the supermarket has at least one product with liquorice in it, and it is usually their best seller. In terms of artisanal chocolates, there are only a few chocolatiers on the island, who make chocolate treats and bonbons with high-quality ingredients (and that will probably cost you a small fortune). The only craft chocolate maker on the island is Omnom Chocolate, whose modern factory is located in the capital Reykjavik's Old Harbour. This company makes chocolate starting from cacao beans sourced in exotic countries and turn them into stylish chocolate bars that have gained international recognition. No matter your personal preferences, be reassured: Iceland is set to satisfy all your sweet cravings.

OMNOM CHOCOLATE

Hólmaslóð 4, Grandi, Reykjavík;
www.omnomchocolate.com; +354 519-5959

◆ Tastings   ◆ Classes   ◆ Cafe
◆ Roastery   ◆ Shop   ◆ Transport

You won't believe the number of travelling chocolate lovers who take a stopover in Iceland just to visit the Omnom Chocolate factory. What used to be an abandoned gas station in the heart of Reykjavik has been converted into a stylish, modern chocolate factory that attracts both chocolate professionals and amateurs from all over the world. Beans arrive here from Madagascar, Tanzania, Nicaragua and Peru to be roasted, cracked, conched and tempered into beautiful, Instagram-worthy chocolate bars. Each cacao origin brings a specific set of flavours mixed with purely Icelandic ingredients like *lakkris* (liquorice), Icelandic milk and sea salt. If you like your chocolate dark, the Tanzania 70% bar brings you notes of apricots and raisins. Prefer something sweeter? Try the Caramel + Milk bar.

THINGS TO DO NEARBY

Whales of Iceland
Ever strolled beneath a blue whale? This museum houses full-sized models of the 23 species of whale found off Iceland's coast, and has helpful audio guides. *www.whalesoficeland.is*

Sægreifinn
Sidle into this charming green harbourside shack for the most famous lobster soup in the capital, or choose from a fridge full of fresh fish skewers to be grilled on the spot. *www.saegreifinn.is*

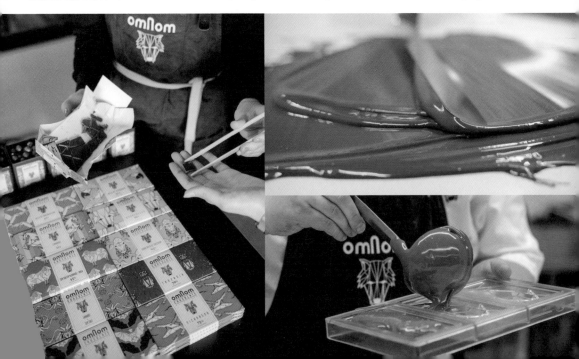

IRELAND

How to ask for chocolate in the local language? *Seacláid* is chocolate in Gaelic.

Signature chocolate flavours? Milk chocolate with caramel.

What to order with your chocolate? Tea.

Do: Be open-minded about milk chocolate despite dark being the foodie's choice.

As a nation, Ireland is third in the world for consuming the most chocolate per capita, an impressive feat when you consider it's beaten only by Switzerland and Germany. Yet it doesn't have the long tradition of chocolate-making of some of its closest neighbours. That has changed in the last few decades, as palates are seeking out inventive, artisanal chocolate taking inspiration from Irish ingredients. The result is small, local chocolate makers creating delicious bars and sweets, often by hand.

More unusual flavours are making their way into the mainstream but one thing will not change: when you think about Irish chocolate, you are thinking about creamy milk

chocolate. While dark chocolate is readily available, local producers take advantage of the unique taste of Irish dairy to make their milk chocolate extra special. With cows grazing on good quality pasture of grass and clovers, their produce has been proven to have better nutritional value, flavour and fat content. The result is melt-in-your mouth velvety chocolate made with lashings of milk, cream or even butter. Even mass-produced international brands often have their own recipe to suit Irish tastes by adding more real milk to their bars.

The richness of Irish chocolate means that caramel and salted caramel are often excellent accompaniments, but if you want to double down on the creaminess, opt for fudge filling. Bars are the most common product to buy, but there is increasingly a plethora of chocolatiers offering a delightfully diverse range of filled sweets to pick and choose from.

Ó CONAILL HOT CHOCOLATE & COFFEE SHOP

16, French Church Street, Cork;
www.oconaillchocolate.ie; +353 21 437 3407

◆ Food   ◆ Cafe

◆ Shop   ◆ Transport

 Ireland's temperate climate means the cosy delights of a creamy hot chocolate are acceptable all year. This independent cafe in the bustling boho quarter of Cork city boasts 120 different varieties, allowing you to create your own drink from a base of dark, milk, white or pure cocoa and mix with any number of flavours, from espresso to spices, praline nuts or essential oils. The chocolate is melted right at the shop counter where you can create your own elaborate concoction or opt for a signature recipe from their menu. Enjoy with a fresh treat from their very own bakery or bring home bars to recreate the hot chocolate in your own home. Sit outside in warm weather or people-watch from the huge windows on colder days.

THINGS TO DO NEARBY

English Market
Continue your local food odyssey with a trip to this iconic food market serving everything from fresh fish and meat to cheese, fruit and homemade preserves.
www.englishmarket.ie

Shandon Bells and Tower of St Anne's Church
On a bright day, a climb to the top will give you a bird's eye view of the city and a chance to ring the bells yourself.
www.shandonbells.ie

SKELLIGS CHOCOLATE FACTORY

The Glen, Ballinskelligs, Co Kerry;
www.skelligschocolate.com; +353 66 9479119

◆ Tastings   ◆ Shop

◆ Cafe   ◆ Tours

 Indulge your sweet tooth in one of the most remote and stunning locations in Ireland. There's no entrance fee to visit Ireland's only fully open plan production factory which is small but incredibly welcoming and all visitors are given a short, informal tour (though there is no production on the weekends). Inventiveness is the key word here, and their normal lineup consists of bars flavoured with gin and tonic, lime and black pepper, and chilli. There are plenty of seasonal goodies to try and the staff are on hand with a friendly welcome and plenty of free tastings including their famous truffles or award-winning alcohol-soaked fruit in chocolate. There's also an added bonus of stunning views on clear days, looking over to the iconic Skellig Michael.

THINGS TO DO NEARBY

Ring of Kerry
This 179km (111 mi) circuit is a dreamily scenic road trip on the Wild Atlantic Way packed with cute villages, beautiful beaches, thrilling surfing spots and hiking routes.

Kerry International Dark Sky Reserve
The only gold tier reserve in the northern hemisphere offers unparalleled stargazing even sans binoculars or telescope.
www.kerrydarksky.com

ITALY

How to ask for hot chocolate in the local language? *Vorrei un cioccolato caldo per piacere.*
Signature chocolate flavour? Hazelnut.
What to order with your chocolate? Glass of *recioto* sweet red wine with *cioccolatini.*
Do: Ask a waiter to sprinkle your cappuccino with cocoa powder.

Italians carry on a passionate love affair, *un amore*, with chocolate, be it a thick dense cup of *cioccolato caldo* that Casanova adored for its aphrodisiac qualities, or iconic bonbons like romantic 'Baci' and the irresistible gold-wrapped Ferrero Rocher, produced at the mind-boggling rate of 24 million per day. While the first person to bring back cacao beans to Europe may have been Italian, Christopher Columbus no less, Italy's chocolate history began on the island of Sicily. In the same way that Belgium discovered chocolate earlier than its neighbours due to being under Spanish rule, Sicily was also part of Spain's kingdom in the 16th century, and was introduced to the wonders of Mexico's *xocoatl* before the rest of Italy. Travel to the baroque Sicilian town of Modica today and chocolate artisans grind a rough, grainy 'cold' chocolate, following the same techniques as the Aztecs, ignoring modern inventions like conching that create the refined, creamy chocolate the rest of the world loves. With an aroma of roasted coffee beans, slightly bitter, these coarse slabs are flavoured with cinnamon, vanilla, chilli and lime, celebrated with an annual festival, ChocoModica.

While Sicily was enjoying the wonders of chocolate, Italy was not even a united country but a series of sovereign states and republics like the Medicis in Florence and the Republic of Venice. One of the most powerful states was the Duchy of Savoy, and its royal city, Turin, was not only the first capital of a united Italy, but the undisputed capital of Italian chocolate. In 1678 the Duke of Savoy granted the first ever royal licence to produce chocolate to a *cioccolataio* in Turin. Elegant cafes soon opened to meet the demand for the new craze of hot chocolate, and then a set of strange circumstances saw Turin change the face of modern choc-olate. While Europe was ravaged by the Napoleonic Wars, cocoa became harder to import and much more expensive to produce.

In the Piedmont countryside around Turin, hazelnut trees grew abundantly, and two Torinese chocolate makers, Ernesto Caffarel and Michele Prochet, had the brilliant idea

5 BEST CITIES FOR HOT CHOCOLATE

VENICE - Caffè Florian
www.caffeflorian.com

TURIN - Caffè Platti
www.platti.it

BOLOGNA - Caffè Terzi
www.caffeterzi.it

TRIESTE - Antica Caffè San Marco
www.caffesanmarco.com

FLORENCE - Caffè Rivoire
www.rivoire.it

DAVIDE BISETTO,
MICHELIN-STARRED CHEF OF VENICE'S ORO AT HOTEL CIPRIANI

'Italians are mad about chocolate like never before, reflecting how our innovative master cioccolatieri *are adapting their artisan creations for a public seeking healthy, ethical, organic chocolate.'*

to replace part of the cocoa in chocolate with a similar but much cheaper, fat greasy ingredient: locally grown hazelnuts. The result was the delicious 'Pasta Gianduja' (a hazelnut-chocolate spread), and Caffarel immediately found fame by using it in the bite-sized *gianduiotto*, named after one of Turin's famous carnival masks. They are still one of Italy's best-loved *cioccolatini*. The ultimate use of this creamy hazelnut-flavoured chocolate spread was discovered by Pietro Ferrero, a baker in the Piedmont town of Alba. In 1946 he made his first Pasta Gianduja, later marketed as Supercrema. In 1964 his son Michele decided to rename it Nutella, and history was made. Ferrero is still based in Alba, where their chocolate empire has extended to Ferrero Rocher, Mon Chéri and Kinder, but their recipes remain top secret, with no possibility of factory visits. The other giant Italian chocolate manufacturer, Perugina in Umbria, has a very different philosophy, opening its doors for the public to visit an on-site chocolate museum and taking part in Perugia's Eurochocolate, a popular celebration that attracts almost a million visitors drawn by chocolate spas, chocolate igloos or the world's longest chocolate bar. Can't make it there? Stop by Rome's famous chocolate factory SAID dal 1923 for a delicious hot chocolate as compensation.

ANTICA DOLCERIA BONAJUTO

Corso Umberto I, 159, Modica, Sicily;
www.bonajuto.it/en; +39 0932 941225

◆ Tastings ◆ Classes ◆ Cafe
◆ Roastery ◆ Shop

The ingredients in Bonajuto's signature bars are satisfyingly simple: cocoa mass, sugar and a dash of cinnamon or pinch of vanilla. The list hasn't changed much since 1880, when Francesco Bonajuto founded this elegant chocolaterie. But their lineage is even longer: they're made the same way chocolate has been made in Sicily for centuries, since Spanish rulers brought the technique from Central America. Beans are ground on stone by hand, then mixed with sugar and natural flavourings. This cold process prevents the cocoa butter separating or the sugar melting,

and the result is a rich, gritty bar that tastes darker than its 50% cocoa and sparkles with sugar granules. Visit in summer to explore Bonajuto's bean-to-bar lab, and all year round to taste its prizewinning products.

THINGS TO DO NEARBY

San Giorgio Cathedral
This baroque marvel is the jewel in Unesco-listed Modica's architectural crown. Revel in its restored tiered tower and white, gold and baby-blue interior.

Accursio Ristorante
Chef Accursio Craparo offers a smart take on Sicilian traditions at his Michelin-starred restaurant. Look out too for his eponymous cafe and cocktail bar. *www. accursioristorante.it*

LA CASA DEL CIOCCOLATO PERUGINA

Viale San Sisto 207/C, Perugia, Umbria;
www.perugina.it; +39 02 45467655

◆ Transport   ◆ Classes   ◆ Cafe
◆ Roastery   ◆ Shop

THINGS TO DO NEARBY

Ipogeo dei Volumni
This underground burial site from the 2nd-century BC is set in a sprawling necropolis from Etruscan times. *www. polomusealeumbria. beniculturali.it/?page_ id = 5291*

Dal Mi'Cocco
A cheap and cheerful trattoria famed for huge helpings and friendly welcome. Enormously popular, it's best to call ahead to reserve.
+39 075 573 25 11

Augusta Perusia
Come here for wonderful artisan ice creams – try Pop Rock, a 'gelato frizzante' – or a pistachio praline from chocolatier Giacomo Mangano. *www. cioccolatoaugustaperusia.*

Umbria Jazz
One of the world's top music festivals, Umbria Jazz attracts the likes of Keith Jarrett and Herbie Hancock for a week of concerts each July.
www.umbriajazz.com

Perugina's 'Chocolate House', just outside Umbria's capital, is a paradise Willy Wonka must have dreamt about. Industrial chocolate makers usually keep their doors firmly closed, and Perugina is owned by Swiss multinational Nestlé. But since 2007, the Casa del Cioccolato offers a unique experience, physically located inside their huge factory, that spans a fascinating museum tour documenting Perugina's history and chocolate production in general, the chance to take a technical class in its chocolate-making school, birds-eye view of production and, of course, a mouth-watering tasting. Ask romantic Italians what their favourite chocolate is and everyone replies Baci (it means kisses): a hazelnut-filled gianduja chocolate with a love note hidden beneath the silver wrapping. They have been buying them since 1922, and today the company produce some 1.9 million a day. Just be prepared to don white overalls and cap to enter the glass bridge walkway that looks down onto the factory floor. At the end of the tour, the *sala degustazione* (tasting room) is pure heaven for chocoholics as you can scoff as many as you like! While most people can't resist Baci, connoisseurs head for the Perugina Nero, an incredibly intense 95% fondente, black chocolate.

CAFFE AL BICERIN

5 Piazza della Consolata, Turin, Piedmont;
www.bicerin.it; +39 011 4369325

◆ Food ◆ Cafe
◆ Shop ◆ Transport

The Bicerin opened its doors back in 1763, originally as an 'acquacedratario' for drinking citronade. In the 19th century, Turin became the place for chocolate and coffee, so the locale was redesigned, and with its ornate mirrored walls, marble-topped tables and slightly rickety chairs, very little has changed since, including the drink that was invented here, served today in every Torino *caffè*. Il Bicerin is a unique mix of espresso coffee, thick chocolate and frothy cream, once tasted never forgotten. Served in a special glass, the trick is never to stir or mix, but sip each ingredient separately, especially the chocolate, slow-cooked for hours in copper pots. And the Bicerin is the perfect accompaniment to their tempting Piedmontese biscuits and a shot of Regale chocolate liqueur.

THINGS TO DO NEARBY

Porta Palazzo
800 stalls pack this pulsating street and covered market where you can find everything from cashmere jumpers and fake jewellery to pungent white truffles and rustic cheeses.

Caffè San Carlo
Turin is the world's aperItivo capital and this its most sumptuous cafe. So order a vermouth and feast off the sumptuous buffet included in the drink's price.
www.caffesancarlo.it

VIZIOVIRTU

Calle del Forner, Castello, Venice, Veneto;
www.viziovirtu.com; +39 041 2750149

◆ Classes ◆ Cafe
◆ Shop ◆ Transport

THINGS TO DO NEARBY

Traghetto
Cross the Grand Canal over to the Rialto market like Venetians on the stand-up public gondola, €2 a trip for tourists and priceless for the memories.

Osteria Al Portego
Rustic wood-beamed bar with delicious *cichetti* (snacks) like grilled squid, and where an *ombra* (glass of wine) only costs €1.
www.osteriaalportego.org

Ospedale Museum
Venice's hospital is housed in a palatial 15th-century building, whose first floor hosts a fascinating museum illustrating the history of medicine. *www.scuolagrandesanmarco.it*

Giovanna Zanella
Irresistible handmade leather shoes by a creative master craftswoman. Choose one of her fantasy designs inspired by the Venice Carnival. *www.giovannazanella.com*

Mariangela Penzo took Venice by storm when she opened the first artisan chocolate shop and cafe 15 years ago, and today her expanded modern 'cioccolateria' and laboratory, just by the birthplace of Marco Polo, is an obligatory stop on any foodie tour of *La Serenissima*, as Venice is known. With the ever-present humidity in this floating city, roasting beans is not possible, but Mariangela and her team create exotic fondant truffles flavoured with everything from pumpkin or wild dill to balsamic vinegar or Mexican chillies, even cigar. Candied fruits are taken to another gastronomic level, as glazed figs, oranges, ginger and plums are coated with intense dark chocolate. Every day there are guided tastings in the shop, explaining the history of chocolate which has been served in the Piazza San Marco at Caffè Florian since 1720, while hands-on workshops in the kitchen teach how to temper chocolate and to make truffles and hot chocolate. This being Italy, you can also pick up some pasta to take home, delicate tagliatelle made with Vizio's artisan cocoa powder. And who can resist their very own Goldoni hot chocolate, named after the Venetian playwright known for his commedia dell'arte works; it's totally sinless too, with no milk or sugar.

NETHERLANDS

How to ask for hot chocolate in the local language? *Mag ik een warme chocolademelk.*

Signature chocolate flavours? *Milk is het beste.*

What to order with your chocolate? *A slice of toast covered with fruit or chocolate 'hagelsag' sprinkles.*

Do: *Ask for Chocomel when ordering chocolate milk; it is Holland's favourite drink, hot or cold.*

The Netherlands may be less renowned today as an artisan chocolate heaven compared to glamorous neighbours France and Belgium, but Holland has played a crucial role in the development of the chocolate that is consumed today. In the 17th century the Dutch were one of

the world's most powerful colonial and trading nations, a major transporter of cacao beans to Europe. But it is easy to forget that, at this time, chocolate was only consumed as a beverage, not in the solid bar form we all know today. That is, until the crucial invention by Dutch chemist, Coenraad Johannes van Houten, of the cocoa press in 1829. Quite simply, this is the process that allows the ground cacao bean paste to be mixed with sugar and cocoa butter to create a delicate, flavoursome cocoa powder, the magic ingredient that gives chocolate bars their creamy, melt-in-the-mouth texture and allows for the production of everything chocolate, from ice cream to milkshakes and cakes. The van

TOP 5 CHOCOLATE EXPERIENCES

Jordino, Amsterdam

It's the best of both worlds: Jordino makes rich chocolates and velvety ice cream and combines the two by scooping the ice cream atop cones dipped in chocolate or caramel. Of its 100-plus flavours, 24 (including fruit-based sorbets) are available at any one time. Other creations include chocolate tulips. *www.jordino.nl*

Hemelse Modder, Amsterdam

This restaurant emphasising North Sea fish and farm-fresh produce is named 'Heavenly Mud' after its signature dark and white chocolate mousse dessert, a must-try. *hemelsemodder.nl/en*

De IJsmaker, Rotterdam

Fresh flavours reign supreme at this artisanal ice cream parlour on Witte de Withstraat and only quality produce is used (that goes for the chocolate too). *deijsmaker.nl*

Van Stapele Koekmakerij, Amsterdam

This teeny cookie shop, located in an alleyway between the Singel and Spuistraat, is the epitome of doing one thing and doing it well. There is often a line out the door, and you'll find out why when you sink your teeth into one of their freshly baked dark chocolate cookies, complete with gooey white chocolate centre. *www.vanstapele.com*

Graaf Floris, Utrecht

Satisfy your sweet tooth with one of the famous apple dumplings along with a hot chocolate from this beautiful cafe. *graaffloris.nl*

Houten factory is still in the suburbs of Amsterdam today, sadly not open to the public, but the Dutch remain loyal consumers of their famed cocoa powder, milk and dark chocolate bars.

Slowly but surely, there is an artisan chocolatier renaissance underway in the Netherlands, seriously committed to ethical trading to end exploitation of plantation workers around the world. For an overall experience of the Dutch chocolate scene, why not visit in February, when for two days the centre of Amsterdam goes choco-crazy with the Chocoa Festival, combining bean-to-bar artisans from around the world with wine, coffee and craft beer.

CHOCOLATEMAKERS

32 Radarweg, Amsterdam; www.chocolatemakers.nl;
+31 (0)6 42765654

◆ Transport ◆ Classes ◆ Cafe
◆ Roastery ◆ Shop

THINGS TO DO NEARBY

Depot
Up to a thousand dance fans cram into this raw warehouse club, where the music ranges from deep house to all-night techno raves. *www. depotamsterdam.com*

Vineyard Bret
Local wine enthusiasts in Sloterdijk have planted a community vineyard just by the new Chocolatemakers locale, which is accessible for visitors.
www.wijnvanbret.nl

Skatecafe
Nearby Amsterdam North's docklands are perfect for skateboarding, but aficionados head to Skatecafe for their indoor skate track, craft beers and eclectic food menu.
www.skatecafe.nl

Het Lab Amsterdam
Industrial Sloterdijk boasts a modern bouldering centre with free climbing lessons for first-time visitors. Casual restaurant serving poke bowls, salads and protein smoothie bowls.
www.hetlabamsterdam.nl

 Imagine a fair trade chocolate maker shipping organic cacao beans from the Dominican Republic to Amsterdam on a magnificent three-masted wooden cargo boat. What's more, the beans are traded from small farmers for genuinely sustainable rates. This is the dream that Enver Loke and Rodney Nickels have made real with Chocolatemakers. Their intense chocolate bars, with little sugar added, may be much more expensive than other options in Holland, but people are obviously willing to pay to support ideals, and the company has just moved into new waterside production premises which are 100% solar powered, loading the bags of beans straight off their boat, the *Tres Hombres*. They also have zero-waste packaging of compostable wrappers. For the moment, visits are limited to one day a week, on Fridays, but it is well worth reserving the short trip out to Sloterdijk. They also import beans from Peru, where they are helping farmers build their own factory, and the Congo, symbolised by their Gorilla bar. Buy one of these and you contribute to a Chocolatemakers project protecting gorillas of the Virunga National Park by assisting villagers plant cocoa rather than cut down the gorillas' already diminishing habitat. This rich, creamy, ethical bar tastes just like the centre of a chocolate fondant.

METROPOLITAN

135A Warmoesstraat, Amsterdam;
www.metropolitan.nl; +31 20 3301955

◆ Tastings ◆ Classes ◆ Cafe
◆ Roastery ◆ Shop ◆ Transport

Kees Raat is one of the pioneers of Amsterdam's craft chocolate scene, and his shop, Metropolitan, located right in the historic heart of the city, is pure bean-to-bar heaven where, each morning, Kees roasts, crushes and rolls beans sourced solely from South America to make his pure chocolate paste.

Passers-by can't resist the seductive aroma wafting out of the roastery, and once ensconced inside this modern cafe-boutique it is easy to be tempted by the 20 different organic ice creams or an old-fashioned waffle smothered with thick hot chocolate. Real ale lovers can sip a cacao beer, made by artisan brewer, de School, while for serious chocophiles, Kees proposes sniffing a line of his homemade cocoa powder.

THINGS TO DO NEARBY

De Oude Kerk
This deconsecrated 14th-century gothic church now hosts art exhibitions and concerts. Next door is another Amsterdam institution, the funky Old Church Coffeeshop.
www.oudekerk.nl

Condomerie
This fun but serious store, billed as 'the world's first condom speciality shop', has been around for 30 years. Customised options even include chocolate-flavoured condoms.
www.condomerie.com

PUCCINI BOMBONI

17 Staalstraat, Amsterdam; www.puccinibomboni.com;
+31 20 6265474

◆ Transport ◆ Classes ◆ Cafe
◆ Roastery ◆ Shop

On first impressions, Puccini Bomboni's sleek showroom resembles a classic chocolatier, with lines and lines of pralines and truffles seductively on display. But on closer inspection it is obvious why a new generation of health-conscious chocolovers are drawn here, as many items contain no butter, no sugar. And while artificial additives are off the menu too, they do use intriguing flavours: pepper, nutmeg, rhubarb, tea, even calvados. The boutique is just by Amsterdam's opera house, hence the inspiration of the great Italian composer. These chocolate bonbons created by Dutch master-chocolatier, Sabine van Weldam – like Fig Marzipan made with a mix of dark and white chocolate – are surprisingly much larger than the norm, because, 'I just feel they should look as good as they taste!'

THINGS TO DO NEARBY

Cafe de Jaren
One of Amsterdam's most beautiful waterside cafes with a great salad bar, overlooking the Amstel river, this former bank has been transformed into the city's favourite meeting place. *www.cafedejaren.nl*

Rembrandt House Museum
Unlike the Van Gogh museum, Rembrandt's home and studio is a much quieter venue. Don't expect to see his masterpieces, but the interiors are lovingly restored.
www.rembrandthuis.nl

TONY'S CHOCOLONELY SUPER STORE

15 Oudebrugsteeg, Amsterdam;
www.tonyschocolonely.com; +31 20 2051200

◆ Roastery   ◆ Transport
◆ Shop   ◆ Cafe

THINGS TO DO NEARBY

Cut Throat Barber
Cut Throat is more than a hip barbershop. After a trim and shave, you can order a Hendricks G&T at their bar, then a burger. It's also open for weekend brunch.
www.cutthroatbarber.nl

Frank's Smokehouse
Frank is a prime supplier to Amsterdam's restaurants, and you can try his renowned smoked fish and meats at this smart deli-restaurant with delicious takeaway sandwiches.
www.smokehouse.nl

Stromma
Just across from Tony's is the embarkment for Stromma's glass-roofed boats, offering everything from one-hour canal trips to cheese and wine or dinner cruises. *www.stromma.com*

Verzetsmuseum
The museum of the Dutch Resistance brings the horror of German occupation in WWII vividly alive. Allow a couple hours to explore.
www.verzetsmuseum.org

Chocolate lovers must be ready for surprises when choosing a bar from zany Tony's Chocolonely; psychedelic wrappers, anarchic chunk sizes to break off, crazy flavours like cherry meringue or popcorn discodip. Their circus-like basement store, full of as many colours as it is overflowing in flavours, is in the tourist centre of Amsterdam, once the historic base of Dutch cocoa trading (with everything that entails on the labour side of things), a perfect location when you read the slogan on Tony's bars: 100% slave- free chocolate.

All their loyal customers know the story of how a Dutch reporter (that would be Tony himself) documented child and slave labour in the world's cacao plantations, then started his own fair trade chocolate company buying beans directly from farmers in Ghana and Côte d'Ivoire. Today, Tony's sells more bars than the likes of Mars and Nestlé in the Netherlands, making it the market leader in the country, and these slave-free bars are on sale from the UK to the USA as well, bringing much-needed visibility to the issues plaguing cocoa production across the globe under a system that sees most of the profits go to the producers rather than to the farmers supplying the raw goods. Not just the chocolate in the bars is carefully sourced; ingredients like sugar are also fair trade certified. Says Tony's, 'We exist to change the cocoa industry and eradicate slavery and stop child labour.'

PORTUGAL

How to ask for hot chocolate in the local language? *Um chocolate quente se faz favor.*

What to order with your chocolate? A piece of *salame de chocolate* that is served in most *pastelerias* (cake & coffee shops).

Do: Track down one of the famous chocolate shops, Arcàdia.

Don't: Throw away the vintage packaging; these are decorations in their own right.

In Portugal, the popular expression *ter cacau* (to have cocoa) means to have a fortune, while *cacau* (cocoa) is slang for money. This stems from the 17th century onwards, when cocoa production was an important part of Portugal's colonial economy, first in Brazil, and later in Angola, Timor and São Tomé and Príncipe. While records suggest chocolate was a luxury consumed as a drink by royalty and rich people (following the Spanish tradition), in the general population it was rarely consumed. Portuguese recipes from convents in the 18th century – considered the country's bibles of cooking – mention cocoa-based concoctions that were mainly savoury, including *figos de chocolate* (chocolate figs) and *porco de chocolate* (chocolate pork).

Throughout the 20th century, several factories in Portugal produced chocolate, mostly in the cooler north of the country. Portuguese companies that are still producing chocolates include Avianense (founded 1914) and Imperial (founded 1932; it owns the popular Regina brand). And Arcádia (begun in 1933), originally from Porto, has shops throughout the country. Here, people consider chocolate as something extra special; for them it's about quality not quantity. Chocolate tends to be a seasonal treat: most of it is consumed over Christmas and Easter. Portuguese pastries and cakes, for which the country is famous, contain small amounts of chocolate only, apart from the *salame de chocolate*, a cocoa and biscuit slice. This is changing, however. Currently, there's a huge resurgence of artisanal chocolaterias that are bringing back chocolates from the past, complete with vintage-style packaging, or which pair chocolate with port, as at Chocolataria Equador in Lisbon.

FÁBRICA DO CHOCOLATE

R do Gontim 70, Viana do Castelo, Minho;
www.fabricadochocolate.com/en; +351 258 244 000

◆ Tastings ◆ Spa ◆ Cafe
◆ Rooms ◆ Shop ◆ Transport

THINGS TO DO NEARBY

Museu do Traje
This costume museum has superb examples of traditional wear from the region that brings past communities to life.

Barcelos
Southeast of Viana do Castelo, this sweet village is home to the original Portuguese rooster, Portugal's unofficial symbol.

Praia do Cabadelo
This gorgeous sandy, dune-backed beach with onshore breezes is the place for watersports. Head there by five-minute ferry boat trip.

Monte de Santa Luzia
A fabulously decorative, neo-Byzantine 20th-century church affords heavenly views over Viana do Castelo and the Atlantic.

Chocolate lovers rejoice! What better way to indulge yourself than at an all-in-one chocolate-themed experience: a hotel, a factory, a chocolaterie and a museum? This 18-room hotel is housed in a former (now converted) chocolate factory that once housed Avianense, the oldest chocolate manufacturer in Portugal.

And this means a sweet feast for the eyes: the exterior maintains the art deco design of José Fernandes Martins (1866–1945), while the accommodation has been stylishly revamped with themes based on all things chocolate. One room is dedicated to *Charlie and the Chocolate Factory*, another to Hansel and Gretel, while the remaining rooms' interiors are a shout-out to the original retro packaging and logos of well-known historic chocolate brands and other chocolate-themed concepts.

If all that chocolate has you in jitters? Immerse yourself in relaxing on-site 'choco-therapies' including chocolate exfoliation and treatment massages.

And it's not over yet. For a nibble on some brain food, don't miss the chocolate museum on-site. The interactive exhibits outline the origins and history of chocolate around the world.

The final treats? Cocoa-based delicacies, including a chocolate fountain, at the on-site chocolaterie. And, for guests or visitors, a themed breakfast. With chocolate-based goodies, of course.

SPAIN

How to ask for hot chocolate in the local language? *Un chocolate caliente de taza por favor.*
Signature chocolate flavours? Dark and thick.
What to order with your chocolate? Churros!
Do: Expect your hot chocolate to be thick and rich and served with little or no milk.

Chocolate-loving Europeans owe everything to Spain. When Spanish ships returned from the Americas from the 15th century onwards, they carried with them all manner of exotic raw materials. One of these, cacao or cocoa, had always been flavoured with pepper and other spices by the farmers who grew it. Unimpressed, the Spaniards instead sweetened it with sugar cane. Its popularity grew, and from the 17th century, chocolate went from being a Spanish delicacy accessible only to the rich to an important import that spread across Europe. It was the Spaniards, too, who first heated the chocolate, and that's still the way Spaniards still like it – dark, thick, hot and in

liquid form. Homegrown chocolate-producing economies grew, most notably around Astorga in the country's north. All the while, chocolate Spanish-style (pronounced with four syllables: *choc-o-lah-tay*) was primarily a drink, loved in its own right or for dunking in churros and other pastries. Chocolate blocks were overwhelmingly dark chocolate, its raw materials imported from the Americas; to this day dark chocolate is considered a mark of good taste in Spain. Recently, Spain's gastronomic revolution, defined by innovation and experimentation, has led to chocolate spiralling in new directions. Traditional forms of eating chocolate continue undiminished, but chocolate boutiques now overflow with flavours that blend salty and sweet, strange confections with balsamic vinegar, and even spicy blends. Today bean-to-bar makers like Catalonia's Pangea and Valencia's Utopick have popped up across the country.

MUSEO DEL CHOCOLATE

Avenida de la Estación 16, Astorga, León;
www.museochocolateastorga.com; +34 987 61 62 20

◆ Tastings ◆ Classes ◆ Cafe
◆ Roastery ◆ Shop ◆ Transport

THINGS TO DO NEARBY

Palacio Episcopal
Astorga is home to this
flight of architectural
fancy designed by Antoni
Gaudí, one of few such
constructions outside of
Barcelona.

Museo Romano
A beautiful Roman city
in antiquity, Astorga still
has a treasure chest of
Roman relics, many at
this excellent museum.
turismoastorga.es/1264-2

**Confitería Mantecadas
Velasco**
Beloved throughout Spain,
Astorga's signature pastry,
the cake-like *mantecada,*
is sold here. *www.
mantecadasvelasco.com*

Restaurante Las Termas
The *cocido maragato* (the
local version of inland
Spain's winter meat-
and-chickpea hotpot) is
especially good here. *www.
restaurantelastermas.com*

On the high meseta (plateau) of northern Spain's
Castilla y León region, the small town of Astorga was
once arguably the country's chocolate capital. Building on
the importation of cacao beans from Spain's colonies in the
Americas, and located along one of Spain's most lucrative
trade routes with gold mines nearby, Astorga oversaw a
chocolate boom in the 18th and 19th centuries. Chocolate
dominated the economy here for more than a century, and
while only small producers remain, this fine museum celebrates that heritage. Arrayed over two floors, the beautifully
presented displays take a holistic approach, carrying you
through the history of chocolate, complete with fascinating
old machines once used in chocolate production, then
detouring into the realm of old posters, advertising and
chocolate wrappers that are now collectors' items.

But pleasure is not forgotten next to the educational
material – just before you get your free sample and enter
the shop (where you can try before you buy), a large panel
lists the health benefits of eating chocolate, among them
the lowering of cholesterol, 'psychological well-being' and
the reminder that chocolate 'is excellent against sadness
and anxiety'. It's the perfect message to encourage your
post-visit snack. The museum is an easy, ten-minute walk
north of the town centre, beyond the old city walls.

© vidalidali / Getty Images

CHOCOLATERÍA DE SAN GINÉS

Pasadizo de San Ginés 5, Madrid;
www.chocolateriasangines.com; +34 91 365 65 46

◆ Cafe   ◆ Food
◆ Transport

THINGS TO DO NEARBY

Palacio Real
Madrid's perfectly
proportioned Royal
Palace overlooks the
supremely elegant Plaza
de Oriente. Take a tour of
the lavish interior or enjoy
the sunset views. *www.
patrimonionacional.es*

Plaza Mayor
Madrid's grandest
public square is a sea of
cobblestones, an epicentre
for city life watched over
by ochre facades and
surrounded by arcades.

Mercado de San Miguel
The former city market,
swathed in glass and
wrought iron, is an
architectural showpiece
filled with tapas and
wine bars. *www.
mercadodesanmiguel.es*

Teatro Joy Eslava
Almost next door to
Chocolatería de San Ginés,
this fabulous nightclub
inhabits a 19th-century
theatre and has opened
every night since 1981.
www.joy-eslava.com

Around since 1894, Madrid's Chocolatería de San Ginés is a city institution devoted to that most Spanish indulgence: chocolate con churros. Nowhere in Spain does richer, thicker chocolate into which you dunk your churros (fried doughnut strips). But this storied place holds a special place in the city's affections for reasons that extend beyond taste. It's always busy here, the chairs and marble-top tables spilling over into one of the loveliest laneway corners of the city centre. And yet, they're open here for 24 hours a day, seven days a week, and that's because Chocolatería de San Ginés is at its most popular in the long hours after midnight when Madrid's streets throng with people heading home or taking a break from a night of revelry – what a kebab or slice of pizza is for night owls elsewhere, *chocolate con churros* does for the all-night crowd in Madrid. They do serve other things at San Ginés – you could order a coffee, while the *porras* (essentially a thicker, flakier version of the churro) do have their devotees. But it's really all about the chocolate here, so rich and delicious, and so thick you could stand your spoon up in it, no matter the hour.

ORIOL BALAGUER

Calle de José Ortega y Gasset 44, Madrid;
www.oriolbalaguer.com; +34 91 401 64 63

◆ Transport   ◆ Food
◆ Shop

This small chocolate boutique in Madrid's upmarket Salamanca neighbourhood elevates chocolate to an art form. Each creation – cakes, pastries, boxes of chocolates – is displayed in a perfectly lit, gallery-like space. And the chocolates here have some pedigree. They're the work of much-awarded Catalan pastry chef Oriol Balaguer, who began his career in the kitchens of world-renowned masterchef Ferran Adrià. Balaguer's many awards include the World's Best Dessert for his Seven Textures of Chocolate, and, at age 23, Spain's Best Pastry Chef (try the croissants).

Choose from more than thirty different flavours across the full palette of salty and sweet, from macarons to marshmallows, from truffles to brownies. Even the packaging is a study in style and good taste. He has Barcelona shops too.

THINGS TO DO NEARBY

Museo Lázaro Galdiano
Salamanca is Madrid's home of old money, and this extravagant private mansion and art collection includes paintings by Goya, El Greco and Constable. *www.flg.es*

Astrolabius
This cross-generational family tapas bar combines grandma's recipes with the grandkids' imaginative flourishes. *www. astrolabiusmadrid.com*

SWITZERLAND

How to ask for hot chocolate in the local language? *Eine heisse Schoggi, bitte* (Swiss German); *un chocolat chaud, s'il vous plaît* (French); *una cioccolata calda, per favore* (Italian).
Signature chocolate flavour? Milk all the way...
What to order with your chocolate? More chocolate! It comes in all forms here: cake, torte, ice cream, fondue, mousse, you name it.
Don't: Don't just stick with the major brands: new-wave chocolatiers are doing great bean-to-bar work, sourcing sustainably and creating palate-awakening flavours.

Every bit as idiosyncratically Swiss as holey cheese, Heidi and snow-capped mountains, chocolate – called *Schokolade*, *chocolat* or *cioccolata*, depending which bit of Switzerland you happen to find yourself in – is more more than just an occasional treat: it's a bona fide national obsession. So much so that the Swiss are champions at eating it, devouring more per capita (10.3kg, or 22.7lb) than anywhere else in the world, and keeping 50% of all they produce to themselves. And frankly who can blame them?

The story, of course, begins with the precious cacao

beans Spanish conquistador Hernán Cortés shipped back to Europe in 1528, but the Swiss didn't really cotton onto its more solid delights until the early 19th century. François-Louis Cailler was the first pioneer, founding a chocolate factory in Corsier near Vevey in 1819. Hot on his heels was Philippe Suchard, who opened a factory in an abandoned mill in Serrières in 1826, and countless others – Rodolphe Lindt (1879) and Jean Tobler (1899) – followed.

Chocolate then, however, bore little resemblance to that of today: it was hard to make and hard to eat (chewy, in fact). The Swiss seized the challenge to refine the art: Daniel Peter added Nestlé condensed milk to his chocolate creations in 1875, then along came Lindt, who in a stroke of accidental genius discovered conching: a method whereby chocolate is stirred and aerated for hours (even days) to get the smooth, creamy melt-on-the-tongue texture that's now the hallmark of Swiss chocolate. The innovation didn't stop there: Nestlé first gave the world white chocolate in the form of Milky Bar in 1930, and to this day the Swiss still like to dabble, with Zürich-based Barry Callebaut recently coming up with the pink and almost-too-pretty-to-eat Ruby chocolate. The Swiss may not have invented chocolate itself, but they certainly had a strong hand in inventing chocolate as we know it, and as such it's an integral part of the country's

From left: © 2020, Funky Chocolate; © Pete Seaward / Lonely Planet; © 2020, Funky Chocolate

TOP 5 CHOCOLATE EXPERIENCES

1. **DURIG**, Lausanne
2. **LOCAL FLAVOURS**, Geneva
3. **CHOCOLATE TRAIN**, Montreux
4. **MILK BAR**, Verbier
5. **TEUSCHER FLAGSHIP**, Zurich

RAMONA ODERMATT,
MANAGER AT MAX CHOCOLATIER

'Switzerland has started moving away from mass production and towards small-batch chocolate that is hand-crafted, sustainable, regional, fresh and tells a story. Each chocolatier has different ideas, but we all share the same passion and the belief that smaller is better.'

history and culinary heritage.

While exact recipes remain closely guarded secrets, there are several factors that set Swiss chocolate apart. First and foremost is the rich milk from cows fed on lush Alpine pastures, then there are the sustainably sourced cacao beans (only the highest quality will do, and more bean is used than butter). Last but certainly not least is the conching technique, where the liquid is rolled, folded and aerated for up to 72 hours to produce a chocolate that is fine and velvety with no hint of bitterness. This being Switzerland, quality is strictly controlled, *natürlich*, by the Association of Swiss Chocolate Manufacturers, Chocosuisse. Chocolate making here is a serious business.

Even before you set foot in the country, some of your first chocolate encounters are likely to be Swiss: purple Milka cows and Lindt chocolate bunnies, not to mention that Matterhorn mountain of a bar, Toblerone. Once you're here you'll find it in on every street corner, hotel pillow and beyond – chocolate spa baths, chocolate trains and chocolate festivals are all in the mix. The Swiss believe that there is no aspect of life that isn't made sweeter by a little of the good stuff, and the ever-growing crop of small-brand chocolatiers here focusing on bean-to-bar, single-origin and weird-and-wonderful flavours certainly all agree.

MAISON CAILLER

Rue Jules Bellet 7, Broc, Gruyères; www.cailler.ch;
+41 026 921 59 60

◆ Tastings ◆ Classes ◆ Cafe
◆ Roasting ◆ Shop   ◆ Tours

One of Switzerland's oldest chocolate makers, Cailler has been making chocolate since 1825, when it was founded by François-Louis Cailler. Its entertaining factory tours take visitors on an extravagant twirl through chocolate history, made even sweeter by generous free samples. Cailler also offers a themed series of one- to two-hour chocolate workshops, some designed for children. These include a factory tour and must be reserved in advance by email or telephone. Find the factory in Broc, just north of Gruyères (famous for its cheese). A cafe is on-site as well. Owned by Swiss chocolate conglomerate Nestlé since 1929, Cailler now produces all of their chocolate from 100% sourced sustainable West African cocoa. And the milk used in the chocolate is sourced directly from Gruyère cows.

THINGS TO DO NEARBY

Fromagerie d'Alpage de Moléson

This 17th-century *fromagerie d'alpage* (mountain dairy) in Moléson-sur-Gruyères makes cheese using old-fashioned methods. At 10am daily you can watch how they do it.

Château de Gruyères

This turreted castle, home to 19 different counts of Gruyères, who controlled the Sarine Valley for 500 years, was rebuilt after a fire in 1493 and has worthwhile tapestries. *www.chateau-gruyeres.ch*

FUNKY CHOCOLATE CLUB

Jungfraustrasse 35, Interlaken; www.funkychocolate-club.com; +41 078 606 35 48

◆ Tastings ◆ Classes ◆ Cafe
◆ Transport ◆ Shop

Run by two passionate chocoholics, Tatiana and Vladimir, the Funky Chocolate is a shop brimming with fair trade and organic chocolate, and even vegan, dairy-free, nut-free and gluten-free varieties are available. You'll also find chocolate fondue, hot chocolate, even pro tools for chocolatiers. To get messy with chocolate yourself and stir up your own creations, hook into one of its four daily workshops to learn the magic of tempering chocolate yourself (kids especially appreciate the decorating). There's also an excellent shop where you can stock up on niche-brand Swiss chocolate and gorge on strawberries with chocolate fondue. Funky Chocolate Club can be a reward for burning calories in the mountains or an escape for the non-sporty. It's a, well, funky way to get to know Swiss chocolate.

THINGS TO DO NEARBY

Harder Kulm
For far-reaching views of the 4000m (roughly 13,100ft) giants, take the eight-minute funicular ride to 1322m (4337ft) Harder Kulm, with many hiking paths and a panorama from above the valley.

St Beatus Caves
Sculpted over millennia, the St Beatus Caves hold dramatically lit stalagmites, stalactites and underground lakes. Lore has it that in the 6th-century the caves sheltered hermit-monk St Beatus.

PHILIPPE PASCOËT

Rue de la Cité 15, Geneva; www.pascoet.ch; +41 (0)22 810 81 899

◆ Food ◆ Classes ◆ Cafe
◆ Roastery ◆ Shop ◆ Transport

Philippe Pascoët might hail originally from Brittany, but the award-winning *maître chocolatier* earned his stripes in Switzerland, with divine melt-in-the-mouth chocolates, pralines, ganaches, bean-to-bars and bonbons. A conjurer of texture and flavour, his unusual taste combinations endeavour to capture moods and moments – the herb garden, say, with rosemary, sage, basil, mint and thyme, or exotic fruits and herbs from far-away places, with passion fruit, yuzu, lime, saffron and jasmine. The flagship boutique is in the quarter of Carouge (Rue Saint-Joseph 12), but more convenient is this chocolaterie-tearoom in Geneva's historic centre. Pop in for a silky smooth chocolat chaud – or in summer a chocolat frappé – and one of the insanely decadent *moelleux au chocolat* (molten chocolate cakes), which come in flavours like caramel-pistachio. Heaven.

THINGS TO DO NEARBY

CERN
The European Organization for Nuclear Research (CERN), west of Geneva, is a laboratory for research into particle physics, where protons accelerate down the Large Hadron Collider. *home.cern*

Palais des Nations
Home to the UN since 1966, the grand Palais des Nations was built between 1929 and 1936 to house the now-defunct League of Nations. *www.unog.ch*

MAX CHOCOLATIER

Schlüsselgasse 12, 8001 Zürich;
www.maxchocolatier.com; +41 (0) 418 70 97

◆ Tastings   ◆ Classes   ◆ Cafe
◆ Transport   ◆ Shop

Entering Max Chocolatier is like falling down the rabbit hole and finding wonderland. Run with globetrotting passion by the König family, this super-stylish chocolatier cuts no corners – everything is handmade and stamped, only sustainably sourced Grand Cru cacao goes into the decadently dark truffles, bean-to-bars and ganaches, made with 100% natural ingredients, and all are chicly boxed and wrapped. But it's the flavours in the single-origin chocolates that will blow you away: black tea, tobacco, vanilla and blood orange, Alpine hay, violet and green pepper; intense spices and flavours mixed with Swiss know-how. There are collections made for each season: elderflower and peach in summer, walnut-marzipan in autumn, all utterly divine and worth the 45-minute tasting.

THINGS TO DO NEARBY

St Peterskirche
Right opposite Max Chocolatier, this striking baroque church has a 13th-century tower visible from afar. Its clock face (8.7m, or 29ft, in diameter) is Europe's largest.

Lindenhof
Just a few minutes' walk north brings you to lime-tree-shaded Lindenhof, a terrace with views out over the rooftops, spires and the snaking River Limmat.

TAUCHERLI

Fabrikhof 5, 8134 Adliswil; taucherli.com;
+41 44 555 86 08

◆ Tastings ◆ Classes ◆ Cafe
◆ Roastery ◆ Shop ◆ Transport

Kay Keusen is one of Switzerland's most creative chocolatiers, bar none. Starting his business in a garage, the small producer swiftly became one to watch, taking the bean-to-bar concept seriously by buying, roasting, grinding and conching the cocoa himself. A must-try specialty is the Taucherli, a praline on a stick that makes the richest, creamiest hot chocolate imaginable when dunked in milk (*taucherli* is local slang for the Eurasian coot, a native waterbird, which appears on the funky pastel packaging). Oddly pleasing flavours swing joyously from chilli and roasted rapeseed oil to popping candy. It's also a great place to pick up chocolate fondue in a tin (what could be more Swiss?) and naturally pink-hued Ruby chocolate, made from unfermented cacao beans. Visits are by appointment.

THINGS TO DO NEARBY

Frau Gerolds Garten
A 20-minute train or tram ride south is the post-industrial Züri-West district. Head to this happening spot for drinks surrounded by shipping containers.
www.fraugerold.ch

Schiffbau
While in Züri-West, stop by the Schiffbau, a strikingly converted factory turned cultural centre, which hosts a jazz bar, restaurant and the Schauspielhaus theatre. *www.neu. schauspielhaus.ch*

UNITED KINGDOM

How to ask for hot chocolate in the local language? English you probably have covered; in Welsh it's a *siocled poeth*
Signature chocolate flavours? That's likely an Earl Grey flavoured chocolate
What to order with your chocolate? In the Highlands, try a tumbler of whisky alongside your treat.
Do: Explore the history of British chocolate in York.

The United Kingdom entered a veritable chocolate craze when the drink first made its way here in the 1650s, a luxury product that caused no little stir in London. Later, John Cadbury would make drinking chocolate a pillar of his new company founded in 1824; his son expanded on the innovation by creating a model village specifically for the company's workers, Bournville. York received its own special imprint from the growth of big-name confectioners, who transported their raw materials into the city via the River Ouse and sold their wares by York's Minster Cathedral. Terry's Chocolate Works, Rowntree's of Kit Kat fame, and

Craven's all flourished here, many run by Quaker owners who promoted chocolate as a wholesome alternative to alcohol. The chocolate industry got a more continental touch with the Bond St opening of what is now the capital's oldest chocolate shop, Charbonnel et Walker, in 1875. London's feast-of-the-senses shop Prestat, founded in 1902 by truffle pioneer and French emigre Antoine Dufour, would even inspire part of Roald Dahl's vision for iconic sweets-romp *Charlie and the Chocolate Factory*.

Today many of the original big hitters such as Bristol's Fry and Rowntree have been subsumed into larger conglomerates, but the artisanal chocolate scene is booming, from London to Wales and the Highlands. According to recent industry studies, British consumers have kept up their chocolate tradition, consuming more per capita than about any other nation: over 8kg (18lb) a year, or three bars a week on average. That makes for 1.5 tonnes in a lifetime, a worthwhile indulgence for this nation of chocoholics.

THE CHOCOLATE BOUTIQUE HOTEL

5 Durley Rd, Bournemouth; www.thechocolatebou-
tiquehotel.co.uk; +44 1202-556857

◆ Tastings ◆ Classes ◆ Cafe
◆ Rooms ◆ Shop

THINGS TO DO NEARBY

Bournemouth Beach
Rent deckchairs or beach
huts from Bournemouth
Pier or stroll the award-
winning 11km (7 mi) of soft
sand with views out to the
Isle of Wight.

Level8ight Sky Bar
Want to sip cocktails from
South West England's
highest bar? Enjoy the
views over Bournemouth
from the 8th floor of the
Hilton Bournemouth Hotel.
www.level8skybar.com

Arbor
One of Bournemouth's best
restaurants, Arbor is a bit
of everything to everyone:
fine dining, Sunday lunches
and afternoon tea with
warm scones on a three-
tiered tree. *www.arbor-
restaurant.co.uk*

Brownsea Island
Take a ferry trip from
Poole Harbour to this
island wildlife sanctuary, a
National Trust site known
for its red squirrels and
abundant bird-watching.
*www.nationaltrust.org.uk/
brownsea-island*

'Bob Geldof's stayed here a couple of times. He
knows quite a lot about chocolate because of Africa.'
Gerry Wilton, owner of the Chocolate Boutique Hotel in
coastal Dorset, southern England, is not just a chocolatier
but a man of many anecdotes. What would you expect
from the former owner of Bournemouth's legendary Jokers
restaurant, founder of the Celebrations Party Bus and the
first person to run a chocolate workshop on a cruise ship?
He was also the largest chocolate fountain distributor in
Europe before purchasing this property, which makes sense
when you learn there's a room upgrade option to have your
own chocolate fountain in your room. Hosting chocoholics since 2007, this 19th-century, Grade II listed Victorian
building declares itself the world's first and UK's only
chocolate-themed hotel. The room names sound enticing
enough: want to wake up in the Chocolate Truffle Suite?
Maybe the Criollo? The Seventy Percent? Try to time your
stay to coincide with one of Gerry's chocolate workshops
where you can make your own truffles from homemade
ganache or even sculpt some chocolate stiletto shoes and
a matching handbag. Or a chocolate self-portrait to hang in
your toilet, which is where Bob Geldof has his (do ask Gerry
for that story if you visit).

CHOCOLATE ECSTASY TOURS

Several locations; www.chocolateecstasytours.com;
+44 (0)20 3432 1306

◆ Tastings ◆ Classes
◆ Transport ◆ Tours

If you're lucky enough to have founder Jennifer Earle leading your Chocolate Ecstasy tour, you'll quickly grasp why she's the perfect person to start such a business. Sip on your welcoming mug of rich hot chocolate at Hotel Chocolat's School of Chocolate, one of many stops on the Soho/Mayfair tour, as Jennifer talks through the history and entire chocolate-making process from bean to bar, with the help of props and illustrations from her visits to cacao plantations around the world. This is one committed chocoholic. Jennifer started taking small chocolate tour groups (max 8 people) in 2005, and while you'll learn a lot about your own preferences through guided tastings, there's a good amount of London's chocolate history thrown into the bargain, which can even surprise locals. What's the

THINGS TO DO NEARBY

Royal Academy of Arts
Burlington House, an impressive Palladian mansion, is home to the Royal Academy of Arts. Run by artists since 1768, it offers splendid exhibitions of art and architecture. *www.royalacademy.org.uk*

Crosstown Doughnuts
What Paul A Young is to chocolate, Crosstown is to doughnuts. Expect quirky seasonal flavours on the world's first yeast-raised, sourdough base and vegan options. *www. crosstowndoughnuts.com*

The Wolseley
Renowned for breakfasts and afternoon teas, the Wolseley is considered to be London's first grand cafe in the European style, with its Venetian and Florentine-inspired details. *www.thewolseley.com*

Liberty London
Trading since 1875, Liberty is not just one of London's famous department stores; the Tudor revival architecture (constructed from timber of two ships) is worth a visit alone. *www. libertylondon.com*

Queen's favourite chocolate? Where's the spiritual home of Roald Dahl? Do you know the story behind the Fortnum & Mason clock? Discounts are offered at all the quality establishments visited, though there is no pressure to buy, and you'll certainly be able to eat your fill of chocolate during the tastings. While there are a variety of tour options and locations, the three-hour traditional Mayfair Chocolate Tour is the most popular.

THE CHOCOLATE MUSEUM

187 Ferndale Rd, Brixton, London;
www.thechocolatemuseum.co.uk; +44 (0)772 3434 235

◆ Tastings   ◆ Classes   ◆ Cafe
◆ Roastery   ◆ Shop   ◆ Transport

THINGS TO DO NEARBY

Brixton Village Market
This vast covered arcade showcases some of London's most multicultural food, with diverse dining and shops for buying rare ingredients. *www.brixtonmarket.net/brixton-village*

Salon
Located within Brixton Village Market, this is the perfect restaurant to sample modern, primarily plant-based British food over set menus of four or seven courses. *www.salonbrixton.co.uk*

Pure Vinyl Records
The owner of Pure Vinyl Records might specialise in soul and reggae, but you can put the needle down on all kinds of musical genres here. *www.thedepartmentstore.com/pure-vinyl*

Brockwell Lido
Fancy a swim? This 50m outdoor pool on the edge of Brockwell Park is a popular spot for families to cool off in Britain's unpredictable summers. *www.fusion-lifestyle.com/centres/brockwell-lido*

You'll likely stroll right past this shop front if you're expecting a museum as grand in scale and design as most in Britain. What looks a little like a colourful classroom (and indeed it is: chocolate-making classes are frequently held here for UK students, as part of their Maya & Aztec Empire curriculum requirements!) is merely the gateway to a whole lot of chocolate history downstairs. Founder and Director Isabelle Alaya, a French artisan chocolatier, opened this independent museum in 2013, which houses a fascinating collection of artefacts and memorabilia, the oldest dating back to 1792. Admire the antique chocolate advertising posters as you take the interactive 'Choco-tale' audio guide through the history of bean to bar. When you're choc-full of history, there are various hot chocolates and cakes to enjoy in the upstairs cafe, with many chocolates made from Isabelle's shop in Peckham called Melange, which she opened in 2008. Anyone can drop in to do the family-friendly truffle-making classes here, no appointment necessary, but you may have to return at a later time if it's busy. Or just linger longer over the historical displays, marvelling at how people used to drink hot chocolate from deep saucers rather than cups.

DARK SUGARS COCOA HOUSE

124-126 Brick Lane, London; www.darksugars.co.uk;
+44 (0) 7429 472606

◆ Roastery ◆ Transport
◆ Shop ◆ Cafe

THINGS TO DO NEARBY

Beigel Bake
Up Brick Lane, this long-standing 24-hour bagel joint is a testament to the area's Jewish history. Bagels can be stuffed with cream cheese, salt beef or chopped herring. *facebook.com/beigelbake*

Tatty Devine
This Brick Lane shop is renowned for its funky laser-cut acrylic jewelry, from nameplate necklaces to dangly lobster earrings. *www.tattydevine.com*

Walking History Tour
Successive waves of immigrants – Huguenots, Eastern European Jews, South Asians – make for rich history, examined on several historical walking tours of Brick Lane and its surrounds.

Spitalfields Market
Find local artisans in this Victorian market hall. Thursdays are all about vintage; weekends mean crafts, clothes and food. *www.spitalfields.co.uk*

At a glance, this Brick Lane shop could be mistaken for an avant-garde jewelry store, it's wares artily displayed on pieces of raw wood. But the smell gives it away: the warm, spicy, roasty scent of chocolate, chocolate, chocolate. From a stall in Borough Market, Dark Sugars has grown into one of London's most innovative chocolatiers. Cacao comes from West Africa, where the owner, Fatou Mendy, learned the trade on her Ghanaian family farm. It's processed in the on-site roastery and turned into fantastical treats. The signature products are the 'pearls', luminous orbs of chocolate in a rainbow's worth of colours, displayed like mermaid treasure in giant scallop shells. Bite into one and release a whoosh of gooey ganache in flavours like mandarin orange, pink champagne and pistachio. For a more adult treat, sample a 'pipette' – a truffle with a tiny squeezable pipette of liqueur suspended on top, for an infusion of booze just before you bite. If you can stay a while, don't miss Dark Sugars' wholly original take on hot chocolate, the velvet liquid topped with a haystack of chocolate shavings. FYI there are two Brick Lane shops in close proximity; the flagship is the one at 124–126.

FORTNUM & MASON

181 Piccadilly, London; www.fortnumandmason.com;
+44 020-7734 8040

◆ Shop   ◆ Food
◆ Transport   ◆ Cafe

 With its classic eau-de-Nil (pale green) colour scheme, the 'Queen's grocery store' established in 1707 refuses to yield to modern times. There are multiple locations, but the crown jewel is the centrally located, luxe flagship on Piccadilly. Its staff – men and women – still wear old-fashioned tailcoats, and its glamorous food hall is supplied with hampers, marmalade and specialty teas. Stop for a spot of afternoon tea at the Diamond Jubilee Tea Salon, visited by Queen Elizabeth II in 2012. An Instagram snap from Meghan Markle's makeup artist Daniel Martin even revealed she serves the brand's chocolate truffles to guests. Seek out their Ruby Chocolate Bar or indulge in a Ruby Hot Chocolate in the Parlour. It's not exactly bean-to-bar, but it's certainly decadent.

THINGS TO DO NEARBY

St James's Piccadilly
This simple edifice is the only church Christopher Wren built from scratch (in 1684), and one of a handful established on a new site. Its baptismal font is by Grinling Gibbons

Beijing Dumpling
Tiny dough pockets ready to be made into soup dumplings are kneaded at speed behind the steamy front window here; order a basket or three.
www.facebook.com/ beijingdumpling

PAUL A YOUNG FINE CHOCOLATES

143 Wardour St, London; www.paulayoung.co.uk;
+44 (0)20 7437 0011

◆ Tastings   ◆ Classes
◆ Transport   ◆ Shop

RHUBARB, PINK PEPPER AND
STEM GINGER CARAMEL
Valrhona 64% Madagascar da...
rhubarb purée, sea s...
crystallised stem...

THINGS TO DO NEARBY

Lina Stores
Some of London's best
handmade pasta is mere
moments away at the
vibrant lime-green Lina
Stores on Greek St. Book
ahead for lunch or early/
late dinners.
www.linastores.co.uk

Chin Chin Dessert Club
Europe's first liquid
nitrogen ice cream parlour
lives up to the hype, with
all its billowing-steam
drama. There's also
award-winning hot cherry
pie on weekends. *www.*
chinchinicecream.com

Bar Termini
Having made the World's
50 Best Bars list three
years in a row, Bar Termini
(inspired by Rome's Termini
train station bar) is negroni
paradise. *www.bar-*
termini-soho.com

Flat White
Claiming to be London's
first home of the flat white
coffee, this Antipodean
trailblazer is the choice
of caffeine addicts and
smashed avocado toast fans.
www.flatwhitesoho.co.uk

You'll understand why Yorkshire chocolatier Paul
A Young's creations are frequently described as
groundbreaking when you visit one of his three boutiques in
London. At the flagship Soho branch of his regally purple-
painted wonderland, customers frequently read the chocolate truffle names aloud in a mixture of awe and intrigue.
Marmite? Yorkshire tea and biscuit? Beer and crisp? Hot
cross bun? Pashwari naan with coconut? It's the innovation
of the limited-edition collections, which are seasonal and
often inspired by Paul's travels, that are attention-grabbing,
but the popularity of his core range underscores the talent
here. Paul worked as head pastry chef for Michelin-starred
chef Marco Pierre White before deciding to specialise
in chocolate. He opened the first of his shops in 2006,
becoming one of the only truly artisan chocolatiers based in
London; everything is made by hand in small batches. You
can really appreciate the skills involved by going behind
the scenes: regular workshops are held in the production
kitchen, such as Easter egg making, beginners' tastings or
more advanced masterclasses with Paul himself. You'll want
to sample everything, but you simply must try his famous
sea salt and caramel chocolate – it has been a Gold winner
in the World Chocolate Awards two years in a row.

PRESTAT CHOCOLATES

14 Princes Arcade, St. James's, London;
www.prestat.co.uk; +44 020 8961 8555

◆ Transport
◆ Shop

THINGS TO DO NEARBY

St James Park
In summer, well-heeled Londoners lounge in deck chairs in the manicured grass of this royal park, as ducks, swans and pelicans glide across the lake. *www.royalparks.org.uk*

Tea at the Ritz
Wander down Piccadilly to this iconic hotel for afternoon teas of warm scones and finger sandwiches served in the mirror-lined Palm Court. *www.theritzlondon.com*

Sketch
This hip, inventively decorated Mayfair restaurant has several different rooms for dining and drinks, each with its own vibe. *sketch.london*

Theatreland
Catch a comedy, drama or musical in one of the splendid playhouses of London's West End, as locals have been doing since the 1600s.

French chocolatier Antoine Dufour may or may not be the original inventor of the chocolate truffle – the history's as hazy as a kitchen fogged with clouds of cocoa powder – but he certainly popularised it in the UK. The nation's poshest of the posh have been nibbling Prestat truffles since 1902, when Dufour opened his first London shop. Visit Prestat's little jewel box in the Princes Arcade in Piccadilly, all periwinkle walls and gilt molding and whimsical chandeliers, enveloped in the velvety aroma of cocoa. Verrry British classics include creamy white chocolate truffles with a kick of gin, wafer-thin Earl Grey rounds and mint chocolates made with heirloom Black Mitcham peppermint. Bright and fanciful candy boxes bear a gold coat of arms signifying that Prestat has a royal warrant to supply chocolate to the Queen (Elizabeth II receives a giant chocolate Easter egg each year; the Queen Mum was said to enjoy Prestat's perfumey violet cremes). Roald Dahl was also a fan – vibrant, enticing Prestat was an inspiration for that classic confectionery novel *Charlie and the Chocolate Factory*. If you can't make it to Piccadilly, the chocolates are also sold in London's grandest department stores – Harrods, Liberty, Selfridges.

YORK'S CHOCOLATE STORY

3-4 Kings Square, York; www.yorkchocolatestory.com;
+44 1904 527765

◆ Tastings   ◆ Classes   ◆ Cafe
◆ Tours   ◆ Shop

THINGS TO DO NEARBY

York Minster
The largest medieval cathedral in northern Europe is this city's most important landmark. Visit its subterranean Undercroft museum to learn about its Roman and Viking links.

Merchant Adventurers' Hall
York's most impressive half-timbered building is now a museum dedicated to its owners, an ancient fraternity of merchant traders. *www.merchantshallyork.org*

Betty's Tea Room
Have a tea and cake session at Betty's, the elegant Yorkshire tea rooms founded by a Swiss immigrant in 1919: no trip to York is complete without it. *www.bettys.co.uk*

Richard III Experience, Monk Bar
Walk York's ancient city walls and stop off at this museum inside a medieval city gatehouse, exploring the life of King Richard III. *richardiiiexperience.com*

There are still York residents who can remember the smell of chocolate wafting down the cobbled streets, and recall that they knew when Rowntree's factory workers were done for the day because the streets would fill with bicycles. Chocolate has been a defining industry of this northern English city since the 18th century and York's Chocolate Story brings to life this chapter of local history. Part museum, part interactive experience, the slick guided tour lasts about an hour and focuses heavily on entertainment as well as education. It starts under a rainforest canopy recreating Mesoamerica, where you'll get to try the world's first drinking chocolate – cold, sugarless and spiked with chilli – and then moves onto the York families who drove the UK's chocolate industry. It was here in York that the Terry's family created the world's first box of chocolates, its All Gold (still on sale today), and the Chocolate Orange. It was here that Rowntree's dreamt up Rolos,

Smarties, Quality Street, Aero and Kit Kat. Some 17.6 billion Kit Kat fingers are still produced every year, many of them from the Nestlé factory in York that took over Rowntree's in 1988. Tours finish in a kitsch world of giant milk bottles, sugar hills and dripping pillars of chocolate with interactive exhibits. Visitors decorate their own lollipop, watch a demonstration on truffle making, then finish in the shop and cafe, selling hot chocolates advertised by geographical region, chocolate fondues and chocolate tasting boards.

YORK COCOA WORKS

10 Castlegate, York; www.yorkcocoahouse.co.uk;
+44 1904 656731

◆ Tastings   ◆ Classes   ◆ Cafe
◆ Roastery   ◆ Shop   ◆ Tours

THINGS TO DO NEARBY

Spark York

Joyously painted shipping containers have been strung together to create this lively base for fledgling food and retail businesses, selling Reubens, buttermilk fried chicken and G&Ts. *www.sparkyork.org*

Shambles

York's most famous street is this crooked line of half-timbered medieval houses. Its bowed shopfronts are said to have provided inspiration for Diagon Alley in JK Rowling's *Harry Potter* books.

Brew York

This microbrewery craft beer hall has rough wooden tables beside ceiling-skimming brewing tanks. Grab a Viking DNA smoked porter to sip on its riverside terrace. *brewyork.co.uk*

York Castle Museum

The recreated Victorian high street is a highlight of this local history museum on the site of the castle erected by William the Conqueror in 1068. *www.yorkcastlemuseum.org.uk*

'Provenance and ingredients are a big part of what motivated me to start the facility here', says Sophie Jewett. Her micro-factory in York's historic centre has brought independent chocolate manufacturing back to a city that in the 19th and early 20th centuries was home to the UK's most prolific confectionery entrepreneurs.

'I got to the stage where I didn't want to buy [mass-produced chocolate] because I don't know what's gone into them in terms of their supply chain. It's about knowing as consumers what goes on in our name', says Sophie. York Cocoa Works, which started as a cafe but became a fully fledged factory in 2018, imports cacao beans direct from farms throughout the equatorial belt, from Uganda and Tanzania to Bolivia, Colombia and even the Solomon Islands. The modern cafe and factory space is designed like a glass box, so that tours can glimpse directly into the processing rooms and follow the journey of the beans,

keeping transparency at the forefront of everything Sophie's team does. Flavour profiling and education is a key component of the walk-throughs, which run three times a day and include six tastings of 63% cocoa solid chocolates from different geographical regions. Bean-to-bar workshops and masterclasses are regular happenings and every Sunday there's the 'Afternoon Chocolatada', a marathon menu of chocolate-themed dishes, both savoury and sweet. Don't leave without trying the decadent Spanish Hot Chocolate.

NEW CHOCOLATE CO

Unit 4, Block B, Kelburn Business Park, Parklea Rd,
Port Glasgow, Inverclyde; +44 1475 743619

- ◆ Tastings   ◆ Classes
- ◆ Shop   ◆ Tours

 Neighbouring Greenock was once Europe's sugar capital, but today Port Glasgow leads the way in sweet success. New Chocolate Co is the new-kid-on-the-block of UK chocolate making (founded 2017) but owners Brian and Joanne have learned their art from the best: World Chocolate Master Ruth Hinks of Cocoa Black. Their slick, modern premises harbour a shop where chocs for sale have a sense of place and a sense of fun: the oh-so-Scottish Irn-Bru ganache, for example, or the tart-tasting palate adventure of the blood orange and passion fruit chocolate.

Factory tours (by appointment) whisk sweet-lovers through every element of chocolate crafting, plus a complimentary treat from their Highland Range, such as a thistle-emblazoned slab bar, or take a hands-on chocolate-making class.

THINGS TO DO NEARBY

Finlaystone Country Estate
This woodsy 202-hectare (500-acre) estate with a venerable 18th-century mansion is home of Clan MacMillan and has hosted the likes of Rabbie Burns.
www.finlaystone.co.uk

Watt Institution
One of Scotland's best provincial museums, just refurbished and replete with wonders collected by former ship captains.

IAIN BURNETT HIGHLAND CHOCOLATIER

Grandtully, Perthshire; +44 1887-840775

- ◆ Food   ◆ Cafe   ◆ Tours
- ◆ Shop   ◆ Tastings

 A riverside Highlands village is the setting for some of Great Britain's most lovingly prepared chocolate. If Iain Burnett's Velvet Truffles cannot be called a labour of love, nothing in confectionery can. These divine spheres, 15 years' worth of development, are preservative-free and often un-enrobed (made mould-free): no easy feat. The best, like the dark velvet truffle, are just cocoa and a particularly nuanced cream from some local cows. Gravitate to the Chocolate Lounge to experience a 'chocolate flight' where tasting guides help you hone your palate as you indulge. Iain is a chocolate master and artisan who wows Michelin-

starred chefs and develops his own machinery to push taste boundaries, and doesn't do corrupt stuff like adulterating chocs with whisky. He has several ranges tailored to complement different Scottish single malts, however.

THINGS TO DO NEARBY

Balllintaggart
This farm near Grandtully in woods-dotted countryside is a highly regarded restaurant with Scottish-themed cooking classes.
www.ballintaggart.com

River Tay Whitewater Rafting
Arguably the UK's best stretch of rapids runs between these two River Tay villages; there are multiple outfitters in the area who run trips.

WICKEDLY WELSH

13, Withybush Trading Estate, Withybush Rd, Haverfordwest, Pembrokeshire; www.wickedlywelsh.co.uk; +44 1437 557122

◆ Tastings   ◆ Classes   ◆ Cafe
◆ Roastery   ◆ Shop

Possibly Pembrokeshire's chocolatiest village, Haverfordwest is your destination for Wales' most hedonistic chocolate experience. It's not just the name. Wickedly Welsh tickles all senses. There is a chocolate factory with regular demonstrations, a chocolate cafe which serves up all sorts of wrong-but-somehow-right dishes like chocolate pizza and chocolate kebabs, and as if that weren't enough, a chocolate deli: chocolate served by the slice. The 'Have a Go' zone lets would-be chocolatiers concoct their own sweet treats. You can't go wrong here with a milk chocolate Anglesey sea salt and caramel bar, or a slab of ganache mingled with Penderyn Distillery's cream liqueur.

THINGS TO DO NEARBY

Picton Castle
A medieval fortress converted into a stunning estate southeast of Haverfordwest, set along the scenic Pembrokeshire Coast Path.
www.pictoncastle.co.uk

Newgale Beach
One of Pembrokeshire's many legendary beaches, a wide, lovely stretch of sand popular with surfers and swimmers, is 14km (9 mi) northwest of Haverfordwest.

10 INTRIC
CHOCO
FLAVOUR F

BEER

Belgium's two most famous exports – rich, silky chocolate and beers galore – make a harmonious match. Savour the full spectrum of flavours by pairing dark chocolate truffles with powerful ales and nibbling milk chocolate alongside raspberry or cherry beers.

MOLE POBLANO

Chocolate is part of the delicate balance of flavours in the centuries-old recipe for mole sauce. Eat this complex Mexican dish slowly: dark chocolate is counterbalanced by zesty tomatoes and fiery chillies, while cloves and other spices deepen those chocolatey notes.

RED WINE

Dark chocolate and red wine both contain resveratrol, which is thought to lower cholesterol and protect brain function. All the more reason to snap off a few squares of chocolate to accompany a brimming wine glass; plummy Argentine merlot is an especially good match for 70% cocoa chocolate.

CURED FAT

Traditional Ukrainian recipes are fond of salo, cured pork fat. Salo coated in chocolate began as a culinary punchline, until restaurants began doing it for real – cloaking chewy morsels of fat in dark chocolate for a decadent sweet-savoury pairing.

ABSINTHE

The 'green fairy' has long been the intoxicant of choice for Europe's literati. While absinthe's classic French preparation, using a spoon and sugar cube, has ritualistic appeal, the drink's anise notes are perfectly balanced by an accompaniment of dark chocolate. In Italy, you'll even find chocolate-absinthe liqueurs...*cin cin*!

GUING
LATE
AIRINGS

Chocolate is a flirty foodstuff, pairing beautifully with flavours sweet and savoury. Raise your chocolate consciousness to new heights with these irresistible, and occasionally odd, combinations.

BEEF STEW

In the southwestern French region of Gascony, dark chocolate is added to boeuf à la Gasconne, a slow-cooked stew of beef and vegetables. Ingredients like mushrooms and thyme give the dish an earthy base, while chocolate and Armagnac liqueur add sweetness.

CRICKETS

Cast aside any thoughts of choking down deep-fried insects at a Thai street-food stall, arthropods are a sustainable foodstuff and they're surprisingly moreish. Crickets dipped in dark chocolate are a munch-worthy match, thanks to their contrasting textures of crunchy and smooth.

BARBECUED PORK

Barbecue is an art form in the USA's southern states, where pork is enhanced by chilli rubs, tangy sauces, and occasionally, chocolate. Roll up your sleeves for a meat crawl across Memphis, where you'll find chocolate-dipped bacon and chocolatey barbecue sauce.

BLUE CHEESE

Pungent cheeses work surprisingly well when paired with the espresso-like richness of dark chocolate. This particular food marriage works well in the UK, where velvety Green & Black's 60% cocoa chocolate harmonises with sharp Stilton.

CAVIAR

Transform any picnic or dinner party into a talking point by matching caviar with white chocolate. Molecular gastronomists swear that salty, tongue-tingling fish eggs are even more delicious with this sweet, creamy accompaniment.

OCE

TOP 3 CHOCOLATE DESTINATIONS

ANIA

SYDNEY, AUSTRALIA

Home to Haigh's Chocolates and Zokoko Artisan Chocolate, Sydney also has its own Chocolate School. No wonder this city has been on the cutting edge of Australia's chocolate wave. Check out Pana Chocolate for raw chocolate, Just William and Belle Fleur for fancy treats, and Josophans outside town in the Blue Mountains.

BOUGAINVILLE, PAPUA NEW GUINEA

You won't find any bean-to-bar manufacturers here (yet) in this DIY-travel spot, still recovering from the armed conflict in its past, but it nevertheless produces some of the world's great cacao. Makers in Australia and New Zealand have paid attention, increasingly sourcing their single-origin bars from the region.

MELBOURNE, AUSTRALIA

From chocolate jaffles at Bad Frankie to a fancy chocolate afternoon tea at the Langham's Aria lounge, plus well-regarded gourmet chocolatier Koko Black and upscale hot choc at Mörk's, you can get every kind of chocolate experience your heart might desire in Melbourne.

AUSTRALIA

How to ask for hot chocolate in the local language? Add a 'mate' on the end to cover your bases.

Signature chocolate flavour? A chocolate Tim Tam.

What to order with your chocolate? A flat white, Australia's favourite coffee drink, or a cappuccino with a cocoa powder topping.

Don't: Underestimate artisanal Australian chocolate.

Over the last decade, Australia has seen an explosion in innovative chocolate-making; the country has even has placed third in a World Chocolate Masters Competition. Consumption rates for chocolate are going up too. Queensland even has its own cacao farms now. Cities have kept up with the pace: Sydney abounds in bean-to-bar makers and handcrafted truffles. In Melbourne, alongside a growing crop of boutique chocolatiers and factories, there are innovative and unexpected chocolate treats to seek out too. Every weekend at the Langham's ARIA lounge, you'll find a Chocolate Bar High Tea: fluffy chocolate-chip scones and endless chocolate desserts, not to mention the famous chocolate fountain. And at Bad Frankie, try the Chocolate Lamington Jaffle (for non-Aussies, that's a type of cake layered in chocolate sauce merged with a toasted sandwich): two slabs of chocolate-soaked sponge filled with hot jam and rolled in coconut. Meanwhile, Adelaide is home to the original, iconic Haigh's Chocolates. Outside big cities, Australia's wine regions of the Margaret River, Hunter Valley and Yarra Valley also boast their own chocolate producers, meaning you can combine wine tasting with chocolate tours. One thing's for sure: Australian chocolate is on the move.

JASPER + MYRTLE

Unit 9, 1 Dairy Road, Fyshwick, Canberra;
www.jasperandmyrtle.com.au; +61 416 182 477

◆ Tastings　　◆ Shop
◆ Roastery

Chocolate and life partners, Li Peng Monroe and Peter Channells had a eureka moment while on holiday in 2015, then returned to Canberra to ditch their day jobs and focus on creating Australia's most internationally awarded bean-to-bar chocolate company, Jasper and Myrtle. The pair sources cacao beans directly from farmers in Bougainville, Papua New Guinea where they also work with the local government to support initiatives improving the chocolate industry. Known for combining interesting and quintessentially Australian flavours, they've produced 15 different bars, four drinking chocolates, and chocolate-coated nuts and ginger. The duo welcome visitors to their Fyshwick facility to discover their intriguing creations, like the wakame (seaweed) and Himalayan rock salt bar.

THINGS TO DO NEARBY

Capital Brewing
Making waves in the Australian craft beer scene, Capital Brewing has 12 beers on tap, all brewed on-site, and serves up one of Canberra's best burgers.
www.capitalbrewing.co

Trench Trail
After 100 years, the Duntroon Trench Warfare school, set up to prepare soldiers for WWI's Western Front, has been excavated and open to the public. It's within Jerrabomberra Wetlands Nature Reserve.

MS PEACOCK

Shop 3B, The Acre, 391-397 Bong Bong St, Bowral;
mspeacock.com.au; +61 0402 917 111

◆ Tastings   ◆ Transport
◆ Shop

Lisa Morley, the creative mind behind Bowral's Ms Peacock, creates exciting products and unique flavours. Opened in 2017, everything is handmade on-site by their tiny team of two, with their creations championing local produce wherever possible. Nuts come directly from nearby growers, their butter is churned by Pepe Saya and the honey that forms their award-winning honeycomb is sourced just an hour away from their opulent shop; the chocolate, however, is sourced straight from France, rich and indulgent. Along with their famous honeycomb, there is a range of filled minibars, caramels, marshmallows and frogs, with a bonbon range coming soon. Try the Joie bar: layers of sea salt butter caramel, peanut butter ganache and chocolate nougat.

THINGS TO DO NEARBY

The Press Shop Cafe
One of the hotspots on the Bowral cafe scene, The Press Shop Cafe, also on Bong Bong St, is a trendy cafe and couture stationery shop in one. *www. thepressshop.com.au*

Biota Dining
Just down the road is one of Australia's top fine dining restaurants, Biota, where Chef James Viles' experimental degustation menu is available for lunch or dinner.
www.biotadining.com

ZOKOKO

3 90/84 Old Bathurst Rd, Emu Heights, Sydney;
www.zokoko.com; +61 2-4735-0600

◆ Tastings   ◆ Cafe   ◆ Food
◆ Roastery   ◆ Shop

THINGS TO DO NEARBY

Arms of Australia Inn Museum
One of the oldest buildings in the area, the inn was built in the early 1800s. Take an evening tour by kerosene lantern. *www.armsofaustraliainn.org.au*

Penrith Regional Gallery
The former home of artists Margo and Gerald Lewers sits on the Nepean River, with art exhibits, gardens and a cafe. *www.penrithregionalgallery.com.au*

Lapstone Bridge Zig Zag Walk
Walk along the former Lapstone Zig Zag railway for spectacular views of the Blue Mountains and the city, ending at the famous **Knapsack Viaduct.**

Royal National Park
This prime stretch of wilderness is at nearby Sydney's doorstep, and includes secluded beaches, rainforest, wallabies, lyrebirds and yellow-tailed black cockatoos.

When you walk into this light-filled, delicious-smelling cafe in the Emu Heights suburb of Sydney, be prepared to have a hard time deciding what to eat. From chocolate cake to chocolate-custard-filled doughnuts to chocolate macarons, everything behind the pastry case is more than tempting, especially when paired with coffee from local roaster Morgan's. And we haven't even mentioned the award-winning bars.

After falling in love with cacao in Costa Rica, owner Michelle Morgan decided she wanted to make chocolate from scratch. In 2009 she started Zokoko, one of the first bean-to-bar makers in Australia and one of the best in the world. Morgan works with high-quality cacao beans from locales like Bolivia and the Solomon Islands, roasting, grinding and smoothening them into chocolate with the help of her vintage Lehmann melangeur (a chocolate mixing machine), which she's nicknamed Molly. (Peek into the factory from a window in the cafe.) Zokoko also stands out for its gorgeous labels, with its single-origin bars in luxurious black packaging and a 'Goddess' line of inclusion bars with colourful illustrations of – you guessed it – female goddesses. Indeed, you might feel immortal after sampling the deliciousness at the cafe. Take the hot chocolate and a few bars for later.

HAIGH'S CHOCOLATES

154 Greenhill Road, Parkside, South Australia;
www.haighschocolates.com.au; +61 08 8372 7070

◆ Tastings   ◆ Tours
◆ Roastery   ◆ Shop

THINGS TO DO NEARBY

TreeClimb Adelaide
Shake off your sugar coma at this grown-up-sized high ropes course, which swings through the treetops of Adelaide Park Lands. The full course takes about two hours to complete.
www.treeclimb.com.au

Adelaide Central Market
Pick up a plethora of gourmet goodies, delicious multicultural dishes and local produce at this sprawling market complex, open Tuesday to Sunday.
adelaidecentralmarket. com.au

Glenelg Beach
A short tram ride from the city centre brings you to the white sands of Glenelg, where crowds gather at sunset to watch the sun sink below the watery horizon.

Cafe Troppo
Sustainability is the name of the game at this charming cafe, from the food on your plate right down to the chair you sit on. *cafetroppoadelaide. com*

Adelaideans speak of Haigh's with a reverence verging on worship – we've heard said they'll do almost anything for a Haigh's chocolate frog – and the small factory just south of Adelaide's CBD is a charming place to get an insight into the family-owned and operated business, which was founded in 1915 by Alfred E Haigh. Alfred purchased the current Parkside site in 1917 and the company flourished even after his untimely death, first under the stewardship of his son Claude, and later his grandson John. John Haigh remains chairman of the board today, while day-to-day operations are handled by fourth-generation Haighs Alister and Simon.

Free 30-minute tours (bookings required) outline the chocolate-making process from bean to bar and offer visitors the chance to watch confectioners at work crafting the varied range of chocolate delicacies. Don't worry: there's also an opportunity to taste the fruits of their labours! Depending on the season, you may see workers carefully wrapping jewel-coloured Easter eggs, hand-painting thousands of Valentines-worthy chocolate hearts or busily packing Christmas hampers. The tours end at the factory store, where you can stock up on the whole Haigh's range; locals swear by the 'aprichocs', soft apricot centres coated in milk chocolate.

THE MENZ FRUCHOCS SHOP

Shop 2/80 Main St, Hahndorf, South Australia;
www.robernmenz.com.au; +61 8 8323 9105

◆ Tastings
◆ Shop

The FruChoc is a South Australian institution. This humble chocolate-coated apricot ball is even listed on the Heritage Icons List of the National Trust of South Australia. And if that's not enough to convince you of its popularity, there's even a FruChocs Appreciation Day. The obsessed gather in the state capital's vast pedestrian shopping hub, Rundle Mall, on 23 August to worship these little balls of bliss. Word to the wise when visiting South Australia: never disrespect the FruChoc.

Discover the joy of the FruChoc at one of Robern Menz's three locations scattered across the metropolitan area. The outlet positioned in the pretty tourist town of Hahndorf pumps out the companies handmade chocolates and is an ideal place to sample the 'icon'.

THINGS TO DO NEARBY

Beerenberg Farm
This Hills favourite offers strawberry picking for eight months of the year (late October to early May). The farm shop boasts 80 + products including jams, relishes and honey.
www.beerenberg.com.au

The Cedars
Set on beautiful acreage, the historic home of one of Australia's most renowned landscape artists, Sir Hans Heysen, is open Tuesday to Sunday, 10am–4:30pm (closed public holidays).
www.hansheysen.com.au

HUNTED + GATHERED

68 Gwynne St, Cremorne, Melbourne;
huntedandgathered.com.au; +61 (03) 9421 6800

◆ Shop ◆ Cafe
◆ Roastery ◆ Transport

A stone's throw from the Yarra River in the creative precinct of Cremorne, Melbourne chocolate maker Hunted + Gathered believes the simplest products are best and usually taste the best too. With a singular mission to explore the depths and flavours of the cacao bean, Hunted + Gathered produces a range of single-origin and inclusion chocolate bars, as well as three varieties of drinking chocolate, all from recipes created by co-founder Harry Nissen, with no more than five ingredients. Their vibrant space was created with transparency in mind, letting visitors enjoy the production process while ordering coffee or sampling delicious chocolate collaborations with Pidapipó Gelateria and Four Pillars Gin. Grab a house-made brownie on the way out: you won't regret it.

THINGS TO DO NEARBY

Top Paddock Cafe
Melbourne breakfast and brunch institution Top Paddock is the perfect spot to fuel you for a busy day, with beautiful interiors and honest, delicious food.
toppaddockcafe.com

Minamishima
A short trip away in Richmond is arguably Melbourne's finest Japanese dining experience, serving authentic, unadulterated nigiri, made by a master.
minamishima.com.au

KOKO BLACK

Royal Arcade, 4/335 Bourke St, Melbourne;
www.kokoblack.com; +61 (03) 9639 8911

◆ Tastings ◆ Transport ◆ Cafe
◆ Roastery ◆ Shop

THINGS TO DO NEARBY

Annam

For the best sweet and sticky oxtail dumplings of your life or lamb ribs marinated in tamarind caramel, head to this Vietnamese restaurant in Melbourne's Chinatown. *www.annam.com.au*

Lune Croissanterie

Its original Fitzroy branch had pastry lovers queuing from dawn and, well, it's much the same at this newer central outlet of some of the world's best croissants. *www. lunecroissanterie.com*

Forum Melbourne

Catch your favourite band playing here or maybe a screening at Melbourne's annual film festival. Or just swoon at the stunning 1920s mosaic floor and marble staircases. *www. forummelbourne.com.au*

Eau de Vie

First-time visitors will need someone to show them the way: a 1920s-inspired cocktail bar in an alleyway with no signage whatsoever. *www.eaudevie.com.au/ melbourne*

Visit the flagship store of this renowned luxury chocolate emporium in one of Melbourne's oldest (1870) Italianate-style arcades and get swept away by all the delicious options. Oh, and it's not just the hundred or so handcrafted Belgian couverture chocolates that'll tempt you. What about a 'dessert degustation' for two or an 'ice cream spectacular'? Open since 2003, Koko Black now has 13 stores right across Australia and prides itself on using native ingredients, such as Tasmanian leatherwood honey and local macadamia nuts. They've also been collaborating with some of the most fabulous food names in Melbourne. Since 2018, Dan Hunter, one of Australia's top chefs whose restaurant Brae has frequently featured in the World's 50 Best listing, has produced an exciting new range for Koko Black. Koko Black X Dan Hunter features the likes of green ant and burnt butter cream or strawberry gum ganache and passion fruit jelly; flavours that are reminiscent of some of his restaurant's desserts.

If you're more into spirits than fine dining or you're looking for a unique Australian gift, try the 16-piece Australian Spirits Collection, with pralines infused with Four Pillars Lemon Myrtle gin, Starward Single Origin Dark Whisky, the Rum Diary Bar's Vanilla Spiced Rum and Melbourne Moonshine's Apple Pie Moonshine.

MONSIEUR TRUFFE

351 Lygon St, Brunswick East,Melbourne;
www.monsieurtruffechocolate.com; +61 (03) 9380 4915

◆ Tastings   ◆ Classes   ◆ Cafe
◆ Roastery   ◆ Shop   ◆ Transport

Situated in East Brunswick in Melbourne's North, Monsieur Truffe is a growing attraction in laid-back Brunswick East. From humble beginnings as a one-man operation at the famous Prahran market in 2007, Monsieur Truffe, headed up by Argentine-born Master Chocolatier Samanta Bakker, creates an endless selection of chocolate delights for all diets, with the creation process best enjoyed through the glass window from East Elevation. Whilst flavour and quality are integral to Monsieur Truffe's mission, the brand prides itself on originality, collaborating with local businesses and artists, as well as its sustainable and ethical approach to the industry, using organic ingredients and wrapping their products in recycled paper packaging.

THINGS TO DO NEARBY

East Elevation
No visit to Monsieur Truffe is complete without a coffee or a bite to eat next door at East Elevation, which has amazing food and a great vibe.
www.eastelevation.com.au

Noisy Ritual
Just 400m (a quarter mile) down Lygon St, urban winery Noisy Ritual is a truly unique experience in Melbourne, and a haven for lovers of good booze, music and food.
noisyritual.com.au

MÖRK CHOCOLATE BREW HOUSE

150 Errol St, North Melbourne;
www.morkchocolate.com.au; +61 (03) 9328 1386

◆ Tastings   ◆ Classes   ◆ Cafe
◆ Roastery   ◆ Shop   ◆ Transport

Uber-hip Mörk is trying to convert Melbourne's caffeine addicts to the wonders of hot chocolate, offering a 'cacao-bean-to-cup' experience using only traceable, ethically sourced cacao. Inside their small, sleek 'brew house', visitors can choose from a lengthy menu of chocolate-flavoured drinks, from an oat-milk-based 'breakfast chocolate' to a frothy chocolate soda. The chocolate is made from cacao beans roasted in the warehouse next door and sourced from small-batch farmers all over the world, from Indonesia to Venezuela to Madagascar. Chocolate lovers shouldn't leave without trying Mörk's signature brew, the theatrical 'campfire chocolate' – a jug of foaming dark chocolate served alongside a wood-smoke-filled upturned wine glass, a toasted marshmallow and charcoal salt.

THINGS TO DO NEARBY

Beatrix
Satisfy your lingering sweet tooth at Melbourne's best cake shop, Beatrix, which is home to a rotating menu of mouth-watering baked goods, like blueberry shag cake.
www.beatrixbakes.com.au

Queen Victoria Market
Operating since 1878, Queen Vic Market (as it's known to locals) is the place to come for local produce, gourmet goods and Australiana knick-knacks.
www.qvm.com.au

YARRA VALLEY CHOCOLATERIE & ICE CREAMERY

35 Old Healesville Rd, Yarra Glen;
www.yvci.com.au; +61 (03) 9730 2777

◆ Tastings   ◆ Classes   ◆ Roastery
◆ Cafe   ◆ Shop

 Nestled in the green heart of the Yarra Valley wine region, this petite chocolate factory, shop and cafe is a lovely spot. Visitors can watch chocolates being handmade on-site through large glass viewing windows, attend workshops and classes, and of course browse and buy all kinds of chocolatey products, from simple bars to elaborate sugar creations. They hold a wide range of events, from a weekly 'Chocolate Story Time' (during term times) to a Brownie Festival. Beyond traditional varieties, interesting products include the Kitchen Garden range, showcasing local produce, and the Bush Tucker range, featuring native Australian ingredients (like chocolate-dipped strawberries).

THINGS TO DO NEARBY

Coombe
Once the estate of Australia's most famous opera singer, Dame Nellie Melba, Coombe is now a world-class winery and restaurant set in stunning landscaped grounds. *www.coombeyarravalley.com.au*

Four Pillars Gin
Taste locally made gin at this stylish cellar door and distillery in Healesville. The uniquely Australian drops are flavoured with botanicals like lemon myrtle and quandong. *www.fourpillarsgin.com.au*

TEMPER TEMPER

2 Rosa Brook Road, Margaret River;
www.tempertemper.com.au; +61 (08) 9757 3763

- ◆ Tastings ◆ Classes TBD ◆ Tastings
- ◆ Cafe ◆ Shop

This wonderland for serious chocolate lovers requires time to meander the 180 shelves of chocolate creativity that charismatic owners Roz and Georgia have dreamed up. Travellers will appreciate the playful Rocky Roads line. The Road Less Travelled is dark chocolate with macadamias and ginger, while the Long & Winding Road has pistachio, orange and blueberries in dark chocolate. The Yellow Brick Road is made from white chocolate with pecans and apricots, Silk Road is milk chocolate with almonds, pistachio and Turkish delight; Route 66 with liquorice and ginger. When not busy coming up with off-the-wall combinations such as Sriracha Strawberry and Lime or a Chocolate Ruby Coconut Pop, the owners are planning classes for the public to learn tempering and truffle making.

THINGS TO DO NEARBY

Margaret River Farmer's Market
Take a Saturday morning stroll through this market, voted one of the best in Australia, with lots of local fruit and flowers.
www.margaretriver farmersmarket.com.au

Stella Bella
Right down the road from Temper Temper is the whimsical Stella Bella winery. Bring food from the Market and buy wine by the glass to enjoy a picnic in the vineyard.
www.stellabella.com.au

© 2020, Temper Temper

NEW ZEALAND

How to ask for hot chocolate in the local language? Gizza hot chocolate (if you don't mind being informal).
Signature chocolate flavours? Whittaker's Peanut Slab.
What to order with your chocolate? Afternoon tea.
Do: Try a Lamington, New Zealand's iconic dessert.

There's no doubt that New Zealanders love their sweets: from pavlova to Jaffas, Kiwis are fiercely proud of their signature confectioneries. Of them all, though, chocolate reigns supreme, the preferred mate to afternoon and after-dinner tea. The treat has a long history in the relatively young country, dating back to the late 1800s when Dunedin-based biscuit-maker Richard Hudson opened the Southern Hemisphere's first cocoa manufacturing plant, which would eventually become the country's Cadbury factory (they closed their doors in 2017, to much public outcry). Shortly after, New Zealand icon Whittaker's began churning out creamy milk varieties, putting this country on the international chocolate map. But the Kiwi chocolate scene is far more than just big names. In the past decade, the country has become a leader in the bean-to-bar movement, where makers roast and mix their own beans rather than start with cocoa paste or liquor like other large manufacturers. While the trend began with Whittaker's (the country's first and largest bean-to-bar manufacturer), at least a dozen small craft chocolatiers have cropped up in cities and hamlets throughout the nation, focusing on fairly-traded cocoa from the rich soils of the Pacific Islands. The country's top-notch dairy means that milk varieties are still the most popular, including Lewis Road Creamery's famous chocolate milk, whose remarkable richness caused a national craze that resulted in an internationally documented shortage in 2014. But now, increasingly more producers are churning out single-origin dark bars without additives, relying squarely on the flavour of the cacao beans, and turning New Zealand into a go-to destination to sample the best chocolate the Pacific has to offer.

BENNETTS OF MANGAWHAI

52 Moir St, Mangawhai; www.bom.co.nz;
+64 9-431-5500

◆ Tastings   ◆ Classes   ◆ Food
◆ Cafe   ◆ Shop

This family-run shop has been a Mangawhai institution since 1998, when Clayton and Mary Bennett left Ireland and brought their three children back to New Zealand, where Clayton grew up. They knew the sleepy town was the perfect place to settle, and to honour their home, they started using ingredients like sea salt from the Mangawhai harbour as well as passion fruit, feijoa, kiwi, tamarillo and quince in their bonbons and bars.

Now their three children, Emily, Harry and Brodie, run the show. At their refined yet homey shop and cafe, you'll find a plethora of pastries, coffee and tea, and breakfast and lunch items as well as plenty of mouthwatering chocolate and even marshmallows. Enjoy the enormous patio as well.

THINGS TO DO NEARBY

Mangawhai Heads
Beaches abound in this part of the world, but this surf beach has made a name for Mangawhai. Get there early to find good parking.
www.mangawhai.co.nz

Te Whai Bay Wines
Enjoy outstanding New Zealand wine at this private boutique vineyard that specializes in Chardonnay, Merlot, Pinot Gris and more. *www. tewhaibaywines.co.nz*

WELLINGTON CHOCOLATE FACTORY

5 Eva Street, Te Aro, Wellington; www.wcf.co.nz;
+64 4-385 7555

◆ Tastings ◆ Transport
◆ Roastery ◆ Shop

Upstart artisan producer Wellington Chocolate Factory (WCF) crafts beautiful, tasty single-origin chocolate bars; it was the first commercial bean-to-bar company in New Zealand. 'Being able to control every part of the process, from sorting to roasting, refining and conching is vital,' says Gabe Davidson, co-founder and director of Wellington Chocolate Factory. 'We only use two ingredients, cocoa nibs and raw organic sugar, so we need to make sure all of these stages are handled with care and attention'. WCF imports whole cacao pods through fair trade or direct trade relationships, and due to New Zealand's location, many cocoa farmers are relatively close at hand.

In 2014, WCF fundraised and completed a sailing journey to bring cocoa pods from Bougainville in Papua New Guinea back to Wellington, a very overt example of direct trade. At their artisan chocolate factory, WCF chefs roast pods to their own specifications. Then the roasted pods are cracked,

THINGS TO DO NEARBY

Wellington Botanic Gardens
These hilly, 26-hectare botanic gardens with great views can be visited via the Wellington Cable Car, although there are several other entrances hidden in the hillsides.

Te Papa Museum
New Zealand's national museum, 'Te Papa Tongarewa', loosely translates as 'treasure box'; the riches inside include an amazing collection of Māori artefacts.
www.tepapa.govt.nz

Weta Workshop
Academy Award-winning special-effects and props company Weta Workshop has been responsible for bringing the likes of *The Lord of the Rings* to life.
www.wetaworkshop.com

Zealandia
This groundbreaking ecosanctuary is hidden in the hills about 2km west of town. Living wild within the fenced valley are more than 30 native bird species.
www.visitzealandia.com

winnowed and ground, making cocoa mass – the typical starting point for many chocolatiers. They then conch and temper the chocolate and form it into bars. The single-origin bars represent the locales from which the cocoa came. It's terroir, for chocolate. Wellington Chocolate Factory also partners with local artists to design colourful wrappers, and the bars are distributed in specialty stores and supermarkets throughout New Zealand. It's a growing collaborative movement with delicious results.

WHITTAKER'S

24 Mohuia Crescent, Elsdon, Porirua; shop at
Auckland Airport; whittakers.co.nz; +64 4-237 5021

◆ Shop
◆ Roastery

THINGS TO DO NEARBY

Pātaka Art + Museum
A bastion of contemporary Māori and Pacific Arts, this cultural hub features impressive rotating displays, a Japanese garden and an education centre.
www.pataka.org.nz

Porirua Saturday Market, Waitangirua
Every weekend, this lively gathering brings a humble mall carpark to life with the sights, sounds and flavours of Asia and Polynesia.
titahibaylions.co.nz

Pukerua Bay to Paekākāriki Escarpment Track
Complete this hike and receive bragging rights that you've done part of the famed Te Araroa Trail.
tearoaroa.org.nz

Onehunga or Shelley Bay, Whitireia Park
Majestic panoramas stretching all the way to the South Island and readily available watersports make this beach one of Porirua's best.

When you think New Zealand chocolate, one name comes to mind first: Whittaker's. Founded in 1890 when James Henry Whittaker began making bars in his Christchurch home, the brand has since become an award-winning, international juggernaut. Despite its success, the company remains true to its heritage. It's owned by James' great-grandchildren, and, unlike other large manufacturers, sees the process through from bean to signature gold-wrapped bar. Most of their ethically sourced cocoa is hand harvested in Ghana and shipped directly to the company's factory in Porirua, where it is transformed via a five-roll refinery process that results in impossibly creamy, rich creations.

While best known for their Peanut Slab, a recipe that hasn't changed since the 1950s, Whittaker's is always innovating, often collaborating with other iconic New Zealand brands like soda-maker L&P for deliciously wacky additions to their signature blocks. Don't leave the country without trying a classic Creamy Milk or Kaitia Fire (dark chocolate made with New Zealand's famous hot sauce). While a trip to Whittaker's Porirua factory is a pilgrimage for chocolate lovers, those hoping for an inside look will be disappointed: due to the company's popularity and relatively small size, they don't offer tours. The good news is their bars are available at any corner store in the country and at their first brick-and-mortar shop at Auckland Airport.

HOGARTH CHOCOLATE

10 Kotua Pl, Stoke, Nelson;
www.hogarthchocolate.co.nz; +64 (03) 5448623

◆ Tastings   ◆ Classes   ◆ Cafe
◆ Roastery   ◆ Shop   ◆ Transport

THINGS TO DO NEARBY

Abel Tasman National Park
This coastal park blankets the northern end of a range of marble and limestone hills extending from Kahurangi National Park. *www.doc.govt.nz/parks-and-recreation*

Tahuna Beach
Nelson's primo playground takes the form of an epic sandy beach backed by dunes, and a large grassy parkland with a playground, an espresso cart, a hydroslide and more.

World of WearableArt & Classic Cars Museum
Nelson is the birthplace of NZ's most inspiring fashion show, the annual World of WearableArt Awards. See entries in sensory-overloading galleries. *www.wowcars.co.nz*

Founders Park
Outside the city centre, this park comprises a replica historic village with a museum, gallery displays and artisan products such as chocolate and clothing. *www.founderspark.co.nz*

If you sneak inside the Hogarth Chocolate factory, you will see dozens of blocks of chocolate put aside to age on tall shelves. Just like fine wine, chocolate can develop more interesting flavours when it's left to rest after conching. Chocolate makers Karl and Marina Hogarth know this well, as they have been crafting chocolate from scratch since 2014 here in Nelson. A former fisherman and sailor, Karl took one bite of rustic homemade chocolate in Guatemala and became enchanted with the art of chocolate making. The cacao beans he uses now come from different countries: Venezuela, Peru, Ecuador, Madagascar, Dominican Republic and, of course, Guatemala.

To the delicate flavours of fine cacao, he adds ingredients proudly sourced locally, from the Italian style coffee blend supplied by a neighbouring coffee roaster, to the honey produced among the native Manuka tea trees that only grow in New Zealand. Once you try his chocolate bars, the growing list of awards he wins every year starts to make a lot of sense: texture is always smooth and creamy (even with the highest cocoa percentages), while all the ingredients are high-quality and perfectly balanced for the ultimate explosion of flavours. The doors of Hogarth Chocolate factory aren't open to the public yet, but you can smell the chocolate around the entire building, and their products are available at the weekly Saturday morning market in Montgomery Square.

OCHO

10 Roberts Street, Dunedin, Otago;
ocho.co.nz; +64 (03) 4257819

◆ Tastings ◆ Shop
◆ Roastery

THINGS TO DO NEARBY

Dunedin Street Art Trail
This 90-minute stroll
around downtown Dunedin
passes 28 vibrant works
representing artists from
ten different countries,
adding a modern twist
to the city's historic
landscape.

Dunedin Railway Station
An outstanding monument
of Edwardian design, this
architectural marvel's
elaborately tiled arches,
stained-glass windows and
blossoming gardens make
it the most photographed
building in the country.

The Otago Peninsula
Take a scenic drive through
this wildlife-watching
wonderland, home to rare
yellow-eyed penguins,
cape fur seals and an
albatross breeding colony,
plus Larnach Castle, New
Zealand's only castle.

Speight's Brewery
Founded in 1876, this South
Island staple serves up
quality ales and hearty
food along with tours of its
historic brewing operation
that has remained intact
for over a century.
speights.co.nz

When Cadbury World – New Zealand's home of the famous British confectioners and one of Dunedin's biggest tourist attractions – announced its closing in July 2017, it left a sugary hole in the country's self-proclaimed 'home of chocolate'. Luckily, it didn't last long. A few months later, OCHO (Otago Chocolate Company) founder Liz Rowe swooped in to fill the gap, organising the country's most successful crowdfunding campaign to date (two million dollars in two days from 3000 individual investors) to turn her garage-housed sustainable chocolate initiative into a full-fledged factory operation.

Now, within the humble waterside building's brick walls, visitors can watch Rowe's bean-to-bar principles in action. There, cacao sourced directly from small producers through-out the Pacific Islands are transformed into intensely dark chocolate bars, the entire process completed under one

roof. OCHO's signature bars feature only two ingredients: cocoa nibs and sugar. Rowe prefers to let the beans speak for themselves, highlighting how the cocoa's origin affects the flavour without any additives. The tastings resemble those at wineries, featuring a flight of samples that allow eager eaters to compare the robust fruitiness of beans from Papua New Guinea to the subtle nuttiness of those sourced from Fiji.

INDEX

ACKNOWLEDGEMENTS

Published in April 2020
by Lonely Planet Global Limited
CRN 554153
www.lonelyplanet.com
ISBN 978 1788 68945 8
© Lonely Planet 2020
Printed in Malaysia
10 9 8 7 6 5 4 3 2 1

Managing Director, Publishing Piers Pickard
Associate Publisher Robin Barton
Editors Nora Rawn, Christina Webb and Lorna Parkes
Art Direction Daniel Di Paolo
Layout Kerry Rubenstein
Illustrations Jacob Rhoades
Image Research Lauren Marchant
Print Production Nigel Longuet

Contributors: Matthew Ankeny, Kate Armstrong, Erica Ayisi, James Bainbridge, Amy Balfour, Sarah Baxter, Andrew Bender, Claire Boobbyer, Celeste Brash, Cathy Brown, Joshua Samuel Brown, John Brunton, Piera Chen, Ann Christenson, Marc Di Duca, Samantha Forge, Bailey Freeman, Max Gandy, Ethan Gelber, Sarah Gilbert, Megan Giller, Anthony Ham, Carolyn B Heller, Michele Herrmann, Cate Huguelet, Anita Isalska, Brian Kluepfel, Abigail K Leichman, Kaelyn Lynch, Emily Matchar, AnneMarie McCarthy, Carolyn McCarthy, Meher Mirza, Karyn Noble, Zora O'Neill, Lorna Parkes, Jessica Phelan, Regis St Louis, Valerie Stimac, Mark Stratton, Sharon Terenzi, Kerry Walker, James Want, Luke Waterson, Barbara Woolsey, Chris Zeiher, Karla Zimmerman

STAY IN TOUCH lonelyplanet.com/contact

AUSTRALIA
The Malt Store, Level 3, 551 Swanston St,
Carlton, Victoria 3053 T: 03 8379 8000

USA
Suite 208, 155 Filbert Street, Oakland, CA 94607
T: 510 250 6400

IRELAND
Unit E, Digital Court, The Digital Hub,
Rainsford St, Dublin 8

UNITED KINGDOM
240 Blackfriars Rd, London SE1 8NW
T: 020 3771 5100

MIX
Paper from
responsible sources
FSC™ C021741

Paper in this book is certified against the
Forest Stewardship Council™ standards.
FSC™ promotes environmentally responsible,
socially beneficial and economically viable
management of the world's forests.